# COMEDY WRITING
# secrets

2nd edition

# COMEDY WRITING

## secrets

the best-selling book on
how to think funny, write funny,
act funny, and get paid for it

### Mel Helitzer
with Mark Shatz

**WRITER'S DIGEST BOOKS**
Cincinnati, Ohio
www.writersdigest.com

Other fine Writer's Digest Books are available at your local bookstore or direct from the publisher.

09  08  07  06  05      5  4  3  2  1

Distributed in Canada by Fraser Direct, 100 Armstrong Avenue, Georgetown, ON, Canada L7G 5S4, Tel: (905) 877-4411. Distributed in the U.K. and Europe by David & Charles, Brunel House, Newton Abbot, Devon, TQ12 4PU, England, Tel: (+44) 1626 323200, Fax: (+44) 1626 323319, E-mail: mail@davidandcharles.co.uk. Distributed in Australia by Capricorn Link, P.O. Box 704, S. Windsor NSW, 2756 Australia, Tel: (02) 4577-3555.

Library of Congress Cataloging-in-Publication Data

Helitzer, Melvin.
  Comedy writing secrets : the best-selling book on how to think funny, write funny, act funny, and get paid for it / by Mel Helitzer with Mark Shatz.
      p. cm.
  Includes index.
  ISBN 1-58297-357-1 (pbk. : alk. paper)
  1. Wit and humor—Authorship. I. Shatz, Mark. II. Title.

PN6149.A88H445 2005                                     2005014368
808.7–dc22                                              CIP

Edited by
**KELLY NICKELL**

Design and Illustration by
**GRACE RING**

Production coordinated by
**ROBIN RICHIE**

fw
F+W PUBLICATIONS, INC.

# A MAGNUS HOPUS

## Dedication
To Linea Warmke
and to
Ethan, his parents' favorite comic.

## ABOUT THE AUTHORS

**MEL HELITZER**, a former Clio award-winning Madison Avenue ad agency president, is now a distinguished, award-winning journalism professor at Ohio University in Athens, Ohio. He was one of the first to teach humor writing at any university in the world. His course led to the publication of *Comedy Writing Secrets* in 1987, and the book is now the largest selling text on humor writing in the country.

Helitzer has written humor for print and broadcast productions as well as comedy material for such stars as Sammy Davis, Jr., Shari Lewis, Art Linkletter, Ernie Kovacs, and presidential candidate Adlai Stevenson. Many of his students are now professional comedians or humor writers for national publications. He is the author of seven books, including a bound-for-Broadway musical, *Oh, Jackie! Her Father's Story*.

**MARK A. SHATZ** is professor of psychology at Ohio University, Zanesville. In addition to teaching humor writing, he has extensive international experience as a teacher, speaker, and seminar leader on various topics such as motivation, death education, and interpersonal communication. Dr. Shatz has published numerous academic papers, including how to use humor to enhance instruction and learning. He is the author of *KISSing Golf: The Keep It Simple (Stupid) Instructional Method*, a humorous instructional book for beginning golfers.

# TABLE OF CONTENTS

# FOREWORD
## And Now a Word From the Prof

Comedy is a lot like professional sports. Past successes are history. You get paid for today's hits. One difference is that in baseball, a .300 hitter gets paid a million dollars and the fans are deliriously happy all season. But a .300 batting average in comedy would get professional performers to go from boos to booze in a week.

With that kind of failure rate, you'd think any person who had reached the age of reason would take up plumbing. But the facts are that writing and performing humor is rising in popularity. And if you're successful, the money in comedy is so abundant that professional practitioners are like well-endowed actors in a porn movie—"You mean I get paid for doing that."

The biggest change in the humor industry in the last ten years has been the need for professional writers. There are just not enough qualified writers today to fill the increasing need. Besides the standard venues, more and more markets are begging for humor material: speeches, business newsletters, advertising, columns, talk shows, sales presentations, and everything from high-tech computer attachments to *Hi, Mom* greeting cards.

Comedy clubs had a ten-year fireworks display. While the worst ones closed from bad management and bad acts, the remainder are solid businesses, and the "I'll do anything to get on stage" neophytes are now secure enough to be unionized.

TV sitcoms also had their vicissitudes of popularity. The great ones lasted into syndication, and the worst ones were pulled after one or two seasons. In the meantime, the number of humor talk shows from Leno and Letterman to Jon Stewart and Conan O'Brien increased. And now every presidential candidate needs to make a guest appearance, not only to be toasted but also to increase his popularity by being roasted.

The formal study of humor in colleges has grown in geometric proportions despite the doubting colleagues who associate facetiousness with frivolity. The president of my university once told me he disdained humor, because he feared failure. "I've heard some of your speeches," I told him. "And I agree with you."

It's the fear of failure, however, that continues to be the biggest drawback. While 90 percent of us claim we have a sense of humor, the number of critics is 100 percent. "I didn't think it was funny."

Go argue.

Milton Berle ended his years appearing before senior citizens in Miami Beach. Once, a little old lady in the front row kept shouting, "That stinks. I've heard it before."

Exasperated, Berle said, "Lady, do you know who I am?"

"No," she said, "but if you'll go up to the desk, they'll tell you."

The net result of all this is that if you really want to take the time and effort to learn how to write (and perform) humor, you've got to have a thick skin to go along with a nimble brain. Learn how to live with people throwing dirt at you.

One day a donkey fell into a well. The farmer couldn't get him out, so he knew he had to cover him up. He called in his neighbors, and they all started to throw dirt down the well, but instead of burying the animal, the donkey would shake the dirt off and take a step up. Pretty soon, the pile of dirt got so high that the donkey stepped over the edge of the well. Moralists use this story to preach that all our troubles can be stepping stones, that we shouldn't give up; instead shake it off and take a step up. Comedians, however, note that as soon as the disdained donkey got to the top he ran over and bit the farmer. Their moral is that if something goes wrong, try to cover your ass. It can come back and bite you.

We hope you'll enjoy this book. It can make you rich in more ways than one. And that's no joke.

**Professor Mel Helitzer**
Ohio University
2005

# INTRODUCTION
## You Can Do It!

### HEY! IS THIS THING ON?

Out of fear that discovery of their superficial tricks will be evaluated rather than laughed at, many famous humorists have sponsored an insupportable fiction that comedians must be born funny. According to Mel Brooks and Woody Allen, for example, you can't teach anyone to be funny. They either have the gift or they don't. Hogwash!

You can teach literate people anything, from Einstein's theory of relativity to how to play shortstop. And compared to humor writing secrets, playing the piano's eighty-eight keys or speaking Greek is a lot harder to learn and a lot less fun. (Which is more beneficial to humanity is debatable.) What is universally accepted, however, is that comedy, a flash of intuition, is more art than science.

Since Eve first admonished her pooped-out partner to be "up and Adam," entertainment has been our kingdom's social pastime, and comedy is the coin of the realm. Theater traditionalists like to point out that one side of their coin is the embossed mask of humor, and the other side, the mask of tragedy. They're wrong again. Humor is tragedy and tragedy is humor. As Mel Brooks once said, "Tragedy is if I cut my finger. Comedy is if you drop into an open sewer and die." As this book will prove, if you can't learn to write humor, kid, that's tragedy!

### HOW THIS BOOK HELPS YOU

Humor style changes dramatically almost every twenty years. This new edition of *Comedy Writing Secrets* has been updated with contemporary methods and formulas. Here are some of the key points the book covers:

- The three Rs of humor
- The secret of the MAP theory
- The beauty of *What if?*
- The THREES theory of humor structure
- Why we laugh at some forms of humor and groan at others
- The natural hostility of humor
- Why humor must ridicule a target
- Why hard-core humor is more shock than funny

The book is divided into three sections. The first part covers the foundations of humor writing, including the theories and principles of humor and why we laugh. The second section describes various humor-writing techniques, such as plays on words, reverses, pairings, triples, and exaggeration. The final section explains how to write humor for popular markets such as greeting cards, speeches, articles, newsletters, and stand-up comedy. This revised edition also includes chapters on humor writing in advertising and the use of humor in education.

Integrated throughout the book are sections titled Showtimes that provide quick exercises that can refine your writing skills. Humor writing demands practice, and it is critical to take the time to complete these writing assignments. If you're not funny by then, demand your money back and don't ever get married.

While this book is an introduction to humor writing, we don't promise it will instantly transform you into a professional. Learning the fundamentals of humor is easy compared with the dedication required to be a successful writer. A woman once rushed up to the famous violinist Fritz Kreisler and cried, "I'd give my life to play as beautifully as you do."

Kreisler replied, "Well, I did."

## NO DEGREE REQUIRED

Since there is no official humor certification organization, there is no such thing as a certified professional humor writer. If you can sell your material or get paid for performing it, you're a professional. But humor writing is commanding more and more attention in higher education.

Approximately sixty universities, including the University of California, Los Angeles, and The New School in New York, offer humor-writing courses and degree-granting programs in humor studies, and more such courses are on the horizon. Many colleges use this book as their primary text.

The first college credit writing course was taught by Mel Helitzer at the Scripps School of Journalism at Ohio University in 1980. Within three years, it had become such a smash hit that the twenty allotted seats were assigned a year in advance. Students for the class are as diverse today as they were more than twenty years ago and range from fellow faculty members to adults from the community—including lawyers, doctors, accountants, homemakers, and even one mortician. (We asked him if, when trying out his material, he killed the audience, and he said, "No, they're already dead when I get there.")

The largest group of current comedy writers for major TV shows and films comes from Harvard, which ironically does not have a humor-writing course. For some reason, there has never been a famous comedian who graduated from Yale or Princeton, that is if you don't count two recent U.S. presidents.

In Chicago, Second City is the country's leading school for improvisational training. Numerous comedy clubs and individual professional writers, particularly in New York, Los Angeles, and San Francisco, offer small clinics.

## THE BIG-PICTURE BENEFITS OF HUMOR

Humor's impact is far reaching. For example, when the editors of *Fortune Magazine* queried human resource directors of Fortune 500 companies as to what qualifications they looked for in middle management executives, the top three answers were: (1) knowledge of the product; (2) respect for the bottom line; and (3) a sense of humor.

Since everyone claims to have a sense of humor, except for an expectant mother in a delivery room, the editors double-checked, "Why a sense of humor?" And the replies were consistent.

A sense of humor indicates leadership. When we smile, it's a sign of confidence, because fear and paranoia are signaled by frowns, not smiles.

Subordinates, associates, customers, and clients like to work with someone with a sense of humor.

## JOINED AT THE LIP: HUMOR AND COMEDY

Academicians, especially English professors, often attempt to draw distinctions between humor and comedy. Humor is considered the broader term that encompasses all types of humor material, such as satire, sarcasm, irony, and parody. Comedy is the performance of humor. The perception is that clever writers write humor while glib comedians do jokes.

 Men say the most important thing in another person is a sense of humor. That means they're looking for someone to laugh at their jokes.

**—Sheila Wenz**

It's true that jokes in isolation are just that—jokes. However, any form of humor writing uses jokes to produce the humor. We take a less elitist position and do not make arbitrary distinctions between humor and comedy. If the result is laughter, then the label is insignificant. Our goal is to help you write funny.

## WHOSE JOKE IS IT, ANYWAY?

Contemporary humor-writing methods are an extension of past techniques. We focus on contemporary humorists, but since today's comedians rip off the greats, knowledge of humor history is not a sometime thing. This book, therefore, includes examples and advice from scores of contemporary comedians such as Jon Stewart, Tina Fey, Billy Crystal, Jay Leno, Chris Rock, David Letterman, Robin Williams, and Rita Rudner, and from humor hall of famers such as Erma Bombeck, Milton Berle, and George Burns, and even from such early American humorists as Mark Twain, Elbert Hubbard, and John Morley.

Unfortunately, credit lines for humor are a researcher's nightmare, like this pairing.

 If you can't join them, beat them.

**—Mort Sahl**

If you can't beat them, arrange to have them beaten.
**—George Carlin**

There are many standard jokes, and they have thousands of variations. No one can swear that any one was his creation. In *Oh, the Things I Know!*, Al Franken stated, "I am not a member of any organized religion. I am a Jew." Franken later noted that he "first heard that joke from a Catholic, who had substituted the word 'Catholic.'" Will Rogers used that same premise—but he substituted the words "political party" and "Democrat"—nearly one hundred years ago.

It's also been proven that such famous lines as Horace Greeley's "Go west, young man," Marie Antoinette's "Let them eat cake," Joseph Addison's "He who hesitates is lost," W.C. Fields's "Any man who hates dogs and babies can't be all bad," and his oft-quoted tombstone inscription, "I would rather be here than in Philadelphia," Mark Twain's "Everybody talks about the weather but nobody does anything about it," Will Rogers's "I never met a man I didn't like," and Franklin D. Roosevelt's "The only thing we have to fear is fear itself," were all previously written by someone else.

If scholars have this problem with historic lines, then giving proper credit for similar jokes, anecdotes, and witticisms can be a never-ending dilemma. So the best we can offer for identification is to list the name that was published in someone's joke collection, but don't bet on its accuracy. Of course, some jokes came to us creditless, and some we wrote ourselves. The ghost of Marlowe will always haunt the library of Shakespeare—and that's not an original line either.

Now, let's get started.

# PART ONE

## The Basics of
## Humor Writing

# CHAPTER 1
## The Importance of Humor Writing

 What is comedy? Comedy is the art of making people laugh without making them puke.

**—Steve Martin**

Humor has tremendous value. It's an art form. But it's not a mystery—it has structure and formula. You can learn this creative art for your own personal enjoyment or for financial gain.

Admittedly, some widely known authors feel that humor-writing skills (let alone the sense of humor) are mystically inherited rather than learned, and likely molded by such factors as ethnic characteristics, early childhood maternal influence, and insecurity.

 Humor is one of the things in life which defies analysis— either you have it or you don't, either you enjoy it or you don't.

**—Ross Mackenzie**

Nobody can teach you humor writing. The secret is passed on from one generation to another, and I will not tell mine, except to my son.

**—Art Buchwald**

But the truth is that anyone can learn to write humor. Although some individuals are naturally funnier than others, just as some individuals are more athletic or more musically gifted, humor writing can be taught and humor-writing skills can be acquired. Humor is not a mystery, because (like stage magic) it is possible to demystify it.

## BUT I AIN'T FUNNY

Let's use a simple humor exercise to illustrate that humor writing is accessible to everyone. Consider the possible uses of two round bar stool cushions. Other than stool cushions, what can they be? For five minutes, use your imagination and plenty of exaggeration. Without being restrained by practicality, scribble down as many possibilities as you can.

Your list of possible uses for two stool cushions might include the following.

- elephant slippers
- oversized skullcaps
- eye patches for a giant
- hemorrhoid pads for a really large person
- Frisbees for the athletically challenged

This humor Rorschach test illustrates the first step in humor conception—imagination. Creativity is the key to comedy's engine, which won't turn over without unbridled imagination. Look at any other common object—an ashtray, a beer bottle, furniture in a room, or parts of the human body. Train your mind to constantly ask *What if?* and brainstorm all the possibilities of what else these objects could be. Don't worry if your ideas seem absurd. The exercise is to get your imagination in gear. To write funny, you must first *think* funny.

 Imagination is intelligence having fun.
**—George Scialabba**

*What if?* imagination allows you to realign diverse elements into new and unexpected relationships that surprise the audience—and surprise makes people laugh.

 What if mother's milk was declared a health hazard? Where would they put the warning label?

What if you actually saw McNuggets on a chicken?

What if alphabet soup consistently spelled out obscene words?

What if the leaning tower of Pisa had a clock? (After all, what good is the inclination if you don't have the time?)

Humorists have one cardinal rule: Don't be inhibited. It's better to take a nihilistic attitude toward sensitive subjects than to pussyfoot around taboos. When writing, write freely. Make uninhibited assumptions. Editing and self-censorship are second and third steps—never the first!

We'll describe later how to fit your ideas into the basic formulas of humor writing. If your internal critic limits your imagination by saying *This stinks*, then you will be left with nothing. Your goal is to tap the full potential of your comedic imagination by remembering this mantra: *Nothing stinks. Nothing does stink!*

 The whole object of comedy is to be yourself, and the closer you get to that, the funnier you will be.

**—Jerry Seinfeld**

Imagination drives comedy, and just about everyone has an imagination—or no one would never get married. So just about everyone can learn the fundamentals of humor. How well you learn them depends on how much effort you're willing to expend.

## THE BENEFITS OF HUMOR WRITING

The benefits of humor writing are the three Rs: *respect, remembrance, and rewards*. The skillful use of humor can

- earn you *respect*
- cause your words to be *remembered*
- earn great financial and personal *rewards*

### Respect: Get Up and Glow

We use humor primarily to call attention to ourselves. Notice how you react when you tell a joke to a small group of friends and, just as you get to the end, someone shouts out the punch line. That person gets the laugh. You don't. You feel victimized. Your glare might be the physical limit of your anger at first—but the second time this happens, you'll try to kill the jerk, and no jury will convict you.

Laughter is to the psyche what jogging is to the body—laughter makes your psyche healthy and bright and vigorous. But unlike jogging, humor (at least in live performance) offers immediate gratification—more so than any other art form. You know within a half-second when your audience is appreciative, because this jury's decision is impulsive and instantaneous.

 Comedy is very controlling—you are making people laugh. It is there in the phrase "making people laugh." You feel completely in control when you hear a wave of laughter coming back at you that you have caused.

**—Gilda Radner**

There are other ways that you can attract attention: You can achieve something outstanding, criticize somebody, or be unconventional, for instance. But you can increase the impact of these things with humor. Humor is more than entertainment or joke telling—it's a powerful social lubricant that eases and enriches communication, interpersonal relations, and education. Humor is a universal speech opener because it immediately earns the speaker respectful attention. It's psychologically impossible to hate someone with whom you've laughed.

When we laugh we temporarily give ourselves over to the person who makes us laugh.

**—Robert Orben**

Humor can also help you gain success and respect in nearly every profession (unless, perhaps, you are a mortician). For example, teachers facilitate instruction with humor, advertising executives use humor to sell products, and politicians rely on humor to promote their candidacies. Humor doesn't just get you attention—it gets you *favorable* attention, and respect.

## Remember: Everlasting Memories

When we're successfully humorous—live or in print—people remember. Our best lines are retained and repeated. An impressive number of sayings in *Bartlett's Familiar Quotations* are witticisms.

 There is a thin line that separates laughter and pain, comedy and tragedy, humor and hurt.

**—Erma Bombeck**

On one issue at least, men and women agree: They both distrust women.

**—H.L. Mencken**

Humor promotes learning and makes it memorable. Studies have found that students who attend lectures that include witticisms and anecdotes achieve higher test scores than students who attend the same lectures minus the humor. When learning is fun, everybody benefits.

 When the mouth is open for laughter, you may be able to shove in a little food for thought.

**—Virginia Tooper**

In and out of the classroom, jokes are probably our best opportunity for immortality—for being remembered.

 I don't want to gain immortality by my humor. I want to gain immortality by not dying.

**—Woody Allen**

### Reward: Show Me the Money

Humor is important in every facet of commercial life. More and more frequently, big-business executives are hiring speechwriters able to make them gag on every line (and you can read that line any way you want to). Many political candidates—in fact, every president since Franklin Roosevelt—have had in-house humorists on their speech-writing teams.

 It really gets me when the critics say I haven't done enough for the economy. I mean, look what I've done for the book-publishing industry. You've heard some of the titles. *Big Lies, The Lies of George W. Bush, Lies and the Lying Liars Who Tell Them.* I'd like to tell you I've read each of these books, but that'd be a lie.
> **—George W. Bush**

Comedy can also be a springboard to lucrative TV and film roles. Robin Williams, Alan King, Chevy Chase, Chris Rock, Billy Crystal, Ellen DeGeneres, Steve Martin, Eddie Murphy, Bill Murray, Mike Myers, Rosie O'Donnell, Jerry Seinfeld, Adam Sandler, and Roseanne Barr are just a few major film and TV stars who started out as comedians. Woody Allen, Mel Brooks, and Carl Reiner began their careers as gag writers for Sid Caesar's TV shows, and David Letterman, Conan O'Brien, and Garry Shandling were TV staff writers before hosting their own TV shows.

 A former girlfriend remembers Bill Gates as having bad breath. He remembers her as not having $100 billion.
> **—Conan O'Brien**

The demand for humor writers far exceeds the supply. One reason for this is that more people want to tell jokes than write them. Opportunities abound for humor writers, who can seek careers as syndicated columnists, speechwriters, greeting card writers, stand-up comedians, Internet and advertising copywriters, and screenwriters for TV sitcoms and film.

Another reason for the high demand for humor writers is that television is a joke-eating shark. It chews up more humor material in a month than all other markets use in a year. Johnny Carson once remarked that television is the only medium that eats its young, because young writers are the ones most frequently hired to feed the shark day after day. Many young humorists are attracted to the eye-popping financial rewards of a career in TV humor writing, but writers are only as good as their last joke, and fatigue causes many of them to burn out after a year. Whatever humor-writing endeavors you choose, you can be financially and personally successful if you develop good humor-writing skills—and staying power.

 The road to success is always under construction.
**—Lily Tomlin**

## THE MAP TO BEING A SUCCESSFUL HUMORIST

The two qualities shared by all successful humorists are (a) consistency and (b) targeted material. If you are consistent, you can make people laugh repeatedly—the ability to write funny isn't a one-time thing.

Once you can consistently make people laugh, it's essential to target your material so you don't waste precious time preparing the wrong material for the wrong performer, to be delivered to the wrong audience. This is as true in print and broadcast humor as it is for stand-up.

 What if you tell a joke in the forest, and nobody laughs? Was it a joke?
**—Steven Wright**

The acronym MAP sums up this second point rather efficiently. MAP stands for *material*, *audience*, and *performer*. MAP is a triangular comedic constellation. Each star in the constellation must relate to both the other stars.

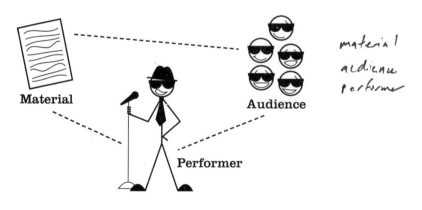

*In order of Sequence*

Successful humor requires all three MAP elements.

*Congruent*

1. **Material.** The material must be appropriate to the interests of the audience, and it must relate well to the persona of the performer.
2. **Audience.** The audience must complement both the material and the presentation style of the performer.

*3 R's*

3. **Performer.** The performer must present the right material to the right audience in the right way.

## Audience: Resisting a Rest

The reason the MAP theory is illustrated by a triangle is that—of the three points—the *audience* is the most important. Every time writers forget this simple piece of advice, they lose the game—and soon the job.

You and the audience have the same goal line. You score when you reach it together. Others can keep score, but ten laughs a minute can be a failed effort if the audience doesn't participate. The first responsibility of every humorist is to evaluate the majority of the audience, whether it's one person or a thousand. (In the next chapter, we'll discuss why people laugh.)

Unless you're prepared with material that obviously and vocally works for a specific audience, you're facing impossible odds of success. There's a distinct audience for every specialized group. They are categorized by hundreds of special interests: color, religion, education, financial and social standing, acumen, geography, politics, fame, and sex. The same material that works for a college audience will not work for a group of lawyers, doctors, or bankers. Dumb-blonde jokes may work for a blue-collar men's audience, but humor that ridicules men's habits and body parts are more popular than ever with women's groups. Youth audiences feel uninhibited language is expected, and senior citizen groups feel young comedians' material should first be exorcised with mouthwash.

Most audiences are more interested in subjects that involve their activities than they are in humor that is all about you, your friends, your pets, and your bar buddies. From the very first day, humor writers are urged, figuratively of course, to throw away the capital letter *I* on their computer. It's true that greats like Ray Romano, Rita Rudner, and Woody Allen talk about themselves, but until you become the equivalent of Ray, Rita, or Woody, it's best to wait. More astute are performers like Jerry Seinfeld, Jay Leno, Chris Rock, and Billy Crystal, who fire round after round of observations of the audience's interests. The best example of all is Jeff Foxworthy's "You know you're a redneck if ..." material, and although he demeans them, his redneck southern audience howls all night.

## Hey, Look Me Over

Once the profile of the audience has been established, the second most important point of the triangle is *performer*. Whether you're writing for someone else or you're the presenter, the audience needs to know who you are in the first thirty seconds. It's in this short window of time that they're going to decide just how comfortable they feel with your comedic persona.

Certain characteristics are mandated by your physical appearance: size, color, accent, sex, and beauty. Performers can enhance their personas with costumes, props, and theatrical projection, but it's best to take advantage of these physical confinements rather than fight them. Michael Richards, of *Seinfeld* fame, looks goofy, and every time he tries to change his character, he fails. Comedian Yakov Smirnoff has maintained a Russian accent even though he lived all his formative years in Cleveland. Red neck comedians wear blue jeans, Las Vegas comics wear suits, and young girls wear black leather pants.

## It's All Material

Only after you know your audience and the characteristics about the performer's persona that need to be consistent, are you ready to start writing the material.

And that's the heart of this book. But learning the fundamentals of humor is easy compared with the dedication required, and you're going to need it.

Throughout the book, we'll show you how to follow the MAP to successful humor writing.

## HUMOR WRITING IS A 24/7 GIG

Writing humor is an all-day—and all-night—assignment. New ideas can (and should!) pop into your head anytime, anyplace. In an issue of *Advertising Age*, journalist Bob Garfield described the idea-collection practices of Marty Rackham, then a beginning comic.

> [Marty Rackham's wallet] is stuffed with miscellaneous business cards, on the back of which he jots random ideas. One says, "Pulling words from a person who stutters." Another, "Jumper cables." Right now, he's working on a bit about continental hygiene: "Did you ever smell a European?" The ideas materialize constantly, in varying degrees of hilarity and sophistication.

The humorist's mind is a wonderful thing to watch. Sometimes you can even see humorists' lips move as they silently try out different ideas. Meet them during off-hours at a social gathering; every fact reported, every name mentioned, every prediction made is grist for humorous association. At the end of a party, if you ask how they enjoyed themselves, they might answer positively only if they've been successful at collecting new material, which they'll write and rewrite all the way home.

 A humorist tells himself every morning, "I hope it's going to be a rough day." When things are going well, it's much harder to make jokes.

**—Alan Coren**

To keep track of ideas and potential material, the humorist's toolbox typically includes the following items: a note pad, index cards, a tape recorder, and a computer with Internet access. If you hope to sell your writing, you'll need a copy of *Writer's Market*, the bible of the publishing industry.

Regardless of the tools you use, you'll need to devise a system for organizing your writing. The traditional method is to organize jokes by topics using some type of filing system. Milton Berle and Bob Hope each had a vault containing more than six million jokes on index cards sorted by topic. The digital alternatives to index cards are database or spreadsheet programs.

*Organize Material*

If you plan to write more elaborate humor (such as columns, articles, or scripts), there are a variety of software programs that can aid your writing. One of the most useful writing development programs is Inspiration. The program allows you to visualize your material and easily manipulate ideas, and its integrated diagramming and outlining environments facilitate brainstorming, concept mapping, organizing, and outlining.

## SHOWTIME

The following activities will help you develop your comedy-writing foundation through listening, observing, reading, and exploring. It's critical that you complete these exercises now, because they will be used throughout the next few chapters.

• List your ten favorite comedians and humorists, and use the Internet to search for jokes or quotes by each of these individuals.

• After you amass twenty jokes, write each joke on an index card. On the back of each card, identify the subject or target of the joke, and explain why you think the joke is funny. This exercise will help you become aware of the format of successful jokes and provide you with insight into your own comedic preferences.

• Collect ten to fifteen cartoons or comic strips and tape each one on a separate piece of paper. As you did with the jokes, identify the target of the humor and describe why the cartoon is funny to you. You may find it helpful to continue building a file of jokes and cartoons that appeal to you.

• In addition to building a joke and cartoon file, you'll need to find new material to use as the building blocks for your humor writing. Most professional humor writers begin each day by reading a newspaper, watching news on TV, and/or surfing the Internet for incidents and situations that might provide joke material. As you read this book and complete the exercises at the end of each chapter, form a daily habit of recording the odd news events that tickle your fancy.

• Everyday life is the main source for humor, so you need to keep some type of personal humor journal. To facilitate psychoanalysis, Sigmund Freud had patients complete a dream diary, and he encouraged them to associate freely during therapy. To be a successful writer and tap into the full potential of your comic persona, you should follow an analogous approach. Record everyday events, ideas, or observations that you find funny, and do your journaling without any form of censorship. The items you list are intended not to be funny but to serve as starting points for writing humor.

# CHAPTER 2
## Why We Laugh

 The first thing I do in the morning is brush my teeth and sharpen my tongue.

**—Dorothy Parker**

Aristotle studied it, and Socrates debated it. Such famous historical figures as Charles Darwin, Thomas Hobbes, and Henri Bergson wrote papers on their humor theories. In the twentieth century, Sigmund Freud, Max Eastman, and even Woody Allen tried to formulate clear explanations of the purpose of humor. In fact, there's been more research on humor in the last decade than in all previous centuries combined. Humor has played an important part in our lives for thousands of years, but scientists and philosophers are still working to understand what laughter means, why we tell jokes, and why we do or don't appreciate other people's humor.

Despite the prowess of the minds that have considered the subject, answers are far from definitive. Like rabbis in the eternal debate over the meaning of the Talmud, every scholar of comedy interprets its subjective phenomena in terms of his own discipline. Today, there is more diversity of opinion than ever.

 So much remains to be done that the student of humor has a real opportunity to make a significant contribution to the field.

**—Jeffrey Goldstein and**
**Paul McGhee**

The only common denominator among the theories is an agreement that humor is so subjective that no one theory can possibly fit in all instances. For those interested in creating humor, there is good news and bad news. The good news is that if humor has so many tangents, it may have an unlimited variety of benefits. Most of them have yet to be discovered. The bad news is that those who create comedy are not sure they know exactly what they're doing. "I work strictly on instinct," Woody Allen admitted. Humor writers therefore have to live with the fear that they won't be able to continue producing humor consistently.

 After being an established writer for fifteen years, I remember staring at the typewriter every morning with a desperate, random groping for something funny, that familiar fear that I couldn't do it, that I had been getting away with it all this time and I would at last be found out. [It was] a painful blundering most of us went through.

**—Sol Saks**

There are few artists more insecure than humorists. They are traditionally suspicious of any attempt to analyze their creative techniques. That's because they develop their formulas through trial and error. They discover comedy batting averages; some techniques work more often than others.

 I think I did pretty well, considering I started out with nothing but a bunch of blank paper.

**—Steve Martin**

## SHOWTIME

Before we discuss how humor works, let's examine your theory of humor. Take out your joke and cartoon collections, and rank each item in terms of funniness.

Next, review the explanations you wrote for the top-rated items to determine common patterns or themes.

Finally, with these patterns or themes in mind, write down at least five answers to the question *Why do people laugh?*

## REASONS FOR LAUGHTER

Few contemporary humor craftsmen agree on any comedic philosophy, except: If it gets a laugh, it's funny. If you want to write funny, however, you must first understand how audiences respond to humor. In short, you must understand why we laugh.

Noted psychologist Patricia Keith-Spiegel identified two primary reasons why we laugh.

- We laugh out of surprise.
- We laugh when we feel superior.

Keith-Spiegel identified six additional motivations for laughter, each of which supports the two main reasons, surprise and superiority.

- We laugh out of instinct.
- We laugh at incongruity.
- We laugh out of ambivalence.
- We laugh for release.
- We laugh when we solve a puzzle.
- We laugh to regress.

The theories of humor discussed in this chapter will provide you with a starting point for analyzing why humor does or does not work. Over time, your personal theory of humor will evolve and influence your writing.

 Analyzing humor is like dissecting a frog. They both die in the process.
**—E.B. White**

Be forewarned—the application of humor theories does have a downside. As you shift into an analytical mindset, you'll spend more time thinking about why something is funny and less time laughing. As we take jokes apart, we must be as unemotional as a coroner during an autopsy.

### Surprise

We laugh most often to cover our feelings of embarrassment. This can be a result of either having unintentionally done or said something foolish, or having been tricked. If we have been tricked, we have been surprised.

Surprise is one of the most universally accepted formulas for humor. A joke is a story, and a surprise ending is usually its finale.

 The guys in strip clubs think because they got a pocket full of dollars they got the power—but the chicks got the power. They spin around the pole and you guys are hypnotized. That's how I look at a dessert case, but at least I get to eat mine.

**—Monique Marvez**

Appreciation of any piece of humor decreases rapidly through repeated exposure, or when the ending is predictable. Clever wordplay engenders grudging appreciation in your peers, but *surprise* wordplay gives birth to laughter. We smile at wit. We laugh at jokes.

The techniques that most often trigger surprise are misdirection (when you trap the audience), and incongruity (which is most effective when the audience is fully aware of all the facts, but someone they are observing is not).

 The universe has come to an end in Houston, where there's a Starbucks across the street from a Starbucks. Is this for Alzheimer's suffers? You finish your coffee and walk out the door and go, "Oh, look, a Starbucks."

**—Lewis Black**

If laughter is the electricity that makes a comedy writer's blood start pumping, then surprise is the power generator. The need for surprise is the one cardinal rule in comedy.

 In West Virginia yesterday, a man was arrested for stealing several blow-up dolls. Reportedly, police didn't have any trouble catching the man because he was completely out of breath.

**—Conan O'Brien**

According to playwright Abe Burrows, the best way to define the construction of surprise is to use baseball terms: A joke is a curve ball—a pitch that bends at the last instant and fools the batter. "You throw a perfectly straight line at the audience and then, right at the end, you curve it. Good jokes do that," said Burrows. To achieve the unexpected twist, it's sometimes necessary to sacrifice grammar and even logic.

 He may not be able to sing, but he sure can't dance.

A key word sets up the surprise. It gets the audience to assume they know the ending. Notice how the word *half* works in the following example.

 My wife and I have many arguments, but she only wins half of them. My mother-in-law wins the other half.

**—Terry Bechtol**

There are many ways to achieve surprise. What's important is to remember that you really can't be funny without it.

## Superiority

There appears to be a strong and constant need for us to feel superior. In many ways, humor satisfies this most basic of needs.

 If you can't laugh at yourself, make fun of others.

**—Bobby Slaton**

"Humor is a reaction to tragedy. The joke is at someone else's expense," wrote anthropologist Alan Dundes. We even laugh when the baby falls down and goes boom. We defend this sadistic release by saying, "That's cute." It's not cute—especially from the baby's perspective. Humor often ridicules the intelligence, social standing, and physical and mental infirmities of those we consider inferior to ourselves.

 You know, you're never more indignant in life than when you're shopping in a store that you feel is beneath you and one of the other customers mistakes you for an employee of that store.

**—Dennis Miller**

But those we consider *superior* to ourselves are not spared. We delight in publicizing and mocking every shortcoming—perceived or real—of people who are in positions of authority, who are richer, more famous, more intelligent, physically stronger, or more admired. The greater the prestige of the victim, the greater our desire to equalize.

# TYPOS: AN ART FULL OF SUPERIORITY

Nothing allows someone to feel superior more than mocking another person's mindless mistake, which is perhaps why typos are such a rich source for contemporary humor and witticisms. Both the original expression or word and the expression or word created by the typo must be so familiar (in other words, part of universal knowledge) that there is no doubt that everyone in the audience can be in on the gag.

 My public relations course had a typo in last semester's course catalog. It was listed as "Advanced Pubic Relations." The registration was 1,500 ... and those were only the faculty wives.

**—Mel Helitzer**

In the 9/11 commission report, they say it was Iran—not Iraq—that was helping Al-Qaeda. So apparently we invaded the wrong country because of a typo.

**—David Letterman**

Humor is social criticism. The object is to deflate. Humor has been an emotional catharsis for every American ethnic minority: Irish, Germans, Arabs, Jews, Blacks, Latinos, etc. There are few joke books on WASPs—but that doesn't mean there aren't jokes about them.

 In a study, scientists report that drinking beer can be good for the liver. I'm sorry, did I say "scientists"? I meant "Irish people."

**—Tina Fey**

I'm a WASP, a White Anglo-Saxon Protestant, and actually, a lot of my people are doing really well.

**—Penelope Lombard**

Humor also reassures the insecure. Even if we believe ourselves to be the "haves" (having power, money, knowledge, or prestige), there is tremendous insecurity about how we got it and how long we're going to keep it. Americans have a tremendous sense of inferiority. We mask it with jokes about our superiority.

 I've been to Canada, and I've always gotten the impression that I could take the country over in about two days.

**—Jon Stewart**

There are two ways to feel superior. The first is to accomplish exemplary work that receives public acclaim. That's difficult. The second (and easiest) way to feel superior is to publicly criticize the accomplishments of others. This diminishes their prestige and focuses attention on us. Regardless of how much the second method might be deplored on ethical grounds, the amount of time and effort exerted to belittle the work of competitors is usually far greater than the amount of time and energy expended to improve our own abilities.

 The penalty for laughing in a courtroom is six months in jail. If it weren't for the penalty, the jury would never be able to hear the evidence.

**—H.L. Mencken**

Our spark of laughter is always ignited by the misfortunes of those we fear. "Humor is the weapon of the underdog," wrote psychologist Harvey Mindess. "We must look for avenues through which we can disgorge our feelings of inferiority by discovering the blemishes of our superiors." In short, we feel superior because their image has been tarnished and because we aren't in the same predicament.

As individuals (regardless of our status), our humor is generally directed upward against more authoritative figures.

In a group setting, our humor is directed downward toward groups that don't conform to our social, religious, national, or sexual mores.

 I worked some gigs in the Deep South ... Alabama. You talk about Darwin's waiting room. There are guys in Alabama who are their own father.

**—Dennis Miller**

Sigmund Freud's explanation of this phenomenon was that "a good bit of humor is oriented to maintaining the status quo by ridiculing deviant social behavior and reassuring the majority that their way of life is proper. It is used as a weapon of the 'ins' against the 'outs.'"

 If you're Black, you gotta look at America a little bit different. You gotta look at America like the uncle who paid for you to go to college but molested you.

**—Chris Rock**

The comic is no El Cid on horseback. If anything, comics are guerrilla fighters—hitting and running, bobbing and weaving. With this kind of an act, they've got to keep moving.

The professional humorist must always be aware that audience members are happiest when his subject matter and technique encourage them to feel superior. The target of a roast smiles only because he knows everyone is watching for his approval. Despite being the guest of honor, he would rather have stayed home with his wife—where he would also have been insulted, but at least he could have saved a clean, white shirt.

Now that we've discussed the two main reasons why people laugh—surprise and superiority—let's examine the six other reasons. These six minor theories overlap one another and either function within or support the two main theories.

## Instinct

Laughter is a born and bred instinct, a phenomenon of evolution. It appears to be a function of the nervous system that stimulates, relaxes, and restores a feeling of well-being. Primates, with little verbal communicative ability, show friendship with a closemouthed smile. They show anger and hostility with an open mouth, exposing all their teeth—despite the fact they could all use orthodontics.

 Scientists believe that monkeys can be taught to think, lie, and even play politics within their community. If we can just teach them to cheat on their wives, we can save millions on congressional salaries.

**—Jay Leno**

For human beings, laughter has evolved as a substitute for assault. Triumph is often coupled with an openmouthed smile followed immediately by a roar of laughter. Watch a pro football player after he scores a touchdown.

If laughter is biologically instinctive, the old adage of never trusting someone who laughs too loudly should be amended to include those who laugh with their mouths open. We laugh and joke not when we need to reach out and touch someone, but when we need to reach out and *crush* someone. It's an attempt to vent our hostility when physical aggression is not practical.

## Incongruity

According to the dictionary, something is incongruous when it is inconsistent within itself. For example, whenever someone behaves in a rigid manner that is suddenly ill-suited to the logic of the occasion, these incongruous antics result in a ridiculous scenario. This comic effect can arise from incongruity of speech, action, or character.

According to philosopher Henri Bergson, one type of comedic incongruity is an unconventional pairing of actions or thoughts.

 There are only two kinds of money in the world: your money and my money.

**—Milton Friedman**

There seems to be more than a Latin semantic root shared by the words *ridiculous* and *ridicule*. And in humor, we *ridicruel*. Many incongruous situations provoke laughter because they allow the observer to feel superior. Some of the best illustrations of this type of comedic incongruity are the practical jokes on such television shows as *Candid Camera* and *Punk'd*. These television programs, by design, encourage us to laugh at people trying to maintain dignity in bizarre circumstances. The audience laughs the hardest when it knows all the facts of the situation—and therefore feels superior to the perplexed victim of the joke.

Allen Funt, the creator of *Candid Camera*, claimed that the talking mailbox gag—a man is mailing a letter when suddenly the mailbox starts to talk to him—was the show's top laugh-getter. The incongruity of a mailbox talking to someone is funny on its own, but the apex of laughter comes when the man calls over his friend and asks him to listen to the amazing conversation. He starts talking to the mailbox. At this point, the mailbox doesn't say a word. As the victim gets more and more exasperated and starts shouting at the mailbox, the camera cuts to a close-up of the friend—who is plainly questioning his buddy's sanity.

Incongruity may take the form of an entire comic plot, rather than a single joke. A common example of an incongruity-based plot in TV sitcoms is when one character hides in the closet moments before someone in authority (a spouse, boss, police officer) unexpectedly enters the room. This plot has a hundred variations, and it's always popular because the audience knows all the facts, and therefore feels superior.

### Ambivalence

This theory is similar to incongruity in its dependence on incompatible experiences. Nervous laughter covers our recognition of rigid conventions that make us appear foolish when held up to a humorist's strobe light. In a dishonest world, honesty is amusing.

 They say you should videotape your baby-sitter, but I don't think you should involve your kid in a sting operation.
**—Dave Chappelle**

Whereas incongruity is the clash of incompatible ideas or perceptions, ambivalence is the simultaneous presence of conflicting emotions, such as the love/hate relationships in families. Holding our ambivalent feelings up for comedic inspection is the powerful shtick of humorists like Bill Cosby, who often played upon the antagonism a parent may often feel for a child.

 Listen to what I'm telling you, damn it, 'cause I brought you into this world, and I can take you out of it.
**—Bill Cosby**

Another common topic under the theme of ambivalence is the mother-son relationship (which makes analysts wealthy).

 My mother never saw the irony in calling me a son of a bitch.
**—Richard Jeni**

Ambivalent humor covers up our guilt feelings or our foolish errors; it's an attempt to maintain dignity. Self-deprecating humor is just a device to set the audience at ease, so you can be in control.

### Release

We laugh in embarrassment when we drop a glass in public or an innocent error of ours has been discovered. In these situations, laughter relieves tension. But laughter as release can also be a planned event, a conscious effort to unlock life's tensions and inhibitions. We attend a Neil Simon play or a Robin Williams concert because we want humor to help us laugh away our anxieties.

 A drunk driver's very dangerous. Everybody knows that. But so is a drunken backseat driver—if he's persuasive.

**—Demetri Martin**

This release is fortified by group approval. Comedy works best when an audience is not only prepared to laugh, but anxious to participate in a shared social experience.

For release humor to work, the audience must be clued to every plot from the beginning. If the audience and the actor don't know what's behind the door, that's mystery. If the audience knows, but someone else doesn't, that's release comedy.

 Did you ever wonder why we sing "Take Me Out to the Ballgame" when we're already there?

One theory of laughter as relief is that, if we feel the need to laugh, it's because we've been whipped by the day's battles and we'd like to hear or see a few others get smacked around. Misery loves company, but only if *we* can laugh at *them* and *they* can't laugh back at *us*. We'll even laugh wildly when a catcher chasing a foul ball wipes out seven guys in wheelchairs.

 I hear blind people are complaining that seeing-eye dogs are expensive, difficult to train, and hard to get. I say, let 'em use midgets. They can use the work.

**—Chris Rock**

That's sadism—and superiority.

### Puzzle Solving

We frequently laugh when disjointed bits of information fall into place: *Oh, so that's the way it works!*

 I learned about sex the hard way—from books!
**—Emo Philips**

We smile, frequently even laugh aloud, when we experience that sudden insight of having solved a mystery, finished a crossword puzzle, or conquered a difficult assignment. Theorists refer to this type of scenario as configuration humor. In configuration humor, we laugh when a riddle encourages us to instantaneously discover some missing—and unexpected—piece of information. If we're successful, we congratulate ourselves by laughing out loud. We are delighted by the solution to the puzzle (surprise), and we want the world to know we're very smart (superiority).

### Regression

Sigmund Freud's theory of humor contended that humor, like sleep, is therapeutic. But even more importantly, he argued, wit can express—in a relatively appropriate way—urges and feelings that can't otherwise be let loose, such as the desire to act on regressive infantile sexual or aggressive behavior. More to the point, Freud believed that a lack of humor can be a sign of mental illness.

 My theory is that women don't suffer from penis envy. Every man just thinks his penis is enviable. Maybe Freud suffered from penis doubt.
**—Bob Smith**

Psychologist J.C. Flugel wrote, "We laugh in order to socially accomplish childish regression without feeling foolish. We adopt a playful mood, excusable as relaxation." This may explain why comic strips are the most universally accepted format of humor among adults, regardless of nationality or culture.

 We're young only once, but with humor, we can be immature forever.
**—Art Gliner**

Psychoanalysts learn a great deal about patients by listening to their humor. And you can learn a great deal about your own psychological makeup by constantly asking yourself (and answering truthfully), *Why did I laugh at this joke and not at others?*

 Every man is a damn fool for at least five minutes every day; wisdom consists of not exceeding the limits.

**—Elbert Hubbard**

Our regression into an infantile state of mind through humor, as suggested by psychoanalysts, is most often experienced in large settings. For group approval, we subjugate our humor preferences to those of authority figures. If the group leaders approve of the humor, we laugh. If the group leaders disapprove, we groan. We rarely enjoy humor if we feel we're laughing counter to the crowd. If we are the first to laugh, we will stifle a hearty *ha-ha* in mid-*ha* if no one joins us. Even when acting childish, our desire is to maintain social approval.

## LAUGH AS I LAUGH

One of the most difficult humor audiences is a room of corporate executives when the big boss is present. Every time the speaker tells a joke, everyone in the room first checks the CEO. If the CEO doesn't laugh, no one else laughs. If the CEO has a good sense of humor and laughs easily, business associates then consider themselves to have permission to laugh. Even though this check for approval only takes a second, it can throw a comedian's timing way off.

Let's not camouflage our true intentions. We don't use humor just to entertain the world. The value of humor in attack is incomparable, because humor is a socially acceptable form of criticism, a catharsis that combines memorability with respectability.

But the only way you'll survive as a humorist is if the audience equally disfavors your target. Understanding what motivates a particular audience is one of the secrets of writing humor. You must maintain surprise and superiority.

## THE SCIENCE OF HUMOR: A MATTER OF WIFE OR DEATH

In 2001, Richard Wiseman, a British scientist and the creator of LaughLab (www.laughlab.co.uk), conducted a global online study to discover the world's funniest joke. He constructed a Web site that allowed visitors to submit jokes and rate the offerings of others. More than forty thousand jokes were received from seventy countries (though two-thirds were deemed inappropriate for posting). Based on several million critiques, the world's funniest joke is:

 A couple of New Jersey hunters are out in the woods when one of them falls to the ground. He doesn't seem to be breathing; his eyes are rolled back in his head. The other guy whips out his cell phone and calls the emergency services.

He gasps to the operator: "My friend is dead! What can I do?"

The operator, in a calm, soothing voice, says: "Just take it easy. I can help. First, let's make sure he's dead."

There is a silence, then a shot is heard.

The guy's voice comes back on the line. He says: "OK, now what?"

The LaughLab joke survey revealed other interesting data. Germans rated jokes the funniest overall, while Canadians gave the lowest ratings. If you like talking-animal jokes, use a duck—it was considered the funniest talking animal. And the most submitted joke was: "What's brown and sticky? A stick." No one found the joke funny.

With the advancement of brain-imaging tools, scientists can now study how the brain processes humor. The typical experiment requires subjects to view, read, or listen to a humorous stimulus, such as an episode of *The Simpsons* or *Seinfeld*, while researchers record brain functioning. Although this type of research is still in its infancy, there is an emerging consensus concerning the brain's reaction to humor. The language-based portion of the brain (the left frontal cortex) "gets" the joke by recognizing the ambiguity, incongruity, and surprise of the humor. The emotional areas of the brain (such as the amygdala) appreciate the humor and trigger laughter.

Eventually, science will be able to explain humor's neural underpinnings. However, the mystery of what, exactly, is "funny" will never be solved. One person considers the Three Stooges to be comic savants, while another finds no humor in Moe's abuse of Curly—this illustrates the individual differences in the perception of what's funny. A sense of humor is as unique as a fingerprint.

## DOES SICK HUMOR MAKE US FEEL BETTER?

Morbid humor arises out of every tragic situation. Within hours after the nuclear accident at Chernobyl, the airwaves were filled with such humor as:

 **QUESTION:** What has feathers and glows in the dark?
**ANSWER:** Chicken Kiev

Do sick jokes, frequently tasteless and insensitive, serve an important purpose? The consensus is that humor is one way of coping with tragedy. The more we're scared, the more we have to create jokes to laugh away the fear.

Many of the most offensive jokes derived from current tragedies are entre-nous humor, told by one person to friends or co-workers, but rarely performed in public.

 Jesus walked up to the registration desk of the Hilton hotel, threw three nails on the counter and asked, "Can you put me up for the night?"

Psychologists have always been interested in explaining human behavior through humor. Humor is an important manifestation of what society really believes, but dares not speak or teach. "We can't confront tragedy directly," suggests Joseph Boskin of Boston University, "so we try to ease ourselves in a humorous way."

Laughing at misfortune frequently replaces negative feelings with positive feelings. This is true whether we're laughing at someone else's misfortune or our own. Sigmund Freud, who studied humor (but not for the fun of it), theorized that jokes allow us to express unconscious aggressive and sexual impulses, to substitute words for what we may not be able to accomplish in deeds.

But when it comes to sick humor, the real reason people tell such jokes is much simpler—to make themselves feel better by getting respect, or at least attention. When we were young, we discovered that we could always get a laugh by dropping our pants or saying some taboo word. We may have grown older physically, but the desire to attract attention and gain approval through audacious humor remains.

Many comedians believe that they don't need sick humor once they've become established. Said motivational speaker and humorist Larry Wilde, "It's mainly done by the young comics anxious to be noticed. As you get older, you find that material on death and disease makes the audience feel uncomfortable."

In other words, a comic has to be brave enough to be clean. It may be coincidental, but a rather significant acronym results from the first letter of the three elements used by those who depend upon sick humor to attract attention: audaciousness, shock, and surprise. Put them all together, they spell *ASS*. Wonder what Freud would have had to say about that?

## SHOWTIME

The following activities reinforce the importance of examining why something is funny.

- Return to your joke and cartoon collections, and reanalyze each item using the two most important humor principles, surprise and superiority. Identify how the element of surprise is used and the ways in which the audience feels superior.

- Select a favorite humor article or column and highlight the funny sections. Examine the writing for how the author uses surprise to deliver the punch.
- Watch a tape of your favorite comedy. Pause after funny scenes and write down how and why the humor worked. Pay particular attention to the two most important principles, surprise and superiority.
- Examine the funny personal stories and anecdotes that you share with your friends to confirm how surprise and superiority play a role in the humor.

# CHAPTER 3
## The Recipe for Humor

 Instead of working for the survival of the fittest, we should be working for the survival of the wittiest, and then we can all die laughing.

**—Lily Tomlin**

There are six essential ingredients in any recipe for humor. With few exceptions, the absence of any one ingredient so disturbs the formula that the humor might not just taste "off," but might deflate like a ruined soufflé. Whether the humor is a one-liner, a lengthy anecdote, or a three-act theatrical piece, these six elements are required.

- Target
- Hostility
- Realism
- Exaggeration
- Emotion
- Surprise

Although the prescribed order may be challenged, in this configuration the first letter of each element forms a memorable acronym: THREES.

The THREES formula focuses on the *what* and *why* of humor. The *what* is the *target*, and the *why* is the *hostility, realism, exaggeration, emotion*, and *surprise* contained in the humor.

## TARGET: AIMING YOUR HUMOR

Our instinctive perception is that humor is fun. It isn't! Humor is criticism cloaked as entertainment and directed at a specific target.

 If there's no corpse, there's usually no joke.

**—Mike Sankey**

The proper selection of humor targets is not just important—it's arguably the most critical factor in writing commercially successful humor. The MAP theory—*material, audience,* and *performer*—postulates that the material must fit the persona of the writer (or performer) and the interests of the audience. A humor target can be almost anything or anybody, but you need to be sure you've focused on the right target for your particular audience.

You can't target an entire audience any more than you can shame the whole world. Humor is an attempt to challenge the status quo, but targeting must reaffirm the audience's hostilities and prejudices.

This means that humor is always unfair. Like editorial cartoons, jokes take a biased point of view. There's no room in one joke for a balanced argument or explanation. As H.L. Mencken put it, "My business is diagnosis, not therapeutics."

 I hate phone solicitors. I'd rather get an obscene call; at least they work for themselves.

**—Margaret Smith**

A neophyte writer often selects humor targets with limited appeal, such as a girlfriend or boyfriend. Here's the problem: Your companion may be the most bizarre or humorous person in the history of the human species, but no one else cares about your partner other than your family members (and even that is questionable). Unless members of the audience can vicariously share your experiences, you might as well perform your material in a bathroom. It will be safer.

Successful humorists select targets with universal appeal. Erma Bombeck wrote about the struggles of being a mother and did not focus on the specific eccentricities of her family. Because she invoked common experiences, Bombeck's humor was appreciated by legions of devoted readers.

Another common mistake when selecting a target is to use general topics rather than specific premises. For example, the way people drive is a broad subject that will not readily lend itself to humor. The target must be more specific, such as how women are able to multitask (put on makeup, talk on a cell phone, etc.) while driving. By narrowing a general target to a specific premise, you increase the likelihood of surprising the audience with the punchline.

Picking a good target isn't a crapshoot. It takes thought, skill, and precision to MAP your way to the right target. Strong targets, as noted above, can range from people to personal beliefs. Let's take a closer look at some of the most common targets: yourself, sex, celebrities, places, products, and ideas.

### Self: Pick on Somebody Your Own Size

By far the least offensive (but most effective) target is yourself. As writer and director Carl Reiner observed, "Inviting people to laugh with you while you are laughing at yourself is a good thing to do. You may be the fool, but you're the fool in charge."

 I'm always getting screwed by the system. That's my lot in life. I'm the system's bitch.

**—Drew Carey**

Many comics open by ridiculing their shortcomings: their physical characteristics, finances, intelligence, and even their success. People are always willing to laugh at someone else, so it's a safe way to warm up an audience. Once the audience is laughing, it's time to move on to hotter issues.

 I plan to become so famous that drag queens will dress like me in parades when I'm dead.

**—Laura Kightlinger**

### Sex: Talk Dirty to Me

Sex is the topic of close to 25 percent of all humor, making it one of the most popular targets. All of us—male or female, young or old—are more ambivalent about sexual activity than about any other single subject. It isn't that we're fascinated by exaggerated acts of sex; it's that we're frustrated by exaggerated reports of adequacy.

 An elderly patient said to his doctor, "Why can't I have sex five times a day?"

"But you're seventy-five, Sam," said the doctor. "Physically you just can't do it anymore."

"But my friend Bernie says he has great sex. He says he can have it five times a day, and he says the most beautiful girls in town are all after him. That's what he says."

"So, Sam," said the doctor, "you say!"

Studies have shown that men's greatest sexual concerns generally center around size, the ability to get an erection, performance, the amount of sex they're having, premature ejaculation, and impotency—pronounced in West Virginia as *im-PO-tan-cy*, because it's real impotent to me! (However you pronounce it, it still means having to say you're sorry.)

 I'm not a good lover, but at least I'm fast.
                                    **—Drew Carey**

In *The Hite Report on Male Sexuality*, Shere Hite reported that while men treasure sexuality, "they also dislike and feel very put upon by it." Her report suggests that men feel trapped by sexual stereotypes. They find themselves unable to speak openly about their sexual angers, anxieties, and desires. Many complain about the escalating pressures to initiate sex, to achieve and maintain frequent erections, to control the timing of ejaculations, and to understand (let alone satisfy) their partner's orgasmic needs. Since the introduction of Viagra, erectile dysfunction jokes have been in sitcoms like *Seinfeld* and *Friends*.

 Cialis warns that if your erection lasts for more than four hours, you should tell your doctor. Hey, at my age, if I have an erection for more than four hours, I'd want to tell everybody!

Research on sexual humor indicates that beginning joke tellers are more likely to select sexual themes that discriminate against males regardless of the gender of the performer or the audience, and that their preferred subjects are those that belittle body parts and sexual performance.

 I once dated a guy who drank coffee and alcohol at the same time. What a prince. Bad breath, limp dick, and wouldn't go to sleep.

**—Kris McGaha**

Many comics use humor based upon deviance from the sexual norm.

 You know you're gay when you bend over and see four balls.

**—Garry Shandling**

Women are also intrigued by ribald humor about sexual activity, because they're as sexually insecure as men about performance and satisfaction.

 I'm just a huge fan of the penis, and they're all different—like snowflakes.

**—Margaret Cho**

During sex, men confuse me. They suddenly start shouting, "I'm coming. I'm coming." I don't know whether they want me there as a partner or a witness.

**—Emily Levine**

## Celebrities: Humor Fodder and Mudder

Celebrities are also popular targets. Celebrity service is a cheap shot, but our appetite for a dash of vinegary gossip about our heroes, icons, and villains is insatiable. Because the public almost indiscriminately idolizes the famous and the infamous, the American media love to create new celebrities in entertainment, sports, politics, and letters. Paradoxically, no sooner do the *idol rich* reach the apex of their media hype than we begin to humble them with gossip and humorous digs.

 This Halloween the most popular mask is the Arnold Schwarzenegger mask. And the best part? With a mouth full of candy you can sound just like him.

**—Conan O'Brien**

## Places: Living in a Crass House

Our need for superiority is the motivating factor whenever we ridicule places: We ridicule countries (France, North Korea); states (West Virginia, New Jersey); cities (New York City, Washington, D.C.); and local spots in the news (a neighborhood, a street, a bar, lover's lane). Every humorist has a favorite dumping ground.

 I moved from New York City to Athens, Ohio. Talk about culture shock. From the city that never sleeps to the city that never woke up.

**—Mel Helitzer**

## Products: Malice in Wonderland

There's a veritable eBay full of products that are favorite humor targets. They run from buildings and automobiles to sports equipment, jewelry, and junk food. The basic rule, again, is that your target be an object of annoyance shared by the entire audience. It's easier to start backwards. Begin with the punchline, but don't finalize your position until you've decided it's *their* position as well. If the audience includes a large contingent of hunters, forget about quoting either of these Ellen DeGeneres bits.

 Stuffed deer heads on walls are bad enough, but it's worse when you see them wearing dark glasses, having streamers around their necks, and a hat on their antlers. Because then you know they were enjoying themselves at a party when they were shot.

I say to a gun owner who owns an AK-47, that if it takes a hundred rounds to bring down a deer, maybe hunting isn't your sport.

## Ideas: Fools of the Game

The list of controversial ideas that can be humor targets is lengthy. Audacious ideas can include subjects such as religion, the meaning of life and death, and politics. Trash-talking politicians is the meat and potatoes of a late night host's opening monologue. Idea topics are the most likely to backfire, because a person's politics and ideologies aren't visible on the outside, like clothes. That's why David Letterman carefully screens requests for his show tickets—to eliminate potential audience members who may not appreciate his sadistic wavelength.

There are no perfect parents. Even Jesus had a distant father and a domineering mother. I'd have trust issues, if my father allowed me to be crucified.

**—Bob Smith**

Although feelings of superiority are essential to humor, you can nonetheless be funny by coming out *for* a topic or idea, rather than against it. "Comedy was born of anarchism," said political humorist Mark Katz, "and now it's moved into advocacy."

 Bisexuality immediately doubles your chances for a date on Saturday night.

**—Woody Allen**

## SHOWTIME

As you've just seen, the list of potential humor targets is nearly endless. Take a moment and list seven to ten possible subjects, topics, or targets of humor. That is, identify things that you want to make fun of.

As noted in the discussion of the MAP theory in the first chapter, the humorist's material must fit the persona of the writer or performer. Each humorist feels more comfortable attacking some targets over others. Return to your list of potential humor targets and identify the three targets that you would feel most comfortable making fun of.

## HOSTILITY: RIDI*CRUEL*

The second ingredient in the THREES recipe for humor is hostility. Humor is a powerful antidote to many of the hostile feelings in our daily lives. All of us have hostility toward some target. That is why, in humor, *ridicule* is spelled ridi*cruel*. Comedy is cruel. The words *cruel* and *ridicule* appear together frequently—where there is one, there is also the other.

All of us have hostility toward some person, thing, or idea—unless we are saints. Did you ever hear a joke about two perfect, happy people? But when a beer-bellied, blue-collar worker walks in the front door and says to his battle-ax of a wife, "Can you spare a few minutes? I need to be taken down a peg"—now, that works as great humor.

Let's discuss some common sources of hostility (and therefore humor): authority, sex, money, family, angst, technology, and group differences.

### Authority: Sock It to Me

While hostility against authority is international, in America, it is a national heritage. Since the Revolutionary days, we've enjoyed pricking the bloated arrogance of authority and watching it bleed. Humor is a great catharsis because it gives the public an opportunity to blow off indignant steam at authority figures both major and minor.

 I looked up the word politics in the dictionary, and it's actually a combination of two words: poli, which means "many," and tics, which means "bloodsuckers."

**—Jay Leno**

One characteristic of this hostility is that invariably we ridicule upward, attacking those we perceive to be superior (or in a superior position).

 The Senate decided they will be smoke-free. They ordained that all public areas in the Senate are now smoke-free. However, the senators themselves will still be allowed to blow smoke up each other's ass.

**—Bill Maher**

Richard Pryor's audiences were easily defined: mostly young black militants, with a fair percentage of young liberal whites. Both the black and white members of the audience held white authority as a common enemy. In the following memorable bit, Pryor shrewdly used this shared hostility to explain his arrest—a front-page story—for shooting his wife's car one night after she threatened to leave him. (Note that Pryor chose the police as representative of white authority.)

I don't want to never see no more police in my life, at my house, taking my ass to jail, for killing my car. And it seemed fair to kill my car to me, right, 'cause my wife was goin' leave my ass in it. "Not in this motherfucker, you ain't. If you leave you're goin' be drivin' those Hush Puppies you got on. 'Cause I'm goin' kill this motherfucker here." And I had one of them big ol' Magnums, you know the noise they make when you shoot something. I shot the car ... boom! And the car went, "Ahhhhhhh." It sounded good to me. So I shot another one ... boom. "Ahhhhhh." And that black car said to me, "Go ahead. Shoot somethin' else." I shot the motor. The motor fell out. The motor say, "Fuck it."

Some readers may view Pryor's work as vulgar, but from the perspective of his peers, he was a comic genius—Pryor was the first recipient of the annual Mark Twain Prize for American Humor.

Hostile humor is usually directed upward. Freshmen ridicule upperclassmen but have little interest in writing humor about their younger brothers or sisters. Faculty spend very little effort on humor directed at students and much more on material satirizing the administration. In the military echelons of command, noncoms gripe about junior commissioned officers, who ridicule the major support staff, who in turn snicker about the general's idiosyncrasies, until—so the story goes—General MacArthur's wife once asked him to convert to a religion in which he no longer believed he was God.

This necessity for hostility bred what is called *nihilistic humor*—humor based on the theory that there is no person or thing so sacred as to be beyond ridicule. Humorists, protected by the First Amendment, enjoy the admiration of audiences that laugh and applaud their unbridled criticism of gods, political leaders, and celebrities. Marty Simmons, who published *National Lampoon*, credited the antiestablishment climate of Vietnam and Watergate with the birth and success of his magazine. But this freedom to criticize must be accompanied by perspective. As one comic admitted, hostility can be nothing more than intellectual masturbation. "There am I criticizing the President of the United States. He lives in the White House, and I'm telling dick jokes in some comedy club basement."

When easily caricatured leaders run for reelection, humorists don't know whether to vote their conscience or their profession. When columnist Art Buchwald was asked when he was going to retire, he said, "Not now, when humor's so easy."

 As they say around the [Texas] Legislature, if you can't drink their whiskey, screw their women, take their money, and vote against 'em anyway, you don't belong in office.

**—Molly Ivins**

## Money and Business: The Loot of All Evil

Men admit they think more about sex than about any other subject, but studies throughout the years have indicated that women worry more about finances than sex. There's little doubt, however, that money is a constant source of irritation and hostility among both sexes.

 Someday I want to be rich. Some people get so rich they lose all respect for humanity. That's how rich I want to be.

**—Rita Rudner**

If you want to know what God thinks of money, just look at the people he gave it to.

**—Dorothy Parker**

Perversely, financial worries only increase as you get wealthier: The more money you have, the more problems. Just buying a new product can multiply anxiety four times: First, you must debate whether you really need the product. Then you must decide on a brand, which means you have to read comparison literature, evaluate alternatives, and physically shop to find the product. Finally, you must haggle over price and agonize over how to finance the purchase. Even after you've acquired a product, you'll be exasperated by breakdowns and the need for repairs.

The concern about financial matters starts with your first cry for someone to give you candy and continues to your last cry—for someone to give you oxygen. Since everyone has personal money problems, focusing hostility on financial matters is one of the best (and least controversial) ways to show the audience you share their problems.

Business practices are more frequently becoming targets of financial hostility. But jokes about business practices actually direct hostility against two subjects at the same time: economics and authority.

 The budget problems with Medicare and NASA could be solved if the country began firing the elderly into space.

**—Al Franken**

Financial humor targets are countless: Executive shenanigans, wages, taxes, investments, gambling, lottery awards, and credit cards are just a few.

 My VISA card was stolen two months ago, but I don't want to report it. The guy who took it is using it less than my wife.

**—Johnny Carson**

### Family Affairs: Coming Home Soon

Hostility against family responsibilities, restrictions, and competing interests needs little explanation as a target of humor. Family members and household affairs like cleaning, paying bills, and cooking have all become popular targets.

 My theory on housework is, if the item doesn't multiply, smell, catch on fire, or block the refrigerator door, let it be. No one cares. Why should you?

**—Erma Bombeck**

The day I get excited about cleaning my house is the day Sears comes out with a riding vacuum cleaner.

**—Roseanne Barr**

I left my wife because she divorced me. I'm not going to live with somebody under those kinds of pressures. But I still love my ex-wife. I called her on the phone today. I said, "Hello, plaintiff ..."

**—Skip Stephenson**

I wanted to be an actress. I said to my mother, "I want to cry real tears. I want to show great emotion for someone I don't really care for." She said, "Become a housewife." She always wanted me to be married all in white—and all virginal. But I don't think a woman should be a virgin when she gets married. I think she should have at least one other disappointing experience. One woman friend of mine told me she hated her husband so much that when he died she had him cremated, blended him with marijuana, and smoked him. She said, "That's the best he's made me feel in years."

**—Maureen Murphy**

Children, especially teenagers and preteens, are common family targets. Even toddlers are targets (they're not just cute but, according to Bill Cosby, exhibit signs of brain damage). Parents are unburdening themselves wittily, even if they can't do it in reality.

 Having a family is like having a bowling alley installed in your head.

**—Martin Mull**

And children are reciprocating, which means *let's give it to our saintly, gray-haired mother and revered father!*

 Mother's Day card: Mom, you're the greatest. At least that's what all the guys at the construction site say!

Children are the most desirable opponents at Scrabble, as they are both easy to beat and fun to cheat.

**—Fran Lebowitz**

## Angst: The Ecstasy and the Agony

Angst is the intellectual observation that fairy tales aren't true—that there is an unhappy end to every happy beginning. Angst has pointed a devil's finger at anxieties so personal that, in the past, we carefully avoided discussing them even in private: A long list of such topics includes fear of death; coping with deformity; deprivations; and neurotic symptoms such as paranoia, insecurity, narcissism, and kinky sexual urges.

 Have you ever dated somebody because you were too lazy to commit suicide?

**—Judy Tenuta**

Woody Allen popularized angst. "I merchandise misery," he wrote. "When I named my movie *Love and Death*, the commercial possibilities were immediately apparent to me: sight gags and slapstick sequences about despair and emptiness; dialogue jokes about anguish and dread; finally, mortality, human suffering, anxiety. In short, the standard ploys of the funnyman."

 They say such nice things about people at their funerals that it makes me sad that I'm going to miss mine by a few days.

**—Garrison Keillor**

### Technology: Now Fear This

Charlie Chaplin exploited frustrations and fears about rapidly growing automation to make people laugh. It's ironic that IBM once used his tramp character as an implied advertising testimonial for computers, because Chaplin's character didn't promote machines—he ridiculed them.

 Computers operate on simple principles that can easily be understood by anybody with some common sense, a little imagination, and an IQ of 750.

**—Dave Barry**

The sense of hopelessness that comes from our apparent inability to control the environment is now a universal hostility. Industrial chemicals can lead to pollution, drugs can lead to suicide, and the advertising drum beats for nonsensical fads. Humor may be our only rational way of coping with the fear of terrorism, an invasion of spooks from outer space, or the chemical mutation of our planet.

 They asked John Glenn what he thought about just before his first capsule was shot into space, and he said: "I looked around me and suddenly realized that everything had been built by the lowest bidder."

### Group Differences: Us vs. Them

Mocking the beliefs or characteristics of social groups is one of humor's most controversial subjects because it caters to our most primitive instincts—prejudice and insecurity. We hope to maintain some sense of superiority by ridiculing abnormal characteristics of others. We're responding to a primitive form of group therapy.

 Sophisticated people have retirement plans. Rednecks, on the other hand, play the lottery. That's our plan. And when we hit the "pick six," we're going to add a room on to the trailer so we don't have to sleep with Grandpa no more.

**—Jeff Foxworthy**

We fear control and intimidation by people of different colors or religions; and so, by derision, we attempt to stereotype their physical appearances, ethnic mannerisms, colloquial speech—any unique characteristic we find odd. We feel the same way about people with different social attitudes about drugs, sex, education, professions—even music, literature, and humor. As long as we're in the majority, humor can criticize.

 I had a cab driver in Paris. The man smelled like a guy eating cheese while getting a permanent inside the septic tank of a slaughterhouse.

**—Dennis Miller**

Do you know how the Amish hunt? They sneak up on a deer and build a barn around it.

**—Tim Bedore**

Humor is often sin without conscience. (A conscience doesn't prevent sin; it only prevents us from enjoying it.) It used to be the blue-collar whites that regurgitated the most hostile ethnic humor. Today, comedians of all backgrounds are sensing both an increasing freedom for public humor and an increasing audience who'll pay to hear it.

 Mexicans don't go camping in the woods, especially during hunting season. Some redneck would say to the judge, "Your Honor, I saw brown skin and brown eyes. He had his hands up. I thought they were antlers. I shot his ass."

**—Paul Rodriguez**

It's time that African-Americans and Korean-Americans put aside their differences and focus on what's really important: hating white people!

—**Margaret Cho**

This is how Cheech and Chong, whose financial successes outstripped that of every other comedy team in film history, described their type of humor:

 Our jokes may be fifty years old, but our audience, the youth, ain't seen shit. To them, it's brand new. If you're white, you can be afraid of people of different color, religious fanatics, but if you're black or brown, you're afraid of other things, like starvation and not having a place to live. By incorporating the basic humor of drugs and poverty into our appeal, it makes it universal—the underdogs against the world. We know the humor of the rough and ready ... we pander to the worst instincts in people—caricaturing swishy gays, dumb blondes, illiterate Mexicans, greedy Jews. We're shameless panderers.

Redd Foxx bragged about his material being "as outrageous as possible. That's the humor I hear in the ghettos. We don't pull punches, and we don't want to hear about Little Blue Boy and Cinderella—and if they don't like my shit, they can fuck off!" The following story, which often reappears as an urban legend, illustrates how ethnic humor can be turned against the majority.

 Four doctors' wives from a small Midwestern city decided to brave a weekend shopping trip in Manhattan. Their husbands were apprehensive about city crime. "If someone wants your pocketbook or jewelry, don't put up a fight. Just do what they say. Promise?"

On their very first morning, as the four were descending in the hotel elevator, a well-dressed black man got on leading a large Doberman pinscher. He looked at the women for a moment, and then commanded the dog, "Sit!" Immediately the four women sat on the floor.

Each writer has his own definition of humor. Shakespeare said, "Brevity is the soul of wit." Somerset Maugham wrote, "Impropriety is the soul of wit." But the soul of wit may just be hostility. When we all think alike, there will be a lot less humor.

## SHOWTIME

Sigmund Freud described depression as anger turned inward. Humor might be viewed as anger turned into profit. Hostility underlies humor, so tapping into your anger is an excellent tool for generating ideas for jokes (and it's less expensive than therapy).

Make a list of people, things, and topics that you feel hostile about. Freely associate, don't censure yourself, and write down why each target is frustrating. Exaggerate your emotional state to the point of being PO'd and fully vent your anger about the target. This exercise can narrow the focus of each target to a specific premise that will be a springboard for writing humor (not venting hot air!).

## REALISM: RAISE YOUR SITES

The third component in the THREES formula for humor is realism. "Most good jokes state a bitter truth," said scriptwriter Larry Gelbart. Without some fundamental basis of truth, there's little with which the audience can associate. But jokes also bend the truth, and the challenge is to learn how to tell the truth (be realistic) while lying (exaggerating).

Since it appears that exaggeration is the logical antithesis of realism, it may seem ludicrous to have both within the framework of one piece of humor. But good humor is a paradox—the unexpected juxtaposition of the reasonable next to the unreasonable—and that creates surprise. Think of the combination of realism and exaggeration as an exercise in lateral thinking, a technique commonly used by business gurus to solve problems and generate new ideas. It's defined as an interruption in the habitual thought process, a leap sideways out of ingrained patterns. Comedy has been doing this for thousands of years.

 Supreme Court Justice Sandra O'Connor went with the other justices to a restaurant for lunch. The waiter asked for her order first. "I'll have a steak sandwich and coffee."

"What about the vegetables?" asked the waiter. O'Connor said, "Oh, they'll have the same."

The basic two-step in humor is to (a) state some common problem, frequently with a cliché, and (b) create an unexpected ending or surprise.

 If you've never wanted to kill your mate, you've never been in love. If you've never held a box of rat poison in your hand and stared at it for a good long while, you've never been in love.
—**Chris Rock**

Incongruous humor, as you may remember from chapter two, is based on the premise of two or more realistic (but contrasting) circumstances united in one thought. Humorist Stephen Leacock wrote, "Humor results from the contrast between a thing as it is and ought to be, and a thing smashed out of shape, as it ought not to be."

 If the world is normal, then how come hot dogs come in packages of ten and hot dog buns come in packages of eight?
—**Robert Wohl**

Dorothy Parker once wrote, "The difference between wit and wisecracking is that wit has truth to it, while wisecracking is simply calisthenics with words." (So, realism fathers truisms, those witty bits of philosophy based upon self-evident and generally accepted facts of life.)

 To entertain some people, all you have to do is listen. But there is nothing quite so annoying as having someone go on talking when you're interrupting.
—**Robert Orben**

The value of realism becomes even more evident when you consider the humor of children. Their combination of truth and simplistic naïveté delights grown-ups because it gives us a feeling of benevolent superiority—if, as is said about benevolent dictatorship, there is such a thing.

 A grandmother was babysitting her four-year-old granddaughter. They both had hazel eyes, so the grandmother proudly asked, "Debbie, do you know where your eyes came from?" The child thought for a moment and answered, "Yes, Grandma, they came with my head."

To be most effective, the "facts" of humor should be logical—the relationship between people should be clear and predictable, the time and the locale of the story should be familiar, the hostility should be common to all the audience members and commensurate to the irritation. Major deviations from reality don't prevent humor, but they may reduce the payoff of uninhibited laughter. In essence, then, humor should be as realistic as possible.

 A priest in New York City was arrested on gun possession. These days, you better be happy that the bulge in his pocket is a .38.

**—David Letterman**

## EXAGGERATION: TALKING UP A STORM

We've already begun discussing exaggeration, the fourth element in the THREES formula for humor. How does realism relate to exaggeration? As we accept poetic license, let's accept a humor license that grants permission to expand on realistic themes with soaring imagination and unabashed metaphors. Audiences rarely counter a joke that the performer has made personal with an admonition "You don't expect me to believe that?"

Only for humor is the public willing to suspend disbelief and skepticism. We permit humorists to utilize hyperbole, blatant distortion, and overstated figures that signal (since the absurd subject matter can't possibly be true): *Hey, it's only a joke.* Therefore, the audience laughs at exaggerated banana-peel acrobatics because the clown will certainly get up. That's comedy! If he doesn't get up, that's tragedy!

An example of the *likely* next to the *unlikely* is the classic story about the newspaper that ran two photos: one of a gray-haired matron who'd just been elected president of the local Women's Republican Club and the other of a gorilla who was a new addition to the local zoo—but the captions got switched. That's *likely*. The second stage of the humor comes from the *unlikely*: The newspaper got sued for defamation—by the gorilla!

## EMOTION: BURST THE BUBBLE

The fifth element in the THREES formula is emotion. Hostility, over- or understated, is not enough. There must be a buildup of anticipation in the audience. This is really nothing more than the writer's skill in using emotion to produce tension and anxiety. It's a trick. Think of hostility as an inflated balloon. When you create tension in your audience, you are effectively adding more and more air to that balloon, building the audience's anticipation over when the balloon will burst. They can hardly keep their eyes off the stunt. The writer's goal is to see that the balloon bursts with laughter, not hot air.

Each performer has a stage personality, called a *persona* or *shtick*. While others can steal material, they can't steal the nuances that make one individual funny. (And an ineffective persona can make a performer unable to tell even a well-written joke). Humorist Larry Wilde said, "There is a melody and cadence to all comedy that is as stringent and disciplined as music."

A great comedic performer must be an actor with boundless energy. The qualities that make a good comedian are over and above those that make a good actor. Many comedians have become good actors in films and sitcoms, but you rarely hear of a good actor becoming a great comedian. In the movie *The Entertainer*, Sir Laurence Olivier played the part of a small-time comic. It was a brilliant, award-winning performance, and when Olivier was asked how he managed to make the comic look so inept, he replied, "I didn't try to do him badly. I played the role as well as I could." Even the best actor may be a flop as a comedian.

The ability to generate emotion is the ability of the speaker to translate the writer's material into entertainment through voice, enthusiasm, and action. The ability to create emotion is also experience: knowing when to pause and for how long, creating a rhythm with inflection, and sometimes nothing more grandiose than making a gesture—called a take, because it *takes* the right gesture.

Woody Allen discovered that "stand-up is a funny man doing material, not a man doing funny material. The personality, the character—not the joke—is primary."

## QUESTION & ANSWER

### HOW DO YOU BUILD EMOTION?

1. The first and most common technique for building emotion is also the simplest—pausing just before the payoff word. This pause is called a *pregnant pause* because it promises to deliver. Even in Henny Youngman's classic, "Take my wife—please!" the slight pause indicated by the dash is essential to the reading of that line. (Try to read it any other way!) The pregnant pause creates tension, which is relieved by the surprise ending.

 I know you want to hear the latest dope from Washington. Well—here I am.

**—Senator Alan Simpson**

Would you be so kind as to help a poor, unfortunate fellow out of work, hungry, in fact someone who has nothing in this world—except this gun!

2. The second technique for generating emotion is asking the audience members a question, thereby encouraging them to become involved. This was one of Johnny Carson's favorite devices.

Anybody see this commercial on TV last night? It claims you can send a letter from anywhere in the country to New York for seven dollars and fifty cents, and it promises next-day delivery. The Post Office calls it Express Mail. I remember when it used to be called the U.S. Mail.

Remember how hot it was yesterday? Well a dog was chasing a cat, and they were both walking.

A common technique used by novice stand-up comics to infuse tension is to ask the audience, "How many here have ever ...?" It's become its own cliché, and the take-offs are even more fun.

 How many here went to grade school?
How many here paid to get in?

3. The third technique is called a build, which is a joke that leads to a joke that leads to another joke. Ultimately, the jokes work together to prepare the audience for one big blast.

4. The fourth way to build emotional tension is by working the audience—a favorite device of today's stand-up comedians. The performer walks out into the audience and throws questions at (what appear to be) randomly selected members. Tension builds in each audience member not from amazement that the comic is able to come up with toppers to every answer, but from the fear that he or she may be the next victim of the performer's ridicule.

Every playwright builds emotion into a scene. A humor writer does the same thing, but because you're working with much smaller units—sometimes just a joke of a few words—you must be able to accomplish more with less. Good humor writers are like professional card cheats. They know how to palm the joker and insert it only when it's needed. When their act is too evident to the audience, they fail— and it ain't pretty.

## SURPRISE: NOBODY KNOWS THE STUMBLES I'VE SEEN

The final element in the THREES formula is surprise. In the previous chapter, we discussed surprise as one of the primary reasons why people laugh. It's no wonder then that it's also one of the primary building blocks for a successful joke. Charlie Chaplin defined surprise in terms of a film scene in which the villain is chasing the heroine down the street. On the sidewalk is a banana peel. The camera cuts swiftly back and forth from the banana peel to the approaching villain. At the last second, the heavy sees the banana peel and jumps over it—and then falls into an open manhole.

It's easy to tell if your surprise works, because a live audience's instant laughter is the most honest of emotions. You can give a bad speech, a poor theatrical or musical performance, and the audience will still politely applaud. If you perform bad humor, you'll get nothing but icy silence (just a preliminary to unsolicited post-show advice).

No matter how well written, jokes don't come off in performance if the comedian telegraphs the surprise. Many performers tip off the audience to the funny line with a lick of their lips or a gleam in their eyes. They hold up their hands and stop the audience from laughing all out ("Hey, listen to this!"), and they prime the audience for a big topper. But then there's no surprise, and no laughter. This can have a domino effect: The performer loses confidence in the material, then starts to press, then loses other laughs because the audience has a sixth sense about *flop sweat*—when a performer is trying too hard.

"Comedy is mentally pulling the rug out from under each person in your audience," wrote Gene Perret. "But first, you have to get them to stand on it. You have to fool them, because if they see you preparing to tug on the rug, they'll move."

 Two roads diverged in a wood and I took the road less traveled by ... state troopers.

## SHOWTIME

Let's see how the entire THREES formula (*target, hostility, realism, exaggeration, emotion,* and a *surprise* ending) works in a story. Identify which parts of the story below correspond with each component of the THREES formula. (At the end of the story, you can rate your answers).

 An elderly truck driver was eating lunch at a roadside diner when three shaggy young hoodlums, sporting black leather jackets garishly decorated with swastikas, skulls, and crossbones, parked their motorcycles and came inside. They spotted the truck driver and proceeded to taunt him, taking his food away, pushing him off the seat, and insulting his old age. He said nothing, but finally got up from the floor, paid his bill, and walked out. One of the bikers, unhappy that they hadn't provoked a fight, said to the waitress, "Boy, he sure wasn't much of a man, was he?" "No," said the waitress, looking out the window, "and he's not much of a truck driver either. He just backed his truck over three motorcycles!"

Did the THREES formula work for the above story? Yes, because the humor contained each of the major components.

**T = TARGET:** The hoodlums, carefully described.

**H = HOSTILITY:** The story exploits public frustration at the escalation of juvenile crime.

**R = REALISM:** There's little doubt that the aggressive actions of the bikers could happen.

**E = EXAGGERATION:** One motorcyclist would have worked, but an element of exaggeration is achieved by including three. Their crude behavior is exemplified not just once, but with three incidents of hostile action. Exaggeration is also present in the truck driver's final action—not a simple thing to do quickly.

**E = EMOTION:** The joke is carefully written to squeeze out every drop of audience hostility: the stereotypical fascist appearance of the bikers, their childish aggression meant just to provoke a fight with an outnumbered, aged opponent. We even feel disappointment when the truck driver appears—for a moment—to be a coward.

**S = SURPRISE:** The climax of the story is withheld until the last two words.

# PART TWO

## Humor Writing Techniques

# CHAPTER 4
## POW: Play on Words

 My wife made me join a bridge club. I jump off next week.

**—Rodney Dangerfield**

Where do jokes come from? Well, funny things do happen to us every once in a while. If we're extroverts, we dramatically recount the bizarre experiences with exaggerated overtones. We get laughs. And we think we're funny.

But professional humorists can't wait for absurd things to happen. They have to produce every day. Two popular ways of doing this are by revamping old material, and by creating new humor from ideas sparked by local, national, or world news.

As a beginner, you can't depend on joke files even if you've got a copy of every joke book written—and dozens of new ones come out every year. Other comics' jokes will rarely fit you. You have to subscribe to the second method: creating jokes from scratch. You start by watching the antics of people in public, on TV, and in films, and you read about them in news stories. You imagine *what-if* situations, and you play with words.

 I just broke up with someone, and the last thing she said to me was, "You'll never find anybody like me again." And I was thinking: I should hope not. Isn't that why we break up with people? If I don't want you, why would I want somebody just like you? Does anybody end a bad relationship and say, "By the way, do you have a twin?"

**—Larry Miller**

More than 50 percent of all humor is based on plays on words (POWs). The POW acronym is reminiscent of a sound effect in superhero comics, and a POW does pack a punch—and a punchline. A POW is a twist on a familiar cliché; aphorism; book, movie, or song title; famous quote; national ad slogan—in fact, any expression widely known by the public. It can make use of double entendres, homonyms, or puns. A humorist twist to the aphorism *The way to a man's heart is through his stomach* is:

 The quickest way to a man's heart is through his chest.

**—Roseanne Barr**

Unlike slapstick humor (which is strictly physical and therefore appeals across cultural and linguistic boundaries), the success of written and performed comedy based on POWs depends on the performer's mannerisms and inflections and the audience's knowledge of the nuances of the language. Punchlines in one language are rarely effective in another.

The POW is a device used by all humor writers, and any successful work of humor will contain a significant number of POWs. Plays on words are the basis of practically all puns, limericks, and clever witticisms. They run the gamut from childish idioms to erudite double entendres. POW practitioners have included S.J. Perelman ("One of our stage-craft is missing," and "Stringing Up Father") and Tom Stoppard ("I have the courage of my lack of convictions"). Writing POW comedy lines is as second nature for humorists as tying their shoelaces.

A common misperception is that plays on words are "old-school" humor. But while POW humor may be considered classic, it certainly can't be considered stale. The successful Austin Powers movies (one of the most successful comedy film franchises in recent years) rely heavily on POWs for character names like Alotta Fagina and Random Task (spoofs of Goldfinger's Pussy Galore and Oddjob), Fook Mi, Fook Yu, and Robin Spitz Swallows.

In George Carlin's three best-selling books—*Brain Droppings, Napalm & Silly Putty,* and *When Will Jesus Bring the Pork Chops?*—POWs account for a large percentage of the humor. Carlin is one of the most serious linguists in comedy. Examples of Carlin's POWs include:

 **UNNECESSARY WORDS**

emergency situation (emergency alone is sufficient)

boarding process (boarding can be used alone as a noun)

**EUPHEMISMS**

uniforms = career apparel

prostitute = commercial sex worker

**MOCK SELF-HELP AND ADVICE BOOK TITLES**

*Where to Hide a Really Big Snot*

*I Suck, You Suck*

*Mock Punk Band Names*

*Tower of Swine*

*Warts, Waffles, and Walter*

Over the next few chapters, we'll explain some of the most important POW techniques.

1. A *double entendre* is the use of an ambiguous word or phrase that allows for a second—usually racy—interpretation.

2. A *malaprop* is the unintentional misstatement or misuse of a word or phrase, or the accidental substitution of an incorrect word for the correct one, with humorous results. Malaprops are effective in part because they allow the audience to feel superior. Malaprops can incorporate clichés and double entendres.

3. An *oxymoron* is a joining of two incompatible ideas in one phrase. It can also be called a contradiction in terms.

4. A *pun* is a word used in such a way that two or more of the word's possible meanings are active simultaneously. A pun may also be a reformation of a word to a like-sounding word that is not an exact homonym.

5. *Reforming* is a process that adds a twist or a surprise ending to a cliché (a predictable, hackneyed phrase) or a common word, phrase, or expression. Other POW techniques, such as double entendres and puns, rely heavily on reforming.

6. The *simple truth* is the opposite of a double entendre. It plays on the literal meaning of a key word in an idiomatic phrase (and will be discussed in the next chapter).

7. The *take-off* is a statement of the standard version of a cliché or expression, followed by a realistic but highly exaggerated commentary, frequently a double entendre. (Take-offs will also be discussed in a later chapter.)

## CLICHÉS IN HUMOR

A cliché is an expression that was clever once but has lost its original impact through overuse. Some people salt every dish, whether it requires salt or not. Clichés are used just as frequently (and indiscriminately). They are sprinkled liberally into every conversation, every letter, every political speech, and (unfortunately) in too many major literary efforts. They're shortcuts to comprehension that we use when we are creatively lazy or mentally bankrupt. But the humor writer uses audacious and surprising interpretations of clichés to shock an audience into laughter.

 I've heard that dogs are man's best friend. That explains where men are getting their hygiene tips.

**—Kelly Maguire**

Laugh, and the world laughs with you. Cry, and the world laughs at you.

**—Caryn Leschen**

A cliché can be reformed with homonyms—words that look or sound the same but have different meanings. In the one-liner below, the humor works when *vein* is aptly substituted for *vain* in the cliché *in vain*. However, it only works in print.

 I tried to give up heroin, but my efforts were all in vein.

**—George Carlin**

Clichés are perfect launch vehicles for the neophyte humor writer because one-liners are the most salable humor form today. Simple cliché humor can be put to immediate use in a wide variety of formats, including photo and cartoon captions, greeting cards, news and advertising headlines, bumper stickers (a rear view of pop culture), titles of books and articles, and monologues.

Frequently, a cliché is used to set the audience's train of thought in motion—so the humorist can derail it. Since the ending phrase of a cliché is predictable, the audience's thoughts head in a predictable direction. The key word here is *predictable*. The easiest way to achieve surprise is to use a vehicle that takes the audience for a ride in a predictable direction—a direction you will change at the last possible moment. It's a last-second switch in the anticipated verbal conclusion. The result is surprise, which produces laughter, the payoff of all comedic effort. As you'll see shortly, there are a number of formulas for altering a cliché so that its final direction surprises the reader or listener.

 Every night I had a strange girl. Same girl—she was just strange.
**—Michael Davis**

In the above example, the audience initially interprets strange to mean "different." The surprise comes when the comedian reveals that the literal meaning of strange is intended.

 When people ask me if I see too much sex in the movies,
I tell them, how should I know? I watch the film, not the audience.
**—Mel Helitzer**

Sex and violence in film and TV is a sensitive topic, so the audience naturally assumes this is what is under discussion in this example. The surprise comes by interpreting the phrase "in the movies" to mean "in the movie theater."

## THE DOUBLE ENTENDRE: AWAY WITH WORDS

*Double entendre* is the French term for an ambiguous word or phrase that allows for a second—usually spicy—interpretation. Double entendres are 40 percent of all cliché humor because they're so easy to construct. Consider these names and slogans.

Tennis store advertisement: What's Your Racquet?

Sign over urinal: Look before you leak.

Art supplies advertisement: Honest, I Was Framed!

The logic behind double entendre humor is as basic as its English translation: two meanings. The audience assumes one meaning; the comic sneaks in another.

 Irving made a lot of money one year in the garment business and decided to buy a racehorse. One day he brought all his friends to the stable as the vet was laboriously working on the horse.

"Is my horse sick?" asked Irving.

"She's not the picture of health," said the vet, "but we'll pull her through."

"Will I ever be able to race her?"

"Chances are you will—and you'll probably beat her, too!"

**—Myron Cohen**

In the above example, the success of the joke relies on the double interpretation of the word *race*. Irving wants to know if the horse will be able to race other horses. The vet comments that Irving himself would win a race against the horse.

Three of the four words in the expression *wire ahead for reservations* have multiple meanings. (This phrase has been replaced in common usage by *call ahead for reservations*, but most people would still instinctively understand its meaning.) By imagining *what-if* scenarios and performing mental calisthenics, the humor writer can recast this common phrase with double entendres.

 The Sioux tribe sent one of their brightest young men to engineering school. After graduating, he returned home and was immediately assigned to install electric lights in all the latrines, so he became famous for being the first Indian to wire a head for reservations.

As new expressions come into the vernacular, the professional humor writer looks for every opportunity to play around with words—the most socially acceptable form of playing around.

We call our maid a commercial cleaner, because she cleans only during commercials.

Be forewarned! Amateurs make the mistake of thinking that, since double entendres are so plentiful, they are easy to cultivate. But you must evaluate them as you would plants at a nursery—if you don't choose carefully, you may wind up with a garden of crabgrass. And there is a second danger to the use of double entendres: They are so often used in humor that even unsophisticated audiences can predict a punchline if it has been telegraphed by the comedian. If the double entendre isn't well hidden, there's no surprise.

### Creating Double Entendres: A Dime a Dozen

The most popular double entendre is the word *it*, which can be used to mean a hundred different things, but is used most often in humor as a synonym for intercourse. For example, *Librarians do it with books*, or *Lawyers do it in their briefs*.

 MC, after bombing with a sexist joke: Boy, am I going to get it when I get home. Or maybe I'm not going to get it when I get home.

The second most common double entendre is the word *in*, which also has an obvious sexual connotation.

 "Isn't it great to be in June?"
"Yes, but her sister, Barbara, was even better."

## KEEPING IT CLEAN

Since the second meaning of a double entendre is frequently considered risqué, broadcast censors examine every word in a script. Mel Helitzer once spent six months arguing with a representative of the National Association of Broadcasters' TV code department for permission to use the jingle line "Two in the bathtub is more fun than one" for a washable doll called Rub-a-Dub Dolly. The censor, an attractive twenty-five-year-old (who, unfortunately, had a five-second broad-cast delay built in to her mind), tried to nix the line with a challenge to its veracity: "Can you prove that two in the bathtub is more fun than one?" Helitzer looked at her for a moment and then said, "You know, I have a wonderful idea!"

The second meaning of the key word or phrase of a double entendre does not have to be racy or sexual.

 He was a millionaire golfer, so he used his chauffeur as his driver.

One man walking his dog met a friend on the street who admired his pet.

"I just bought him for fifteen hundred dollars," said the owner.

"Isn't that a lot of money for a mutt?" his friend asked.

"Why, he's not a mutt! He's part Airedale and part bull."

"Yeah, what part is bull?"

"The part about the fifteen hundred dollars."

More sophisticated forms of double entendre make use of irony and sarcasm. Irony is notoriously difficult to define (though there seems to be a general agreement that, despite Alanis Morissette's words to the contrary, rain on your wedding day is not ironic). For the purposes of the current discussion, irony is a statement that is the opposite of what is intended. Sarcasm is defined similarly, but sarcasm usually has more of a bite, the sting of open ridicule. In an excellent example of irony, Bob Hope once walked into the ward of a military hospital and shouted to the wounded GIs, "Please, don't get up!"

Irony can be expressed in many ways, but it's often the result of evoking an absurd meaning from a standard phrase.

 Hillary Clinton said she once got a dog for Bill. She said it was the best deal she ever made.

## EVERYBODY SHOULDN'T DO IT: OBSCENE LANGUAGE AND DOUBLE ENTENDRES

Many funny double entendres are made up of words that have a sexual connotation. There are endless possibilities—all obvious. Through frequent use, some double entendres that were originally shocking—such as he sucks—have become acceptable. Richard Pryor popularized making mother half a word in an act that still represents one of the greatest creative performances in contemporary comedy. And often, a play on the double meaning of a word can lead to powerful spontaneous humor, as illustrated by a classic interview on *The Tonight Show*.

 Zsa Zsa Gabor appeared as a guest while holding one of her prized felines. As she was sitting there, she suddenly turned to Johnny Carson and asked, "Would you like to pet my pussy?"

"Sure," said Carson, "but first move the cat."

Given the abundance of double entendres with sexual connotations, beginning humor writers often abuse them through overuse. The professional humorist recognizes that the problem is not to find them but avoid them. They're just too easy a joke. Many audiences think they are adolescent and cheap—a sign of an amateur.

We'll take a closer look at obscenity in humor in chapter eleven.

## SHOWTIME

As a warm-up exercise, let's do it: Practice the art of double entendres with the word *it*. Complete the following sentences, then compare your responses to those at the end of the chapter.

- Comedians do it …
- Dancers do it …
- Bankers do it …
- Math teachers do it …
- Publishers do it …
- Carpet layers do it …
- Bowlers do it …

## MALAPROPS: AN ERROR OF THEIR WEIGHS

A malaprop (sometimes called a malapropism) is an unintentional misstatement or misuse of a word or phrase, or an accidental substitution of an incorrect word for a (similar) correct one—to humorous effect. These examples of twisted language only qualify as malaprops if the person speaking them is unaware (or appears to be unaware) of the mistake. Malaprops were the staple of George Burns and Gracie Allen's comedic act for more than thirty years and were used abundantly by various sitcom characters from Archie Bunker of *All in the Family* to Joey of *Friends*. Today, entertainment columns are good sources of celebrity witticisms-turned-malaprops. Publicity agents, when they can't find something positive to say about their clients, create modified clichés that turn into malaprops. Movie mogul Samuel Goldwyn was quoted in the entertainment columns so often with examples of mistaken grammar that a malaprop became known as a *Goldwynism*.

 A verbal contract isn't worth the paper it's printed on.
Every Tom, Dick and Harry is named William.
Include me out.

Baseball managers Casey Stengel and Yogi Berra were credited with malaprops that helped to cemented their immortality in reference books.

 You wouldn't have won if we had.
**—Yogi Berra**

If people don't want to come to the ballpark, nobody can stop them.

**—Casey Stengel**

Baseball is 90 percent mental. The other half is physical.

**—Yogi Berra**

That restaurant is so popular, nobody goes there anymore.

**—Yogi Berra**

Humorists bless politicians who make their jobs easy by fracturing the English language, as did former Vice President Dan Quayle. His malaprops include:

 If we do not succeed, then we run the risk of failure.

What a waste it is to lose one's mind. Or not to have a mind is being very wasteful. How true that is. (A malaprop based on the United Negro College Fund slogan A Mind Is a Terrible Thing to Waste.)

It isn't pollution that's harming the environment. It's the impurities in our air and water that are doing it.

President George W. Bush's habit of misspeaking spawned several books' worth of malaprops known as Bushisms. They include:

 Rarely is the question asked: Is our children learning.

They misunderestimated me.

I promise you I will listen to what has been said here, even though I wasn't here.

A time-honored rule in comedy is never to do more than three jokes on one topic, and some comedy writers will argue that two is plenty. The same rule applies to using the same technique several times within one joke, as in the next example. The following radio commercial for City National Bank in Los Angeles uses the malaprop technique seven times, holding the audience's interest through the cute twist at the end.

 **[PHONE RINGS]**

**YOUNG DAUGHTER:** Smith residence.

**FATHER:** Hi ya, sport. Let me talk to Mom.

**DAUGHTER:** Hey, Mom! It's Dad.

**MOTHER:** Ask him what he wants, hon. I've got my hands in dishwater.

**DAUGHTER:** What do you want, Dad? Mom's got her hands in fish water.

**FATHER:** Just tell her I've been to City National.

**DAUGHTER:** He's been pretty bashful, Mom.

**MOTHER:** What about?

**DAUGHTER:** What about?

**FATHER:** About the trust.

**DAUGHTER:** About the truss.

**MOTHER:** Truss? What truss?

**DAUGHTER:** Which one?

**FATHER:** The life insurance trust, kiddo. The one from City National.

**DAUGHTER:** The lighting shirt's truss, Mom.

**MOTHER:** The lighting shirt's truss?

**FATHER:** The one that keeps the tax man from being one of my beneficiaries.

**DAUGHTER:** The one that keeps the Pac-Man from eating bony fishes.

**MOTHER:** Ask him what in the world he's talking about, honey.

**DAUGHTER:** What in the world are you talking about, Dad?

**ANNOUNCER:** Come in and talk to a City National trust officer. We'll show you how a truss can protect your lighting shirts.

**DAUGHTER:** That's "life insurance."

Note that malaprops give the audience a chance to mock the speaker's confusion with English, and thereby feel superior. As you remember, the feeling of superiority is a prime motivator for laughter.

---

## OXYMORONS: PRETTY UGLY

Another category of incongruous expressions goes by the suggestive name of oxymoron—an oxymoron is a contradiction in terms that provides a gold mine of humor material, particularly for greeting cards and T-shirt copy. Consider the following.

- found missing
- living dead
- good grief
- working vacation
- larger half
- soft rock
- extinct life
- Microsoft Works
- plastic glasses
- alone together
- exact estimate
- taped live
- small crowd
- even odds

## SHOWTIME

Words are the instruments of humorists, and mastering the subtleties of language is a necessary step to becoming a successful humor writer. Use the following exercises to practice your POWs.

- Search a dictionary for ten words that you do not know the definitions for. Don't look at the definitions! Write each word on an index card, and on the back of the card, create a logical but whimsical definition.
- Search the Internet for clichés, proverbs, or common phrases that relate to the potential humor targets you identified in the last chapter. Compile a list of ten items. Using the techniques described in this

chapter, reform the clichés into jokes by changing the original ending or adding on to the phrase.

Writing humor starts with an audience of one. If your goal is to write commercially successful humor, you must expand your audience. To begin testing your writing, use e-mail to showcase your material. Many people attach to their e-mail messages something called a signature, which contains contact information, a quote, or a "thought of the day." Instead of relying on the words of others, you can punch up your e-mail messages using the exercises you just completed.

- Use your fictitious definitions for a "word of the day."
- Attribute your reformed clichés to a celebrity to create a "quote of the day."
- Reform famous quotations and credit new authors for the quotes. For example, transform Freud's famous line *Sometimes a cigar is just a cigar* to a Bill Clinton quote: *Sometimes a cigar is more than a cigar.*
- Create a series of fictitious names (I. M. Sane, Anita Prozac) to use as the authors of your clichés, definitions, or quotes.

## A BARREL OF PUN

A pun is created from the intentional confusion of similar-sounding words or phrases. Puns, which overlap with double entendres and homonyms, can be used as the basis for a joke or to reform an expression or cliché. They work better when spoken or heard than they do in print, because the ear transmits to the mind the most familiar interpretation of each word. (Actually, *here* is one of the most popular words to use, because it can sound like *hear, hair,* and *hare*: *An adolescent rabbit is a pubic hare. Hair today, gone tomorrow.*)

Puns are very versatile and can be used in a number of formats. They can take the form of riddles.

What do you call a smelly chicken?
A foul fowl.

What does a grape say when you step on it?
Nothing. It just gives a little whine.

Or they can be simple quips.

 Asphalt, another word for rectal problems.

With friends like you, who needs enemas?

She was chaste, very chaste. Of course, sometimes they caught her, too.

**—Norm Crosby**

Often, several puns can be made around the same topic. Here's how Halloween-themed puns would sound in a dialogue between two phantoms.

 "Witch way ghost thou?"
"My house."
"Haunted?"
"Of corpse."
"Howl you go?"
"Broom."
"May I ghoul along?"
"Sure. Always broom for one more."
"What'll I wear?"
"Shroud."
"Why?"
"Because behind every shroud is a shiver lining."
"Sounds frightfully expensive."
"Ya' gotta take scare of yourself, Halloween."

Notice that, in the above example, the puns were based on near homonyms, reformed words that sound similar to the original, but are not exact homonyms: *howl* for *how will*, *broom* for *room*.

Puns can also be used to create "daffy definitions."

What's a Fahrenheit? A moderately tall person.

What's an ICBM? Eskimo doo-doo.

What's an infantry? A very young sapling.

What's fireproof? A tenured professor.

Content: Where prisoners sleep while on a camping trip.

Detail: The act of removing a tail.

Arbitrator: An Arby's cook who leaves to work for McDonald's.

Eyedropper: A clumsy ophthalmologist.

Some puns can seem pretty obvious, but they're not easy to create from scratch. It is said of second-rate comedians that they know a good joke when they steal one. If you practice enough, it becomes instinctive to look for words that can form double entendres or that have homonyms or near homonyms.

For example, try reforming words using homonyms from one subject group (like fish names), just for the pun of it. Next, use your puns to create reformed clichés or standalone jokes. (Did you hear about the Norwegian who brought his harpoon to Israel because he knew he'd be visiting the Wailing Wall?) Or string all the puns together in one sentence: I got a haddock herring that tuna blow "salmon chanted eel-ing" and, upon my sole, he did it on porpoise.

## SHOWTIME

Many newspapers, magazines, and Web sites hold POW contests in which readers are asked to submit entries. The *Washington Post*'s annual contest requires readers to select any word from a standard dictionary; change, add, or delete only one letter; and then provide a new definition. (This type of construction, popularized in books by Rich Hall, is often called a sniglet.)

Here are some submissions from the *Washington Post*'s contest (without accompanying definitions). Change, add, or delete one letter in each of the following words, then write a definition for the new word. (The reformed words and definitions originally submitted by *Washington Post* readers are listed at the end of the chapter.)

- foreplay
- sarcasm
- inoculate
- hepatitis
- libido
- ignoramus

## REFORMING

An invaluable POW technique, reforming is the process of altering a word, expression, phrase, or cliché to arrive at a twist that cleverly changes the point of view. There are several ways to reform a cliché or expression.

**1. TRANSPOSE WORDS.** The first way to reform a phrase or cliché is to transpose the words to create a new, related thought. Drama critic Walter Winchell did this in a review of a season opener: "Who am I to stone the first cast?" Then there's the classic drug joke: "I'm not as think as you stoned I am."

**2. REPLACE A FEW LETTERS IN A KEY WORD.** The second and most frequent type of reforming is replacing one or two letters in a key word of an expression in order to achieve a surprise turn of phrase.

 I will not cut off my nose to spite my race.

**—Golda Meir**

**3. USE A HOMONYM.** The third way to reform a cliché is to use a homonym, a similar-sounding word with a second possible interpretation. Reforming with homonyms often creates double entendres or puns, as in restaurant names like *Wok 'n Roll, Mustard's Last Stand, Blazing Salads*, and *Aesop's Tables*.

That restaurant inspired the TV show *That's Inedible!*

The things my wife buys at antique auctions are keeping me *baroque.*

**—Peter De Vries**

### Homonyms and Fractured Clichés

Homonyms are strictly defined as words that are spelled and pronounced alike, but that are different in meaning (*bore a hole* vs. *bore someone to death*). However, homophones (words pronounced alike but spelled differently, like *bough* and *bow*) and homographs (words spelled alike that differ in meaning or pronunciation, like *bow* in *tie a bow* and *bow and arrow*) often fall under the rubric of homonym.

Homonyms are particularly popular in print advertisements, T-shirts, signs, and store names. The bumper sticker "I owe. I owe. It's off to work I go!" uses a homonym effectively, as do the following store names.

 Fishing supplies: Master Bait and Tackle

Towing service: Dyno-Mite Hooker

Glass repair: A Pain in the Glass

Here are some homonyms as signs.

 Bird Food—Cheep

Boats for Sail

Lenten Special—Filets of Soul

Your Money Tearfully Refunded

In skits and humorous short stories, you'll often find homonyms and puns in character names.

 Air traffic controller: Ulanda U. Lucky

Customer care representative: Kurt Reply

Funeral director: Hadley Newham

Compassion coordinator: Ophelia Paine

Copyright attorney: Pat Pending

Dessert chef: Tyra Meesu

Dry cleaner: Preston Creases

Loan officer: I.O. Silver

There's no limit to the number of POWs you can have in one sentence. In fact, the paired word humor form (which will be discussed in greater detail in chapter twelve) requires two homonyms in one joke.

 Then there's the overweight jogger who ignored advice and panted himself into a coroner.

**—Bert Murray**

Definition of a stockyard: flesh in the pen.

**—Robert Fitch**

Do under others as you would have them do under you.

No nukes is good nukes.

Some newspaper bloopers—known as typos—form serendipitous puns.

 Our paper carried the notice last week that Mr. Herman Jones is a defective in the police force. This was a typographical error. Mr. Jones, of course, is a detective on the police farce.

*—The Ootlewah Times*

**(Tennessee)**

One common reform process using homonyms is called *split-reforming*. Split reforming involves separating—or fracturing—one word into two to get a surprise double meaning.

 An eighty-six-year-old lady was being interviewed by the quizmaster on TV. "You look wonderful," he said.

"Yes," said the old lady, "I've never had a sick day in my life."

The MC was astonished. "You've never been bedridden even once?" he asked.

The old lady said, "Oh, many times. And three times in the haystack."

One of the most common split-reforms begins with a word that starts with the letter *a* (*alone, around, abreast, abroad, apparent, apiece, ahead*). The initial *a* is detached, and the second half of the word is allowed to stand alone.

Two partners on a sinking boat are thrown into the sea.

"Can you float alone?" one asks the other.

"I'm drowning," says the other partner, "and he's talking business."

**—Larry Wilde**

This example not only illustrates split-reforming but also uses *loan* as a homonym of *lone*. Note that the success of the joke depends on the audience, when it hears *alone*, interpreting the word to mean *on your own*. In writing, this joke succeeds because you read *alone*, and the alternate meaning doesn't occur to you until the last few words of the joke.

 "Would you like to play around?" the young man asked his girlfriend.

"Are you asking that as a lover or as a golfer?" she replied.

The first line in the above example could be written as it appears here, or with a split-reform as *Would you like to play a round?* If you were already talking about golf or were addressing an audience of golfers, the audience would probably infer that you meant *a round*. In that case, you might want to reverse the order of the words *lover* and *golfer* in the last line. Outside the context of golf, however, the audience would probably assume you meant *around*, and the meaning of the split word would not occur to them until after the girlfriend's mention of golf.

 One actor to another: I was abroad myself for two years, but fortunately a psychiatrist fixed me up.

This joke depends on the audience assuming that *abroad* means *overseas*. The split-reform occurs when the audience mentally separates *a* and *broad* after the punchline.

Other common types of split-reform are the addition, deletion, or separation of a prefix (such as *a-*, *an-*, *pre-*, *un-*, and *in-*) from a word.

An elderly man and a woman meet for the first time at a Miami Beach social: "And how's by you the sex?" asks the woman.

"Infrequently," replies the old man.

"Tell me," demands the woman, "is that one word or two?"

**—Myron Cohen**

An atheist is someone who has no invisible means of support.

At Ohio University, students owe so much money they changed the initials of the college from OU to IOU.

**—Mel Helitzer**

Plagiarism: the unoriginal sin.

**—Roy Peter Clark**

Split-reform can include changing suffixes or interpreting suffixes as homonyms (such as -*ize* for *eyes*).

 "Do you want this pasteurized?"

"No! Just up to my mouth'd be fine!"

Split-reform also includes the separation of a compound word into two.

 Juggler to audience: Don't worry. I've got a backup system. Everybody, back up!

Another category of split-reform reinterprets an -*er* ending as the word *her* (*catcher, licker, freezer, player*), or capitalizes on words that begin with the *her* sound (*harass*). Words that contain a *him* sound (*vitamin, Himalayan, hemisphere*) work as well.

 One frosh to another: I can hardly wait to read the book the English prof assigned us—J.D. Salinger's *Catch Her in the Rye.*

"I was a diesel fitter in a shoe store."

"They don't have diesels in shoe stores!"

"Sure they do. I stood around and said, 'Dese'll fit 'er.'"

## SHOWTIME

Think of one of the humor targets you identified in chapter three, and write down some words that relate to that topic. Pick one, and write down as many soundalikes as come to mind. Then write a joke based on these soundalikes.

For example, *hormone* sounds like *whore moan, her moan,* and *harmony*. Now, it's not difficult to write such bits as Tom Padovano's "Hormone could be heard clear across campus," or that old classic "How do you make a hormone? Don't pay her."

Okay, so far so good. But how many homonyms can you make from the following words? Two is fair, four is good, five or more is excellent; if you can't come up with any, take up accounting.

| | |
|---|---|
| • Caesar | • bore |
| • Dewey | • bigamy |
| • Tudor | • maker |
| • read | • hoarse |
| • fowl | • wurst |
| • liquor | • bare |
| • atoll | • Hebrew |
| • Czech | |

## PRINT REFORMS

Because the sound difference in reformed homonyms is so subtle, some puns and reformed clichés work better in print. That's why they're so popular on signs and graffiti. But spoken aloud, they may cause puzzlement in the audience, rather than laughter.

I know a transsexual who only wants to eat, drink and be Mary.

**—George Carlin**

A zebra is twenty-five sizes bigger than an A bra.

Humor writers prefer gag lunches.

Celebrity in snowstorm talking to reporter: If I had a good quote, I'd be wearing it!

The boy had a lot to be spankful for.

Familiarity breeds attempt.

Note from meter maid to ticketed car owner: Parking is such sweet sorrow.

Young boy to star baseball player walking out of DA's office during drug investigation: Say it ain't snow, Joe!

## WRITING A REFORMED CLICHÉ OR EXPRESSION

In the summer of 1985, two Czechoslovakian tennis stars—Ivan Lendl and Hana Mandlikova—won the U.S. Open men's and women's tennis championships, respectively. The fact that they were both Czech gave writers of photo captions, cartoons, headlines, and newscasts a homonym field day.

Imagine you are a newspaper or magazine editor. You have a photo of the two winners, each holding a U.S. Open trophy and a huge prize check. Your assignment is to come up with a photo caption or headline. A POW using homonyms is an obvious choice.

First, write down all the homonyms associated with the sound of the word *Czech*. A sample list would include all those connected with bank checks.

- bounced check
- bad check

- good check
- rubber check
- cashed check
- deposited check
- big check
- paid check
- returned check
- endorsed check
- cancelled check
- the check is in the mail

But the word *check* has many other meanings. The terms *check* and *checkmate* are used in chess. There's the game of *checkers*, and the clichéd expression "check and double check." In ice hockey, one player *body checks* another. In a roll call, one *checks off* names with a *check mark*. You can ask for *separate checks* in a restaurant. And when you've completed this list, be sure to *check it out* completely!

Next, substitute the word *Czech* in all the above expressions and determine if one of the captions or headlines syncs with the specific picture you have. How many different captions can you come up with? (You should be able to generate five to ten possibilities from the above list. For instance, *Czech-mated* or *cashed Czechs*.) Only after examining many possibilities would you select the best one.

It seems like a lot of work for one photo caption. It is. But before long, your mental computer will have a file of all the different possibilities, and you'll be able to call them up at a moment's notice.

Do all those steps really become automatic? To continue the tennis theme, think of all the moves a tennis pro has to make while setting up for a tennis shot. As the ball approaches, he decides to move diagonally forward or backward, left or right. At the same time, he is getting his racket back, planting his feet properly while keeping both eyes on the ball to judge its speed and spin. He now makes decisions on his shot: the velocity of his swing in order to block, punch, or slam the ball. With his peripheral vision, he determines where his opponent is and guesses where he'll go. A tennis ace does all this and more in less than a second while the ball is traveling nearly a hundred miles per hour—for every shot. If this type of thing can become automatic, so can the creation of POWs.

Compared to a champion tennis player, you have a lot more time to run through your gamut of double entendres and homonyms. The second time you perform this exercise, it will not only be easier but will generate better results. The five thousandth time will be easier still.

Let's try it again. In this case, you'll be a copywriter writing an advertisement to encourage the public to use your bank for personal loans. Again, we'll go through similar steps.

**STEP ONE:** Locate the important word or phrase you would like to reform. In this case, concentrate on the word *loan*. Then write as many words as you can think of that rhyme with or sound similar to *loan*. Go for quantity.

**STEP TWO:** Select the words from your list that seem to have possibilities as double entendres. You might choose *groan, lone, moan, phone, postpone,* and *own.*

**STEP THREE:** Now, start eliminating. *Groan* and *moan* have negative associations. *Postpone* is the opposite of what you wish to recommend. But we still have *lone, own,* and *phone.* That's not bad!

**STEP FOUR:** Write as many POWs as you can with the word *loan* or *lone* in it, and try some reforming based on changing the spelling. Humor permits us to take some liberties with the language, so our list (which would be much longer than this) would include:

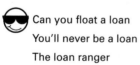 Can you float a loan
You'll never be a loan
The loan ranger

**STEP FIVE:** With a little reforming, the Lone Ranger and Tonto can become the *loan arranger* supported by his loyal sidekick, *pronto.* Now you have an ad headline that suggests action.

Santa Monica Bank
Phone the loan arranger—and pronto!

To appreciate the innumerable variations possible with homonyms, let's examine POWs on the title of Stravinsky's famous ballet *The Rite of Spring*. Okay, the sound rite can be spelled in the following ways: *rite*, *write*, *right*, and *wright*. Each spelling, singular or plural, contributes to a variety of humor possibilities, such as these examples of newspaper photo headlines.

 Over a photo of a high school commencement: The Rite of Spring

Over a photo of a book on spring gardening: The Writes of Spring

Over a photo of the Wrights' annual garden party: The Wrights of Spring

In addition, the word *spring* can now be replaced with one of the following eighteen words that rhyme with it.

| | |
|---|---|
| bing | bring |
| ding | cling |
| fling | king |
| ling | ming |
| ping | ring |
| sing | sling |
| sting | string |
| swing | thing |
| wing | wring |

Thus, a picture of a coach instructing hitters at training camp could carry the headline *The Rites of Swing*.

By multiplying those nineteen words by the four variations on the sound *rite* (the other three were *right*, *write*, and *wright*), we now have a total of seventy-two possible variations on one phrase. And we're not finished! Just as we did with *spring*, let's take the word *rite* and replace it with one of the twenty-three words that are close in sound. Here your rhyming dictionary will be of help.

---

| | | |
|---|---|---|
| bright | brite | cite |
| dike | dyke | fight |
| flight | height | hike |
| knight | like | mike |
| might | pike | plight |
| sight | site | spike |
| strike | tight | trike |
| tyke | white | |

This changes the options for rite from four to twenty-seven, and with the eighteen spring variations, we now have the possibility of 414 variations—from just one expression! Of course, only a handful of these combinations could ever be used, but you never know when odd opportunities will turn up: a college president named Ping shows up at his child's birthday party, so now you can have a news photo caption that reads: *The Tykes of Ping.*

## THE ANSWER MAN

Here are some possible answers for the Showtime exercises on page 70.

 Comedians do it standing up.

Dancers do it to music.

Bankers do it with interest.

Math teachers do it with unknowns.

Publishers do it by the book.

Carpet layers do it on their knees.

Bowlers do it with balls.

Here are the *Washington Post* reader submissions that correspond with the Showtime exercises on pages 76–77.

 foreply: Any misrepresentation about yourself for the purpose of getting laid.

sarchasm: The gulf between the author of sarcastic wit and the person who doesn't get it.

inoculate: To take coffee intravenously when you are running late.

hipatitis: Terminal coolness.

glibido: All talk and no action.

ignoranus: A person who's stupid and an asshole.

# CHAPTER 5
## More POW: The Simple Truth and the Take-Off

 I spilled spot remover on my dog—and now he's gone.

**—Steven Wright**

Many English phrases, expressions, and clichés are idiomatic, which means they can't be taken literally: *I got up on the wrong side of the bed*; *I had a change of heart*. Other phrases and expressions are understood within a context of logical assumptions. When you tell someone you are getting your hair cut, it's logical for them to assume you mean hair in the plural sense, not the singular.

 Grandchild: Grandpa, I love running my fingers through your hairs.

The simple truth is a technique for creating humor by considering the implications of the *literal* meaning of such expressions—without their context of logical assumptions. The simple truth is just that—simple and true. By taking the literal meaning of a key word, you surprise the audience members, who have automatically interpreted the cliché with its traditional meaning. The simple truth makes logic illogical. It's commonly referred to as the "Call me a taxi" or "Call me a doctor" formula. ("Call me a taxi." "Okay, you're a taxi"; or, "Call me a doctor." "Why? Are you sick?" "No, I just graduated from med school.")

 I was trying to get back to my original weight—seven pounds, three ounces.

**—Cheryl Vendetti**

I got some new underwear the other day. Well, it's new to me.

**—Emo Philips**

How long was I in the army? Five foot eleven.

**—Spike Milligan**

The take-off is the most traditional of all humor techniques. Like the simple truth, the take-off begins with a standard expression or cliché. But it continues with an outrageous commentary, often containing a double entendre.

 I say live and let live. Anyone who can't accept that should be executed.

**—George Carlin**

If truth is beauty, how come no one has her hair done in a library?

**—Lily Tomlin**

My mind wanders a lot, but fortunately it's too weak to go very far.

**—Bob Thaves**

Let's examine the logic and construction behind each of these two techniques.

## THE WHOLE TRUTH
## AND NOTHING BUT THE TRUTH

The construction of a simple truth depends on an almost childlike comprehension. One of the ways to understand this technique is to think like a child.

 Grandma Elden was baby-sitting, and every five minutes Adrienne had another request to keep from going to sleep. Exasperated, she said to her four-year-old granddaughter, "Adrienne, if you call Grandma one more time, I'm going to get very angry." Five minutes later she heard Adrienne say quietly, "Mrs. Elden, can I have a glass of water?"

Another way to craft a simple truth is through a childish riddle.

 "I bet you I can say the capitals of all fifty states in less than thirty seconds."

"Impossible. It's a bet. Ready, set, go!"

"Okay. The capitals of all fifty states in less than thirty seconds. I said it. You lose!"

The innocence of children is an easy set-up for the simple truth in humor.

 A six-year-old asked her mother: "Ma. Tell me the truth. Where did I come from?" The flustered mother thought, "Must I really start explaining the details of sexual reproduction already?" So she asked, "Tell me, Debbie, why do you want to know?" And Debbie said, "Cause the kid next door said he came from Detroit. I wanna know where I come from."

As we mature comedically, simple truth techniques permit a whole series of formula jokes.

 I went to a bookstore and asked the saleswoman where the self-help section was. She said if she told me it would defeat the purpose.

**—Dennis Miller**

It's no wonder illiterate people never get the full effect of alphabet soup.

**—John Mendoza**

## Simple Truth Construction: It Ain't Simple

On the surface, the mechanics of the simple truth seem easy to understand and structure, and therein lies the danger. To create a simple truth, reexamine every major word in a phrase, reject its most common meaning within its context, and reinterpret it literally. This is not a simple task.

 I slept like a log last night. I woke up in the fireplace.

**—Tommy Cooper**

When I got divorced, I missed my husband, but I'm getting to be a better shot.

**—Sheila Kay**

Because the simple truth is so juvenile, it's frequently denigrated as a smart-ass remark (which used to be called smart-aleck until they discovered that Aleck had nothing to do with it).

 "What would you say to a martini?"
"Depends on what the martini said to me first!"

**—Sophia in *The Golden Girls***

Let's take a peek under the comedy tent to see how the simple truth works. Remember that the goal is to create the element of surprise.

 I like a girl with a head on her shoulders. No neck!

Try not to be restricted by the logic of the original idea. Comedy writers are not philosophers. In the simple truth, we are linguistic specialists concerned with exactly what the literal logic of a word conveys. You might try to visualize a phrase or cliché to help you get past the standard interpretation. If you visualize a girl with a head on her shoulders, you can see that what's missing is her neck.

Once you've spotted the simple-truth potential in a phrase or cliché, you may come up with a variety of related punch lines.

 I like a girl with a head on her shoulders, because I hate necks.

**—Steve Martin**

Let's illustrate the construction of a simple truth by examining the double entendre possibilities of the word *join*. Join has three possible definitions: (a) to cooperate, to become a member, to enlist; (b) to unite, to bring together, to touch; and (c) to argue, to quarrel, to engage in battle. In humor writing, the choice is always up to you.

When a friend asks, "Will you join me?" the obvious understanding is that he's using the first definition ("to get together"). But if you base your answer on the second definition ("uniting"), your reply can create humor by surprise: "Why, are you coming apart?"

---

If, on the other hand, you're asked, "Please join me in a cup of coffee," the incongruity of the first definition allows you to respond, "Only if there's enough room in the cup."

The following examples play on the multiple meanings of the word *nurse*.

 I majored in nursing. I had to drop it. I ran out of milk.

**—Judy Tenuta**

I was at a bar nursing a beer. My nipple was getting quite soggy.

**—Emo Philips**

Such elementary simple-truth jokes will always get a physical reaction: either a laugh or—more likely—a kick in the pants. In any case, remember that one of the rewards of humor is attention, and that people will admire your courage (maybe).

The simple truth can also be effective in physical comedy. In several Mel Brooks movies and in his Broadway musical *The Producers*, the hero and his cohorts ask the heroine, "How do we get there?," And the beautiful hostess says, "Walk this way." Then she swishes and sways across the set and the men imitate her feminine walk.

In a basic simple-truth construction, the first part of the sentence or paragraph is a cliché. The second part (the punchline) is an unexpected interpretation because it is realistically literal.

 Doctor: I don't like the looks of your husband.
Wife: Neither do I, doctor, but he's good to the children.

**—Larry Wilde**

Boss to employee: I'd thank you, Harrison, but yours is a thankless job.

**—Frank Modell**

I bought a new Japanese car, I turned on the radio. ... I don't understand a word they're saying.

**—Rodney Dangerfield**

With practice, your ear will find countless opportunities to make humor using the simple truth.

 **WIFE:** You never look out for me!

**HUSBAND:** Of course I do. And when I see you coming, I run like hell.

**THE PRESIDENT OF THE SYNAGOGUE ADDRESSED THE CONGREGATION:** Lefkowitz just lost his wallet with six hundred dollars in it. If anyone finds it, Lefkowitz says he'll give a reward of fifty dollars.

**A VOICE IN THE REAR:** I'll give seventy-five!

**CLERK TO JUDGE:** The bar association wondered if you'd like to contribute ten dollars to a lawyer's funeral?

**JUDGE:** Here's a hundred. Bury ten of them.

Actor Edmund Kean, on his deathbed, said, "Dying is easy. Comedy is hard." In the same vein, reading about joke construction is easy, but creating original humor material using these methods is not. You must find the perfect construction—and that's difficult.

 I bought Odor-Eaters. They ate for a half-hour and then threw up.

**—Howie Mandel**

The proper setup for a simple-truth joke is essential. If someone asked you, "Can you tell me how long to milk a cow?," a humorous simple-truth response would not be obvious. But if you reword the question to "Can you tell me how long cows should be milked?" you now have a long cow. An answer could be: "The same way as short cows."

George Carlin, who uses the simple truth in his monologues, examines words closely for incongruous variations.

 How come my book of free verse costs twelve dollars?

Sometimes they say the wind is calm. Well, if it's calm, they're not really winds, are they?

When you step on the brake, your life is in your foot's hand.

Can placebos cause side effects? If so, are the side effects real?

Why don't they have waiters in waiting rooms?

Research reports and statistics are excellent sources for simple-truth humor material.

 If a single dolphin has as many as two thousand babies, can you imagine how many she'd have if she were married?

Old joke, old punchline:

 Every six seconds in the U.S., some woman gives birth. So what we've got to do is get hold of that woman and stop her.

Old joke, new punchlines:

 **MARRIED DAUGHTER TO MOTHER ON PHONE:** Ma, I gave birth to triplets. Isn't that exciting? You know, triplets are conceived only once in every three million times!
**MOTHER:** My heavens, Linea, when did you have time to do housework?

**PROFESSOR:** Every fifteen minutes in the U.S., some student is contracting VD.
**STUDENT:** I think I know him.

## A QUICK LESSON IN WORD ECONOMY

In many literary forms, embellishment might enrich a piece; but when writing humor, less is better. A joke is not a short story. It's a small story—often a single-sentence story—told in as few words as possible.

Professionals constantly rewrite jokes to remove unnecessary words, especially in the punchline. The following Mitch Hedberg joke is a picture of such high-impact shrinkage.

I'm against picketing, but I don't know how to show it.

Beginning writers, on the other hand, tend to fluff up a joke with unnecessary words. For example, the novice might write the same joke in the following ways.

 I'm against picketing, but I don't know if I should protest it with a sign or whatever.

I'm against picketing, but I'm not exactly sure what ways to demonstrate it.

I'm against picketing, but I don't know how to let other people know that I'm against it.

Each of the alternative tag lines delivers the same general idea, but the punch of the POW is lost in the verbiage. Professionals call the use of too many words in a punchline frosting the flake or stacking the wack.

Your goal is avoid extra words and get to the joke as soon as possible. Brent Forrester defined this as the Humor and Duration Principle, which, simply put, states that the less time you take to get to the joke, the funnier the joke will be. Embellishing a setup or punchline diminishes the funniness of a joke.

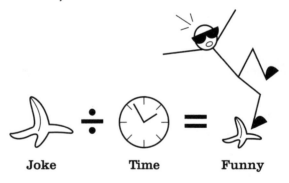

Joke      Time      Funny

## Top This: Combining Simple Truths

A good humorist doesn't deliver just one gag and then tax the audience's patience by developing a new setup. Once you've got the audience laughing or on a roll, it's better to stay with toppers—a series of three or four punchlines, each related to the previous one.

 A girl phoned me the other day and said, "Come on over, there's nobody home." I went over. Nobody was home.

**—Rodney Dangerfield**

Here are a few examples: The first contains one simple-truth punchline, while the second—a variation on the same joke—tops the first punchline with a second simple-truth punchline. The length of the pause between the two punchlines in the second joke is a matter of judgment. Knowing how long to pause separates the amateur from the pro.

 The forest ranger approached an Indian riding his horse up the steep canyon trail, his aged squaw trudging slowly along behind him. "Chief, I've been noticing for months now that you always ride up the trail and your wife always walks. How come?"

"Because," said the Indian solemnly, "she no gottum horse."

Here's the topper version of the same story. Note how the change in locale keeps the simple-truth punchline realistic.

 In Iraq, a GI approached an Arab who was riding his donkey along the military highway. His aged wife trudged along ahead of him.

"Hey, Abdul," said the GI, "I've been noticing for months that you always ride and your wife always walks. How come?"

"Because," said the Iraqi, "she no got donkey."

"But why does she always walk ahead of you? Arab politeness?"

"No! Land mines."

## SHOWTIME

Now try to finish some on your own. Read the following expressions and clichés, and see if you can come up with a simple-truth tag. To help you get started, the key word with the best possibility for a double entendre is underlined. Check your payoff lines with the ones suggested at the end of the chapter.

 Boy: Are you <u>free</u> tonight?

My girlfriend was faithful to the <u>end</u>.

We never <u>serve</u> women at the bar.

Cleanliness is <u>next</u> to godliness.

Judge: The <u>court</u> awards your wife $200 a week for support.

## SIMPLE TRUTHS AND MISPRONUNCIATION-BASED DOUBLE ENTENDRES

There are thousands of words in the English language that can become simple-truth double entendres by simple mispronunciation. Every humorist has his own favorites. Most people consider such constructions to be terrible puns. To overcome this conception, professional humorists put simple-truth double entendres in the mouths of children. Art Linkletter used them on his *House Party* TV show, and so did Stu Hample's books, such as *Children's Letters to God*. Everyone is familiar with take-offs of lines in the Bible (*Lead me not into Penn Station*) and fractured Christmas carols (*On the first day of Christmas, my tulip gave to me ... and ...*). You can collect your own mispronunciation double entendres by reading the words in the dictionary aloud. Once you find one, your cleverness must add the punchline.

I bought a product for erectile dysfunction and the box said Cialis. I've been looking for her for the last three months.

Did ya hear about the Buddhist who refused novocaine when he went to the dentist because he wanted to transcend dental medication?

I'm not as concerned with euthanasia as I am with kids in this country.

It wasn't my fault, it was the asphalt.

My mother makes our family eat so much salad, I wish she'd lettuce alone.

## SHOWTIME

The simple-truth double entendre technique works in oral presentation, but every once in a while it works best in print. Which method—oral or print—would work best for the examples below?

 The Paul Revere computer virus protection program warns of impending hard disk attack—once if by LAN, twice if by C:/>.

When George W. Bush was campaigning during an Ohio primary, he and an assistant dropped into a small luncheonette.

"Oh, Mr. Bush," smiled the attractive waitress. "We're so honored. Have anything on the menu on us. What would you like?"

Bush studied the menu for a few moments and then said to the waitress, "You know what I'd like, honey. I'd like a quickie."

The waitress slammed her pad on the table and said, "I don't care if you are running for President, no one talks that way to me." And she walked away.

"I don't know what she's so huffy about," said Bush. "It says right here on the menu: quickie."

"Mr. Bush," said his assistant. "It's pronounced quiche."

If you guessed print for the first example and oral for second, you guessed right.

---

## Simple Truths and Non Sequiturs

Another category of simple-truth humor is the non sequitur, an illogical statement that is humorous because of the juxtaposition of two unrelated elements. "One must have some grasp of logic even to recognize a non sequitur," warned author and professor John Allen Paulos.

 I shot an elephant in my pajamas. How he got in my pajamas, I'll never know.

**—Groucho Marx**

A hundred years from now, the works of the old masters will be a thing of the past.

**—A. Grove Day**

Roadhouse sign: Clean and decent dancing every night but Sunday.

Store sign: "Big Sale—Last Week!" Why are they telling me this? I already missed it.

**—Yakov Smirnoff**

## Simple Truths and Non Sequiturs on Stage

Many professional comedians use simple truths and non sequiturs from time to time in their monologues. Several use non sequiturs most of the time, including stand-up comedian Steven Wright. Here's a sample; by now, you should be able to quickly anticipate most of the humorous conclusions.

 I bought some batteries, but they weren't included. So, I had to buy them again.

I had some eyeglasses, and as I was walking down the street, the prescription ran out.

I parked my car in a tow-away zone. When I came back, the entire zone was gone.

If you're sending someone some Styrofoam, what do you pack it in?

I used to work in a fire hydrant factory. You couldn't park anywhere near the place.

I walked into a restaurant. The sign said "Breakfast Served—Anytime." I ordered French toast during the Renaissance.

A lot of people are afraid of heights. Not me, I'm afraid of widths.

I like to reminisce with people I don't know.

Survey these bits from Mitch Hedberg, and anticipate the humorous conclusions.

 Once you understand Morse code, a tap dancer will drive you crazy.

I don't wear a watch because I want my arms to weigh the same.

It's dangerous to wave to people you don't know, because if they don't have hands, they'll think you're cocky.

I used to do drugs. I still do, but I used to, too.

## SHOWTIME

Try to finish each joke, then compare your answers to the ones listed at the end of the chapter.

 And I hate it when my foot falls asleep during the day ...

I woke up one morning and my girlfriend asked me if I slept good. I said ...

At the gym they have free weights, so ...

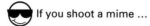 If you shoot a mime ...

If you saw a heat wave ...

I got my hair highlighted, because ...

On the other hand ...

---

## THE TAKE-OFF:
## DO UNTO OTHERS ... THEN TAKE OFF

The idea behind the take-off, one of the most popular formulas in humor writing, is to draw a humorous conclusion from the intended meaning of a standard cliché. Because the take-off is based on the intended meaning of the phrase, a take-off is the opposite of the simple truth, which interprets the cliché or expression literally. In the take-off, the phrase or cliché can either start the joke or be the punchline, but the cliché is typically used as an introduction, and the surprise take-off is the big payoff at the conclusion of the joke.

 An invisible man married an invisible woman. Their kids were nothing to look at either.

Nobody knows the trouble I've seen, but I keep trying to tell them.
**—Mignon McLaughlin**

Let a smile be your umbrella—and your hair will be a big mess.

Where there's a will, there's a family fighting over it.
**—Buzz Nutley**

The hands on my biological clock are giving me the finger.

**—Wendy Liebman**

Animals may be our friends. But they won't pick you up at the airport.

**—Bobcat Goldthwait**

---

A fool and his money were lucky to get together in the first place.
**—Harry Anderson**

Whatever goes up must come down, but don't expect it to come down where you can find it.
**—Lily Tomlin**

Comedy is in my blood. Frankly, I wish it were in my act!
**—Rodney Dangerfield**

Sign on hot chestnut stand: I don't want to set the world on fire. I just want to keep my nuts warm.

Honesty is the best policy, but insanity is a better defense.
**—Steve Landesberg**

The race isn't always to the swift, nor the battle to the strong— but that's the way to bet!
**—Damon Runyon**

The take-off construction is more difficult when the standard phrase is the second clause or sentence. A groan is the most frequent reaction to this construction, so it's not as popular with stand-up comedians (they get enough groans without scheduling them).

 The dog's breath smelled terrible, so his bark was worse than his bite.

If you don't want the dentist to hurt you, keep your mouth shut.

I believe Dr. Kevorkian is on to something. Suicide is our way of saying to God, "You can't fire me. I quit."
**—Bill Maher**

I know a guy who called up the Home Shopping Network. They said, "Can I help you?" and he said, "No, I'm just looking."
**—George Miller**

I stuff my bra. So, if you get to second base with me, you'll find that the bases are loaded.
**—Wendy Liebman**

You can combine humor techniques in one joke. Here's an example (inspired by author S.J. Perelman) that combines reforming (as discussed in chapter four) with a take-off (note that the cliché comes second).

 The hooker was chasing the comedian down the street—a case of the tail dogging the wag.

You can also put more than one cliché in a take-off. It doubles the work, but it also doubles the fun.

 Immortality is a long shot, I admit. But somebody has to be first.
**—Bill Cosby**

Give a man enough rope and he'll get tied up in the office.

Some girls fight against being kissed. Others take it lying down.

Why do people groan rather than laugh at outrageous puns? No one has the slightest idea.

 A pun is the lowest form of humor—unless you think of it first.
**—Oscar Levant**

Whether you put the cliché first or second in a take-off depends on which ending holds the surprise to the last possible moment. You may perform the joke with the cliché first, but remember that humor is written backwards. That means you must first find the cliché you want to work on, then build a story around it. The trick is not to telegraph the punchline. Here's a take-off that was so obviously stretched, it looks more like good taffy than good humor.

 A construction worker discovered his wife in the back seat of a Yugo making love to another guy. He got into his cement truck, drove up to the car, and dumped an entire load of concrete all over it. Then, he drove away thinking, "The longer they go, the harder it gets."

This example is a labored anecdote, but it does follow one essential rule: Make sure the joke is the last possible thought, and don't add other words to the sentence after the joke. If you do, the audience will think that your take-off was only a setup for a topper—and they'll be disappointed when that topper doesn't pop up.

## Take-Offs on Stage

One of the great masters of the take-off was Rodney Dangerfield, who used the technique to emphasize his self-deprecating stage persona of the man who gets no respect.

 I looked up the family tree and found out that I was the sap.

I said to my wife, "All things considered, I'd like to die in bed," and she said, "What, again?"

My father never liked me. For Christmas, he gave me a bat. The first time I tried to play ball with it, it flew away.

When I was a kid my parents moved a lot, but I always found them.

I could tell my parents hated me. My bath toys were a toaster and a radio.

When I was born, the doctor said to my father, "I'm sorry, we did everything we could, but he still pulled through."

My mother didn't breast-feed me. She said she just liked me as a friend.

The Deep Thoughts book series by fictional author Jack Handey also uses the take-off. Each "deep thought" typically begins with a cliché or common phrase, and takes off with a bizarre, off-the-wall conclusion.

 It takes a big man to cry, but it takes a bigger man to laugh at that man.

Dad always said that laughter is the best medicine, which is why several of us died from tuberculosis.

If a kid asks where rain comes from, I think a cute thing to tell him is "God is crying." And if he asks why God is crying, another cute thing to tell him is "Probably because of something you did."

Children need encouragement. So if a kid gets an answer right, tell him it was a lucky guess. That way, he develops a good, lucky feeling.

## SHOWTIME

Let's analyze the saying that has more variations than any other in comedic literature: If at first you don't succeed, try, try again.

 If at first you don't succeed, try, try again—she expects you to.

**—Guido Stempel**

If at first you don't succeed, then quit. There's no sense being a fool about it.

**—W.C. Fields**

If at first you don't succeed, don't think of it as a failure. Think of it as time-release success.

**—Robert Orben**

If at first you don't succeed, then skydiving isn't for you.

Sometimes it isn't even necessary to use the full cliché. Often, just a suggestion or variation of the cliché is enough. Here are some classic Homer Simpson lines, also known as Homerisms.

 If something's hard to do, then it's not worth doing.

Kids, you tried your best and failed miserably. So, the lesson is, never try.

How to weasel out of things is important to learn. It's what separates us from the animals ... except the weasel.

Write the opening words for this cliché (If at first you don't succeed), then create take-offs that have a surprising ending. A result of ten take-offs is average; twenty is outstanding.

## THE ANSWER MAN

Here are some punchline possibilities for the exercises on page 98. How do yours compare?

 **BOY:** Are you free tonight?
**GIRL:** Of course. Have I ever charged you?

My girlfriend was faithful to the end.
Unfortunately, I was the quarterback.

We never serve women at the bar.
You'll have to bring your own.

Cleanliness is next to godliness.
No, I looked in the dictionary, and go-getter is next to godliness.

**JUDGE:** The court awards your wife $200 a week for support.
**DEFENDANT:** Gee, that's very nice of you, Judge. I think I'll throw in a few bucks myself.

Here are the professionals' conclusions to the jokes on pages 101–102.

 And I hate it when my foot falls asleep during the day, because that means it's going to be up all night.
**—Steven Wright**

I woke up one morning and my girlfriend asked me if I slept good. I said, "No, I made a few mistakes."
**—Steven Wright**

At the gym they have free weights, so I took them.

—**Steve Smith**

If you shoot a mime, should you use a silencer?

—**Steven Wright**

If you saw a heat wave, would you wave back?

—**Steven Wright**

# CHAPTER 6
## POW Brainstorming Techniques

 Writer's block is a fancy term made up by whiners so they can have an excuse to drink alcohol.

**—Steve Martin**

Like most creative people, humor writers spend a lot of time looking for the right figure of speech. Occasionally, the blank "I'm thinking" gaze progresses to the comatose state known as writer's block. Unfortunately, humor writers can not only suffer from writer's block, but also from humor block: unavoidable moments when the comedic juices stop flowing. As comedian Marty Feldman overstated, "Comedy, like sodomy, is an unnatural act."

Even when a writer's imagination is going full steam, the rule of ten in, nine out applies: For every ten jokes written, only one might be acceptable. The high ratio of successful to unsuccessful jokes explains why most late-night talk shows, such as *The Tonight Show* and *Late Night*, employ teams of gag writers. A five-minute monologue may be written by as many as six writers.

There are ways to jump-start the creative process. The most common brainstorming methods are association and listing. These techniques allow you to generate multiple options for humor, thereby improving your chances of uncovering a successful play on words (POW). Brainstorming can be time-consuming, and most of the items you come up with will be discarded, but brainstorming is nonetheless an invaluable tool for writing humor. It also explains why humor writers are better at wordplay than foreplay.

### ASSOCIATION

A humorist's funny bone is like an athlete's muscles or a singer's vocal cords. It works best when it's warmed up first. Writing instructors insist that students do fifteen to thirty minutes of brain-stretching exercises each morning to clear the mind. Developing new associations is a creative-writing technique that can help you discover humor in unexpected relationships, and create POW jokes.

Association is putting two activities that haven't been previously associated into a plausible but audacious scenario. Association is a more formal word for teaming, humor's variation on metaphor. You combine two simple elements that are logical alone but impossible together. The humor comes from the unexpected, offbeat relationship.

Associations have several formats. One type of association begins with a cliché or expression that the audience is likely to interpret one way, but then the performer gives an illustrative example that reverses the anticipated meaning.

 My opponent has done the work of two men: Laurel and Hardy.
**—Governor James A. Rhodes**

Another type of association is the teaming of two clichés. This technique is the backbone of improvisation.

 Wife to friend: I call Herb's salary a phallic symbol even though it only rises once a year.

A third type of association is the Tom Swifty, the teaming of a quotation with a verb or adverb of attribution that puns on the meaning of the quotation.

 "I want to renew my membership," Tom rejoined.
"I hope I can still play the guitar," he fretted.
"All the twos are missing from this deck," she deduced.
"You're burning the candle at both ends," he said wickedly.
"I think he's dead," she said mournfully.
"I'm as tired as a sled dog," he said huskily.

Robert Orben, one of the most prolific humor writers, warms up by writing twenty-five POW jokes inspired by the morning paper. Then, he gets to work. Others like to imagine funny captions to news photos. Humor lecturer Art Gliner gets his seminars going with a POW association exercise. He has attendees write down words that might describe how tired firefighters, police, dogcatchers, plumbers, etc. feel when they get home at night. For example:

**FIREFIGHTER**

| | |
|---|---|
| burned up | alarmed |
| torched | fired up |
| like a plugged nickel | steamed |
| like a ladder day saint | not too hot |
| like he had made an ash of himself | |

**POLICE OFFICER**

| | |
|---|---|
| beat | flat-footed |
| half-cocked | run down |
| blue | shot |
| charged | holed up |
| badgered | it was a riot |
| that's the ticket | |

**DOGCATCHER**

| | |
|---|---|
| muzzled | bone tired |
| bitchy | run down |
| pooped | hounded |
| licked | dog tired |
| collared | the paws that refreshes |

**GARDENER**

| | |
|---|---|
| hosed | potted |
| plowed under | bogged down |
| bushed | raked over |
| mulched | dug up |
| seedy | all wet |
| rocky | |

Comedy writer Gene Perret likes to associate puns on famous names. First, find a name with homonym possibilities. Then, write an anecdote to fit.

Before she became Madonna, she was a pre-Madonna.

**—K.C. Conan**

An Italian-American farmer erected a tombstone for his beloved wife, Nellie, that read: "Here Liza Minnelli."

Take pity. I'm Jung and Freud-ened.

"I just can't Handel the Messiah."

"Then you'd better go into Haydn."

"Oh, get off my Bach, or I'll give you a karate Chopin the neck."

A microcomputer that draws geometric patterns on the screen is called a Micro-Angle-O.

Here are some slogans (based on the same principle) for famous artists.

 Seurat: Que Seurat, Seurat.
Monet: A lasting impression.
Van Gogh: Lend me your ear.
Warhol: The new Warhol—uncanny.
Gauguin: Here we Gauguin.
Goya: You can be Jewish and still love a Goya.

**—Advertising Age**

Humorists take only themselves seriously, no one else. The more you can combine realism and exaggeration, the more humorous you will be. That's why disrespectful association of the rich and famous with book or movie titles is a frequent POW warmup for professionals.

 Britney Spears in *Once Is Not Enough*
Dick Cheney in *Raging Bull*
Hillary Clinton in *Cold Mountain*
George W. Bush in *Lost in Translation*

Associating the last names of two different celebrities is another exercise in association.

If Isadora Duncan had married Robert Donat, would their child be a Duncan Donat?

If Betty White had married Soupy Sales, would they have called her Betty White Sales?

If all this is just the first step in humor writing, you're probably reminded of the ancient warning: Watch out for that first step—it's a bitch! But with patience and practice, you'll soon be skipping down the sidewalk without missing a crack.

## REVISING FOR SURPRISE

It takes a good deal of testing to create a joke with a surprise ending. So much so that jokes aren't written—they're rewritten. Precision and brevity help make a surprise ending effective. A well-constructed joke:

- uses as few words as possible
- does not reveal key words in the setup
- preserves the funniest word until the end

When you write humor, your first draft can be as long as you wish. The second draft should cut every nonessential phrase. The final draft should cut every nonessential word. No machine has needless parts, and no good comedy routine has needless words. Your mantra should be: *Make every word work.*

As you're revising, trim redundant phrases—such as *old adage, exact same, really essential, continue on, four short years, absolutely necessary, advance planning, brief respite, future plans,* and *interact with each other*—down to the one necessary word.

If surprise is home plate, good humor writing runs the bases as fast as possible. Normal speech is clocked at two and a half words per second, so if you can erase just twenty redundant words from your final draft, you'll save eight seconds that will help keep your audience alert.

Let's analyze three different endings to the same joke. Which would you select as the most effective?

 He was complimented when the editor called his work sopho-moric because he had flunked out of college his freshman year.

He had flunked out of college in his sophomore year, so he was complimented whenever anybody called his work sophomoric.

He had flunked out of college in his freshman year, so he was complimented whenever anybody called his work sophomoric.

The first joke is less effective because, after you've written *sophomoric*, the surprise goes past the payoff window. The second joke loses its punch because the word sophomore in the middle of the sentence fore-shadows the surprise word, sophomoric, at the end. The last joke works best, because the surprise word—sophomoric—is held to the last instant.

The constant attention to editing may seem extensive, but the con-struction of a joke is as important as its content. Word economy and holding the surprise until the end are two major characteristics of a well-written joke, and humor writers spend considerable time ensuring that they maintain those characteristics.

Consider the following example.

### First draft

 On the road into town there was a sign in an empty field that said, "Three miles ahead, lots for sale." So I went to the loca-tion, but to my surprise, there was nothing there.

At two and a half words per second, the audience has to wait four sec-onds between hearing about the sign and getting to the punchline. This period is too long and asks too much of the audience.

### Second draft

 I saw this sign: "Lots for sale." And when I went there, I must have been too late, because there was nothing there.

This joke still contains too much unnecessary information.

**Final draft**

 I saw this sign: "Lots for sale." But there was nothing there.

## LISTING: AN EXPLODING MIRTH RATE

The concept of listing seems simple enough: You break down a topic of your choice into groups of related activities, then create smaller and smaller subgroups. Regardless of your humor assignment, the technique is the same. Let's imagine you need to write material on golf, a favorite topic for speech humorists because so many clients play golf.

**STEP ONE: LIST GROUPS AND SUBGROUPS.** The first step is to chart the subject. On paper, divide the main subject into different headings. For example:

1. golf equipment
2. golf course
3. golf play
4. golf players

Now add as many subheads as you can think of, and keep adding to the list every time you have another brainstorm. Don't censor yourself. The quantity of ideas is important here; quality comes later.

### GOLF EQUIPMENT
Under golf equipment you might list:

| | | |
|---|---|---|
| argyle socks | bag | ball washer |
| balls | caddy | cap |
| cart | clothes | clubs |
| flag | glasses | gloves |
| hats | head covers | lucky ball |
| optic yellow | pencil | rake |

| scorecard | shoes | socks |
| spikes | tees | towels |

Now break down the subhead clubs even further:

| drivers | woods | irons |
| wedge | putter | |

Even the woods and the irons can be listed by numeric designation: two wood, nine iron, etc. And that's only category one—golf equipment.

## GOLF COURSE

Now do the same with category two, golf course.

| apron | ball wash | bunker |
| clubhouse | country club | divots |
| dogleg | driving range | eighteen-hole course |
| fairway | green | groundskeeper |
| lake | locker room | men's tee |
| nine-hole course | nineteenth hole | out of bounds |
| practice green | pro tee | rough |
| sand trap | shower | trees |
| water hazard | women's tee | woods |

## GOLF PLAY

And now category three, golf play:

| birdie | bogie | championship |
| chip | double bogie | drop ball |
| eagle | "fore" | foursome |
| handicap | hole in one | hook |
| lost balls | mulligan | par |
| play through | pro-am | score |
| shank | skyball | slice |
| stroke | tournaments | trophy |

## GOLF PLAYERS

Finally, category four, golf players:

| amateurs | betting | bragging |
| cheating | curses | disgust |
| double up | duffer | exercise |
| expense | fanatics | foursome |
| hackers | hobby | hooker |
| hustler | lessons | Nassau |
| opponents | pair | partners |
| pros | sandbagger | slicer |

**STEP TWO: LIST CLICHÉS**. The next part of the chart is a comprehensive list of clichés or POWs associated with each entry. For example, in category one (golf equipment) you could list:

**CLUBS**

| got a new set of clubs | he hit a three-hundred-yarder |
| make a six-footer | practice swing |
| she knows how to putt | |

**BALLS**

| they've gotcha by the balls | kiss his balls for good luck |
| she addressed the ball | he lost his balls |
| keep your eye on the ball | don't stand too close to the ball |
| hit a pair of beautiful balls | |

**BAG**

| that's not his bag | she's a bag lady |
| in the bag | |

And in category two, golf course, a list of cliché expressions might include:

| name of the game | how many strokes per round |
| let's play a round | great way to meet people |
| she gave the caddy a tip | a rich man's sport |

In categories three, golf play, and four, golf players, you might include:

| he knows the score | it was a playable lie |
| it's a gimme | she got out of the trap |

| | |
|---|---|
| I lie three | he's a poor sport |
| she moved heaven and earth | what's par for the hole? |
| that shot was a prayer | she shoots in the low seventies |
| he's a scratch player | he's a hooker |
| she's a slicer | she's a weekend hacker |
| the woods are full of them | he got out of a hole |
| he got distance off the tee | how do you like the greens? |

**STEP THREE: ADD THE POW.** As you read over the list, you can already see a number of humor possibilities, particularly with double entendres. Now is the time to list double entendres, synonyms, antonyms, and homonyms that have a connection with golf. Here's a sample list.

### DOUBLE ENTENDRES

| | | |
|---|---|---|
| a six-footer | bag | ball |
| ball wash | birdie | game |
| handicap | hole | hole in one |
| hooker | lie | long ball hitter |
| lost ball | lucky ball | make |
| nine holes | out of bounds | play |
| play through | putt | rough |
| score | scratch | slicer |
| socks | sport | stroke |
| swing | tip | trap |

### SYNONYMS

| | |
|---|---|
| away = longest distance | bar = nineteenth hole |
| club = sticks | drive = tee-off |
| gimme = concede | good shot = beauty |
| green = carpet | hat = cap |
| lake = drink | locker room = showers |
| oath = curse | par = scratch |
| putt = tap | tip = gift |

## ANTONYMS

birdie = bogie

eagle = double bogie

hold head down = hold head up

match play = lowest score

opponent = partner

stand close = stand away

wager = friendly game

country club = public links

flubbed = on the nose

lost ball = found ball

men's tee = women's tee

play = practice

tip = advice

## HOMONYMS

fore = four, for, foreplay, foursome

course = enter course (sign), intercourse, curse

play a round = play around

caddy = caddy (Cadillac)

seventies (score) = seventies (Fahrenheit temperature)

putts = putz

**STEP FOUR: CREATE THE JOKES.** Use all this research to come up with humorous material for your monologue, sketch, or speech on golf. Remember that, to be funny, the final line of the story or joke must be a surprise. Depending on the speed of the performer, four jokes a minute is maximum, and two jokes plus one anecdote in a minute is average. So if you need five minutes of material, at the maximum you need twenty one-liners, or seven anecdotes, or twelve one-liners and three anecdotes, etc.

The beginner writes the minimum to fill the time. The professional writes three times what's needed (as many as sixty different bits for this example), and tries them out on small groups (but never on her own family), rewrites, discards, rewrites some more, then finally settles on the twenty that work best for that specific audience.

Let's try a few jokes based on the golf lists above. For this exercise, let's stick with just one scenario—the dialogue between golfer and caddy—so we can concentrate on humor technique. These stories would all benefit from personalizing—substituting a VIP's name for the golfer or the caddy, for instance. Many of these jokes would work whether the hacker was male or female.

## CATEGORY ONE (GOLF EQUIPMENT)

 **CADDY TO HACKER:** No matter how you slice it, sir, it's still a golf ball.

**HACKER:** I got some new clubs for my wife.
**CADDY:** I know your wife, sir, and that wasn't a bad trade.

**CADDY:** I don't get it, sir. First, you slice your ball into the woods. Then you hook it onto the highway. Now you top the same ball into the water. And you still insist on my finding it?
**HACKER:** Of course. It's my lucky ball.

**HACKER:** I hit two beautiful balls today.
**CADDY:** The only way you could do that, sir, would be to step on a rake.

**CADDY:** Here's a lost ball I found on the golf course.
**HACKER:** Gee, thanks. But how did you know it was a lost ball?
**CADDY:** Because they were still looking for it when I left.

**HACKER:** This is my first time playing golf. When do I use my putter?
**CADDY:** Sometime before dark, I hope.

## CATEGORY TWO (GOLF CLUB)

 **HACKER:** I'm moving heaven and earth to do better.
**CADDY:** Try just moving heaven. You've already moved plenty of earth.

**CADDY:** The traps on this course are certainly annoying, aren't they, sir?
**HACKER:** Yes, and would you please shut yours?

**HACKER:** How does one meet new people at this country club?
**CADDY:** Easy. Try picking up the wrong ball.

---

CATEGORY THREE (GOLF PLAY)

 **HACKER TO CADDY:** I play golf in the seventies. When it gets hotter, I quit.

**HACKER:** Golf is sure a funny game.
**CADDY:** It wasn't meant to be, sir.

**HACKER TO CADDY:** This hole should be good for a long drive and a putt.
**CADDY (AFTER HACKER FLUBS HIS FIRST SHOT):** Now for a helluva putt.

**HACKER:** Any ideas on how I can cut about ten strokes off my score?
**CADDY:** Yes, quit on hole seventeen!

**CADDY:** How come you're not playing with Mr. Anderson today, sir?
**HACKER:** Would you play with a man who lies, cheats, and moves his ball?
**CADDY:** No, sir!
**HACKER:** Well, neither will Mr. Anderson.

**CADDY:** Sir, you're teeing off from the ladies' tee.
**HACKER:** Shut up, willya? I lie three here.

**HACKER:** With my score today I'll never be able to hold my head up.
**CADDY:** Why not? You've been doing it all afternoon.

**PRIEST:** I wonder if it would help me if I prayed each time I teed off?
**CADDY:** Only if you prayed with your head down.

**CADDY:** Father, is it a sin to play golf on Sunday?
**PRIEST:** The way I play, it's a sin on any day.

**HACKER:** Ever seen such a long ball hitter as me?
**CADDY:** Sure, the woods are full of them.

CATEGORY FOUR (GOLF PLAYERS)

 **HACKER TO CADDY:** My wife says if I don't give up golf, she'll leave me. And you know, I'm going to miss her.

**HACKER:** What do you think I should do about my game?
**CADDY:** Well, sir, first I'd relax, then stop playing for six months, then give it up entirely.

Now let's see how several anecdotes are used to construct one golf joke.

 A young man in his twenties went to Las Vegas, met a girl, had a fabulous night, got drunk, got married, and woke up the next morning. He said to her, "Look I've got a surprise for you. Last night when I said I don't have a handicap, I meant I am a no-scratch golfer. I spend all my time out on the golf course, and you're the first girl I ever went out with." The girl said, "Well, I really have a handicap. I'm a hooker, and I can't stop." So, the kid took out one of his clubs and said, "Look, I can help. Next time, before you swing, just put your right hand high on the shaft. You'll do fine."

**—Bob Hope**

## Why Work So Hard?

This seems like an awful lot of labor just to create a few one-liners. Well, it is. No humor writer will deny that associations are laborious, tedious, time-consuming, and frustrating when it doesn't come out right. (And just as you're about to find that last elusive punchline, your spouse will come up and say, "As long as you're not doing anything, take out the garbage.")

### FOUR MORE BLOCK BEATERS

Here are four more tools for busting through humor block.

**1. WORK BACKWARDS.** Create the last line—the punchline first. Then write the anecdote or setup that best prepares the audience for the punchline. For instance, you might accidentally discover a unique literal interpretation of a cliché (which can happen easily when you accidentally make a whittle typo). But creating setups isn't easy; you might try half a dozen before the best one is apparent. Then you may spend hours changing words and paring the joke down, whittle by whittle. To get out of the habit of starting with the setup, take a trip to a greeting card store and read some of the humorous cards backwards. Start with the inside (the punchline) of the card, and then guess the line on the outside (the setup).

**2. LOOK FOR OPPOSITES.** One key method of creating surprise is associating two dissimilar things. Choose a topic, then brainstorm for people, places, things, phrases, clichés, and words that are dissimilar to this topic.

**3. TALK INSTEAD OF WRITING.** Put down the pen and start talking out loud. Use a voice recorder to capture ideas, which may come faster than you can write.

**4. IMAGINE INSTEAD OF WRITING.** Albert Einstein recognized that the mind's visual powers greatly exceed its verbal abilities, and he used visualization to discover many of his famous theories. Whenever you need to kick-start your imagination, close your eyes and let your mind create a mental movie of you telling jokes to a receptive audience.

## SHOWTIME

Aggressive editing is important. Remember that a good joke:

1. uses as few words as possible
2. preserves the funniest part of the joke until the end
3. does not reveal key words in the setup, and does not contain words after the funniest part of the punchline

If the three criteria for a good joke are not met, a potentially good joke will become lame. Complete the following exercises to practice aggressive editing.

Aggressively edit the POW jokes you have written. First, remove any unneeded words. Second, identify the funniest word or phrase in each punchline, and if any words appear after the funniest part, rewrite the joke to get rid of them. Third, make sure that key words that telegraph the surprise ending are not used in the setup.

Now do the same with one of your favorite funny stories. How can it be aggressively edited to be even more effective?

# CHAPTER 7
## The Next Giant Step: Reverses

 My boyfriend and I broke up, even though we're still deeply in love. He wanted to get married and I didn't want him to.
**—Rita Rudner**

The term *reverse* has many definitions in humor writing, but one of the best is "a device that adds a contradictory tag line to the opening line of a standard expression or cliché."

 I couldn't wait for success, so I went ahead without it.
**—Jonathan Winters**

Other writers call it *the old switcheroo*; a technique that switches the characters and setting of a standard humor bit to fit the existing situation.

 We were incompatible in a lot of ways. Like for example, I was a night person, and he didn't like me.
**—Wendy Liebman**

The most common definition of a reverse is "an unexpected switch in the audience's point of view." Surprise comes from a basic change in direction—a reversal of habitual thinking or activity. To maintain the element of surprise, the writer must drop at least one prominent clue to mislead the audience, to push the audience in a false direction. See if you can spot the misdirection in the example below.

 A man and woman are making passionate love in the bedroom. Suddenly, the apartment door opens, and a man comes in and shouts, "Darling! I'm home." He walks into the bedroom, sees the naked couple and says, "What is she doing here?"

Did you spot it? The misdirection is the man shouting, "Darling!" The audience thinks he's calling to the woman. The unexpected change in point of view occurs in the last line: "What is she doing here?"

In each of the following examples, the writer wants you to be thinking predictably. Despite the careful step-by-step analysis above, you may be so accustomed to the logical thought process that many of these reverses will still catch you by surprise.

 **BOY:** Can I take your picture in the nude?

**COED:** Absolutely not! You'll have to wear your socks and a tie.

A junior executive walks into his boss's office. "I'm afraid I'll have to leave early today, sir. I've got a terribly sore neck."

The boss says, "Whenever I get one, I go home and my wife makes love to me. She knows how to massage every muscle in my body, and when she's finished, all the tension is gone. You should try it, and that's an order."

The next day the boss walks over to the young executive: "Did you try what I told you?"

"Yes, I did," says the young man, "and it worked just fine. By the way, you have a beautiful house, too!"

The standard reverse, then, is a simple statement setting up a point of view that is effectively cancelled out by the last few words. Pro writers sometimes spend hours polishing that important last line. In the examples below, the setup statements have been underlined.

 I sold my house this week. I got a good price for it—but it made my landlord mad as hell.

**—Garry Shandling**

I stayed at one of the crummiest hotels in town. In the middle of the night, I called the desk clerk and said, "I've got a leak in the bathtub." He said, "Hey, you paid for the room. Go right ahead."

When the old Sheraton hotel was being renovated, they sold the ripped-out fixtures, so I bought the two front doors for my house. After they were installed, I pointed them out to a friend, "These came from the Sheraton hotel." He was astonished, "Most people just take soap and towels."

## REVERSES AND THE ART OF SURPRISE

Why humor reverses continue to surprise us is a mystery. After all, the ending is logical (if not realistic). A magician is able to use physical misdirection to accomplish his sleight of hand, while the comic has only words—and the hope that the audience goes off on the wrong train of thought.

 I understand that the doctor had to spank me when I was born, but I really don't see any reason he had to call me a whore.

**—Sarah Silverman**

When I was young, I thought that money was the most important thing in life. Now that I'm old—I know it is.

**—Oscar Wilde**

Effective humor is carefully scripted to ensure the surprise ending remains hidden until the writer is ready to reveal it. Each phrase, idea, or fact is carefully designed so that when the performer reverses the train of thought, the audience is totally surprised. If they can see the reverse coming, they're not surprised, just smug.

 I made a killing in the stock market. My broker lost all my money, so I killed him.

**—Jim Loy**

In the following routine, comedian Emo Philips plants clues that encourage the audience to think along predictable lines.

 One day I was playing—I was about seven years old—and I saw the cellar door open just a crack. Now my folks had always warned me: Emo, whatever you do, don't go near the cellar door. But I had to see what was on the other side if it killed me, so I went to the cellar door, pushed it open and walked through, and I saw strange, wonderful things—things I had never seen before—like … trees, grass, flowers, the sun—that was nice!

Note how he built up the reverse by playing on the audience's assumption that he is outside the cellar.

I was about seven …

A child could be forbidden to enter the cellar. He might fall down the stairs, or the cellar might contain something dangerous.

 I saw the cellar door open just a crack.

The parents have warned Philips away from the door, so the audience thinks there is something dangerous in the cellar. When the door opens just a crack, tension is created in the audience (who is still thinking that Philips is outside the cellar).

 My folks had always warned me … whatever you do, don't go near the cellar door.

The cellar is beginning to sound like some mysterious, horror-filled dungeon.

 I had to see what was on the other side if it killed me.

The word *killed* further builds tension.

 I saw strange, wonderful things—things I had never seen before.

Now the audience is sure that the mysterious cellar is filled with relics from King Tut's tomb.

 Like …

This is a necessary long pause, which is the apex of tension in preparation for the surprise ending—Philips revelation that he was in the cellar, looking out.

## SHOWTIME

A reverse should not be easy for the audience to spot in advance. Write a reverse for each of the following setups, and then compare your best efforts with the pros' versions at the end of the chapter.

Condoms aren't completely safe. A friend of mine was wearing one and …

My wife insists on turning off the lights when we make love. That doesn't bother me. It's the …

We have a presidential election coming up. And I think the big problem, of course, is …

After twelve years of therapy, my psychiatrist said something that brought tears to my eyes. He said …

## THE ANECDOTAL REVERSE

An anecdote—like the Emo Philips routine just discussed—is a short story with a sudden climax. The setup includes just enough information to encourage the audience to proceed automatically in a direction the performer reverses at the end.

 "Let me tell you about my big-spending husband," one woman said to another. "It was our anniversary, so he took me to the most famous restaurant in town and told me to order the most expensive dish on the menu. I did … a Big Mac."

Two old men were watching a Great Dane lick his balls. One turned to the other and said, "All my life, I've wished that I could do that!" The second one said, "Better pet him first, he looks mean as hell."
**—Billy Crystal**

The trick to creating a good anecdotal reverse is to lay out the plot line of the story so realistically that the reverse isn't expected—even a little bit—by the audience.

 A man was driving on a narrow, winding mountain road when he almost collided with a car that wildly careened around a blind curve. "You stupid fool," he shouted at the other driver. The other car came to a dead stop. A woman rolled down the window, looked at the man and yelled, "Pig! Pig! Pig!" and then quickly drove off. Furious at the insult, the man slammed his car into gear, roared around the mountain curve—and slammed head-on into a giant hog standing in the road.

The reversal in this anecdote works so well because the events leading up to it are completely believable—they could happen to anyone.

Films and sitcoms can lay the groundwork for surprise endings with seemingly insignificant dialogue sprinkled throughout an entire scene. But jokes can't take a half-hour, so clues using the minimum number of words must be dropped seamlessly into anecdotes. Only after audience members have been fooled by the magician are they anxious to analyze what really happened. When your audiences retrospectively analyze your anecdotes, make sure they can note the cleverness of your construction.

 A worker on a construction site would wait until the end of the day, then walk out with a wheelbarrow filled with dirt. Management was positive he was stealing supplies, but every security check of the wheelbarrow accounted for nothing but plain sand. After the job was completed and the worker collected his final paycheck, the foreman walked up to him and said, "Mike, I know you were stealing something. Tell me the truth, what were you takin'?"

And Mike said, "Wheelbarrows!"

## WRITE, DON'T TELEGRAPH

Telegraphing—inadvertently cluing the audience in to the upcoming surprise—is a sign of a beginner. Telegraphing can take the form of a too-detailed introduction, making the setup so obvious that the audience can anticipate the ending of the story. Here's an example: Jack Ellis, a former fund-raising director, was being given a testimonial dinner. One speaker told the following story.

 A carnival strongman wet a towel and then squeezed every drop of water out of it. Then he offered to bet anyone in the audience fifty dollars that they couldn't squeeze out just one more drop. Up sprang our guest of honor, and sure enough, he squeezed out three drops. "Who in the devil are you?" asked the strong man. And the man said, "I'm a fund-raiser for Ohio University."

There is an unwritten law in humor that only one reverse is permissible in any one anecdote. Two is pushing it, and the audience can usually predict a third reverse in advance. The following joke successfully withholds the single reverse until the end of the anecdote.

 A man finds a chimp in the middle of the street. A police car drives by and the man asks the cop, "Hey, what do you think I should do with him?"

"Take him to the zoo," yells the cop.

The next day the police notice the same man with the same chimp.

"I thought I told you to take it to the zoo," said the cop.

"I did," said the man, "and we had so much fun, today I'm taking him to Disneyland."

A Texan, visiting Vermont, asked a farmer how much acreage he had.

"Oh, I've got a big farm," said the farmer. "More than 150 acres."

The Texan swelled up and said, "You know, mister, I get into my car in the morning, I drive all day, and I still can't get to the end of my property."

The farmer said, "I know what you mean. I've got a car just like that."

If they are too obvious in their layout, reverses can be telegraphed even in the shortest anecdotes.

 "Sorry to hear your wife ran away with your gardener."

"Oh, that's all right. I was going to fire him anyway!"

After two drinks, my wife turns into a screaming bitch. After five drinks, I pass out completely.

## HIDE AND PEEK

Hiding is the opposite of telegraphing. Hiding is successful when the audience believes the setup to be a straightforward statement. After a short pause, the humorist reveals the surprise ending—since the audience wasn't expecting anything further, the punchline is even more of a surprise.

 Ohio University was founded in 1804 and opened with a freshman class of twelve students. And this year, eight of them graduated.

## REVERSES ON STAGE

Reverses are common techniques for all stand-up comedians.

 I divorced my first wife because she was so immature. I'd be in the tub taking a bath and she would walk in whenever she felt like it and sink my boats.

**—Woody Allen**

The doctor enters the examination room and says, "Okay, lay down." I say, "Buy me a drink first, pig."

**—Judy Tenuta**

When I went to college, my parents threw a going-away party for me, according to the letter.

**—Emo Philips**

My mother buried three husbands … and two of them were only napping.

**—Rita Rudner**

Every day people are straying away from the church, and going back to God.

**—Lenny Bruce**

To me, clowns aren't funny. In fact, they're kind of scary. I've wondered where this started and I think it goes back to the time I went to the circus, and a clown killed my dad.

**—Jack Handey**

My husband and I didn't sign a prenuptial agreement. We signed a mutual suicide pact.

**—Roseanne Barr**

My grandfather is hard of hearing. He needs to read lips. I don't mind him reading lips, but he uses one of those yellow highlighters.

**—Brian Kiley**

I don't believe in reincarnation, and I didn't believe in it when I was a hamster.

**—Shane Richie**

I was with this girl the other night, and from the way she was responding to my skillful caresses, you would have sworn that she was conscious from the top of her head to the tag on her toes.

**—Emo Philips**

## OPPORTUNITIES FOR REVERSES

One delight of the reverse is that it can be used in speeches to make a serious point, not just tell a joke. As a result, it's an excellent technique for sermons as well.

 Two manufacturing competitors were roommates at an industry association outing at a mountain resort. The first night, they heard scratching outside their cabin door. One went to look, came back, and started to put on his running shoes.

"What's the trouble?" asked his roommate.

The competitor said, "There's a giant bear outside who's so hungry he's gonna smash his way right into this room."

"Well," said the other, "why put on sneakers? You can't outrun a bear." "I know," said the other, "but all I need to do is outrun you."

MCs are notorious for incorporating reverses into their brief introductions.

 We usually go for the best in live entertainment. But, tonight we have to settle for ...

Is everybody having a good time? Well, we'll put an end to that right now!

Reverses can occur in physical humor as well. During an appearance on David Letterman's late-night TV show, Jack Hanna, then director of the Columbus Zoo, was displaying a toucan. Letterman was tossing grapes to the bird: "One, two, three," toss. The bird caught each grape to the roaring approval of the audience. Suddenly, Letterman said to Hanna, "Jack, why don't you try one?" "Fine," said Hanna. "Here we go," yelled Letterman, and he began tossing grapes into the air for Hanna to catch in his mouth. "One, two, three," toss.

Reverses are also very practical for deflecting insults. If the critic isn't carefully specific, the target has the thrill—and it is a thrill when that opportunity comes—to reverse the point of view and change the critic's javelin into a boomerang.

 I don't like country music, but I don't mean to denigrate those who do. And for the people who like country music, denigrate means "put down."

**—Bob Newhart**

Goldie Hawn is funny, sexy, beautiful, talented, intelligent, warm, and consistently sunny. Other than that, she doesn't impress me at all.

**—Neil Simon**

People say to me, "You're not very feminine." Well, they can just suck my dick.

**—Roseanne Barr**

**HUSBAND TO WIFE:** You are not only beautiful, but stupid.
**WIFE TO HUSBAND:** Well, God made me beautiful so you would be attracted to me. And he made me stupid so I'd be attracted to you.

## SCHOOL DAZE: REVERSING A CLICHÉ

Now that we've discussed the uses of reverses and how reverses are constructed, let's write a reversal of a cliché. For the target, let's use the beginning of the school term, when summer is over and parents everywhere happily send their children back to school. Just writing *We all feel relieved when our kids go back to school and the house is quieter and neater* is not wit. Your first efforts to reverse a cliché may look something like these.

 **TOO OBVIOUS**

When my kids go back to school, I go back to sanity.

For parents, Thanksgiving takes place in September—on the day school starts.

**BETTER**

When school starts, my kids think they're going back to hell, and I think I'm going back to heaven.

The meaning of "life, liberty, and the pursuit of happiness" gets a lot clearer the first day my kids go back to school.

**BEST**

September is the month when millions of beautiful faces radiating happiness turn toward school. ...

They all belong to mothers.

It helps to work backward from the reverse. The most obvious reverse might be to make a point about mothers when the audience thinks we're talking about the children.

This type of joke would be a fun opening for a speech to a PTA-type group because the audience members are likely to share a parent's ambivalence toward children.

 When school is out, there's always the tearing up of homework, screeching, and giggling. You would think professors would act more dignified!

**—Paul Sweeney**

# SHOWTIME

The "news" reports on shows such as *Saturday Night Live* and *The Daily Show With Jon Stewart* commonly include reverses in the form of one-sentence news headlines followed by contradictory tag lines. Write a reverse for each of the following setups, then compare your responses to the pros' versions that appear on the next page.

 A Harvard Medical School study has determined that rectal thermometers are still the best way to tell a baby's temperature.

The University of Nebraska says that elderly people who drink beer or wine at least four times a week have the highest bone density.

A man in France was arrested today for using his car to run down a pedestrian he thought was Osama bin Laden.

# THE ANSWER MAN

Here are the pros' conclusions for the reverse setups on pages 128–129.

 Condoms aren't completely safe. A friend of mine was wearing one and got hit by a bus.

**—Bob Rubin**

My wife insists on turning off the lights when we make love. That doesn't bother me. It's her hiding that seems so cruel.

**—Jonathan Katz**

We have a presidential election coming up. And I think the big problem, of course, is someone will win.

**—Barry Crimmins**

After twelve years of therapy, my psychiatrist said something that brought tears to my eyes. He said, "No hablo ingles."

**—Ronnie Shakes**

Here are the conclusions for the headline news setups on page 136.

 A Harvard Medical School study has determined that rectal thermometers are still the best way to tell a baby's temperature. Plus, it really teaches the baby who's boss.

**—Tina Fey**

The University of Nebraska says that elderly people who drink beer or wine at least four times a week have the highest bone density. They need it—they're the ones falling down the most.

**—Jay Leno**

A man in France was arrested today for using his car to run down a pedestrian he thought was Osama bin Laden. Even though it was a mistake, it still ranks as France's biggest military victory.

**—Jay Leno**

# CHAPTER 8
## The Harmony of Paired Elements:
## Phrases, Words, Statistics,
## and Aphorisms

 She was an earthy woman, so I treated her like dirt.

**—George Carlin**

Humor is a feat of verbal gymnastics, and paired elements are examples of the type of clever writing that is commonly used in political addresses, sermons, academic oratory, and toasts. A paired element consists of two grammatical structures (words, phrases, clauses, or sentences) that are similar in construction and that play off each other in meaning.

Paired elements appear in humor formats as varied as ad slogans, bumper stickers, and Shavian wit. You might find paired elements in the "thought for today" in your desk calendar.

There are three varieties of paired elements.

1. paired phrases or sentences
2. paired words
3. paired numbers

### PAIRED PHRASES AND SENTENCES

To be most effective, paired phrases or sentences must be parallel—equal in grammatical purpose, structure, and rhythm. Some need an introductory setup line; most do not. In most cases, the first unit in the pair is a simple declarative statement. The carefully crafted second unit of the pair echoes the first, but a key word may be altered, or the order of the words may be reversed to change the meaning. Aphorisms, which will be discussed later, often contain paired phrases, which are almost lyrical in repetition, and valuable because they make the words easy to remember.

 Ask not what your country can do for you. Ask what you can do for your country.

**—John F. Kennedy**

Better a witty fool than a foolish wit.

**—William Shakespeare**

When the going gets tough, the tough get going.

Figures don't lie, but all liars can figure.

Imagination compensates us for what we are not. Humor compensates us for what we are.

As a humor technique, paired phrases with word reverses are facile but not necessarily simple. The basic rule, common in most humor writing, is that the last line is written first—the last line is the one that makes the point and is most easily remembered. Then, you try to reinforce the theme by reversing the words so the first line introduces the cadence.

 Nobody cares how much you know until they know how much you care.

Pilot over intercom to impatient passengers: We're having a short delay for engine repairs. Aren't you glad you're down here wishing you were up there, rather than up there wishing you were down here?

**—Joan White Book**

Paired phrases are popular with clichés, which afford many opportunities for take-off humor—the line after the paired phrase.

 Boss to new employee: "Relax, Bitler. You have nothing to fear except fear itself. And me, of course!"

**—Robert Mankoff**

Paired elements are frequent applause-getters, and writers know that the audience is more stimulated by the turn of phrase than by its logic. Homonyms get laughs even when they don't make much sense.

 It is better to have loved a small man than never to have loved a tall.

**—Mary Jo Crowley**

As a general rule, you don't want the audience to be able to fill in your punchline for you. You want to surprise them, because they won't appreciate the humor if it's predictable. But audience participation—mentally engaging the audience—can also be an excellent technique for increasing appreciation. If you can create a strong, fresh, paired-element joke, it may not be necessary to state the second part of the pair if the audience can deduce it from the first. You can flatter the audience members by letting them complete the thought themselves. Then they will applaud not only your cleverness, but their own perspicacity.

 The difference between herpes and mono is that you can get mono from snatching kisses.

Each sentence in a paired-sentence element contains one of two paired phrases. In a joke format, each sentence is usually attributed to a different person. The final impression is of a snappy comeback—the audience appreciates the responder's ability to reverse the order of the words and toss them back in the originator's face.

 **TELEGRAM FROM PLAY PRODUCER TO GEORGE BERNARD SHAW:** Send manuscript. If good will send check. **SHAW'S REPLY:** Send check. If good will send manuscript.

A creditor enclosed a picture of his four-month-old daughter in a collection letter to a customer, pleading: "This is why I need the money." The customer replied with a picture of a voluptuous blonde in a bikini. His note: "This is why I don't have the money."

## SHOWTIME

Review your jokes from chapters four and five and rewrite seven to ten of your favorites as paired phrases or sentences.

## PAIRED WORDS

Most paired words fall into one of four classifications: synonyms, homonyms, antonyms, or groupings. No professional humor writer is without a dictionary of synonyms, antonyms, and homonyms.

### Synonyms

Synonyms are different words that share a meaning (horses sweat, gentlemen perspire, ladies glow). Synonyms are popular word pairings. There are so many words in the language that have a similar meaning that there are countless double entendre opportunities. One simple technique for pairing synonyms is to express an idea in one line or phrase, then include in the second line or phrase a synonym for a key word in the first. But the synonym should evoke a different and unexpected meaning of the key word in the first phrase.

 **SHOE SALESMAN:** Don't worry about the shoes. They'll stretch.

**WOMAN:** Then don't worry about the check. It'll bounce.

**—Rita Rudner**

In the example above, the paired words are *stretch* and *bounce*. Although *stretch* and *bounce* aren't strict synonyms, their close relationship (something that can stretch may be likely to bounce) allows them to work together in a play on words.

In each of the following examples, the second phrase features a highly exaggerated synonym for a key word in the first phrase.

She wasn't just throwing herself at him. It was more like taking careful aim.

He only acts mean. But down deep in his heart, he's thoroughly rotten.

The paired synonym take-off, like any take-off, begins with a cliché or standard expression and includes a synonym with the unexpected insight in the punchline.

 I love mankind. It's people I can't stand.
**—Charles M. Schulz**

Redneck against women's lib: I told my wife to stick to her washing, ironing, sewing, cooking, and cleaning. No wife of mine is going to go to work!
**—John Boblitt**

## Homonyms

Homonyms are words that sound the same but are spelled differently or have a different meaning (see the full discussion of homonyms in chapter four). Our language is rich with words that are pronounced alike. Take gene, for instance. Gene can be a scientific term or a man's name, but when spoken, it can sound like pants made of denim (jeans) or a woman's name (Jean).

 One DNA molecule to another: Those genes make me look fat.
License plate of sheep rancher: EWEHAUL.
She was a girl who preferred men to liquor.
Ad for telephone system: From high tech to hi, Mom.

## Antonyms

While synonyms are words or phrases that share the same meaning, antonyms are words or expressions that mean the opposite of each other: hot vs. cold, tall vs. short. Paired antonyms generate humor because they are the simplest form of a reverse. The first word of the phrase starts you in one direction; the antonym flips you in the opposite site. When *Saturday Night Live* was having a bad season, critics were quick to dub it *Saturday Night Dead*.

There are good and bad politicians in the government: Some are trying to clean it up; some are trying to clean it out.

**—Robert Orben**

Young boy to friend: If I'm too noisy they give me a spanking. If I'm too quiet, they take my temperature.

The use of antonym pairs is compatible with humor based on double entendres and puns. Since laughter frequently arises from the appreciation of clever word play, even antonym non sequiturs can get laughs.

 Let's get out of these wet clothes and into a dry martini.

**—Robert Benchley**

It's no wonder foreigners are confused by our language. Here a slim chance and a fat chance mean the same thing.

**—Joyce Mattingly**

Three most frequently used antonym pairs are (a) good and bad, (b) right and wrong, and (c) good and lousy.

 **FATHER TO PRETEEN DAUGHTER**: "There are two words I want you to stop using. One is swell and the other is lousy. Promise?"
**DAUGHTER**: "Sure, Dad, now what are the two words?"

Your manuscript is both good and original, but the part that is good is not original and the part that is original is not good.

**—Samuel Johnson**

Antonyms can exist as two words that mean the opposite of each other (hot vs. cold), or one word can form its own antonym by the addition of a prefix such as un- or in- (sensitive vs. insensitive). There are hundreds of words that become their own antonyms just by the addition of a prefix—uninteresting is the antonym of interesting, and impatience is the opposite of patience.

 I left journalism because I met too many interesting people at an uninteresting salary.

The reasonable man adapts himself to the world. The unreasonable man persists in trying to adapt the world to himself. Therefore, all progress depends on the unreasonable man.

**—George Bernard Shaw**

### Brainstorming Paired Antonyms

The first step of brainstorming humor is association, as discussed in chapter six. When brainstorming antonyms, you must dredge up every related combination. For example, when you think of the antonyms right and left, you think of the directions *right* and *left*, and perhaps the political perspectives of the right and the left. But good humorists would notice that the word *right* is also an antonym to the word *wrong*. Some of the most sophisticated (and appreciated) humor combines the meaning of a word from one antonym pair with the meaning of a word from another antonym pair.

 Most bankers recommend that you wait until you've completely paid for the right running shoe before you plunge in and buy the left.

**—Dave Barry**

In comedy, antonym pairs need not fit the dictionary definition of an antonym perfectly. As long as the suggestion of an opposite is inferred, the humor can work.

 This administration brags that it has developed a new balance of trade: Young people go south of the border to buy drugs and senior citizens go north of the border to buy drugs.

**—Mel Helitzer**

A new patient was asked by his doctor to list all the prescriptions he was taking. The doctor looked at the long list of different medications and said, "You know, Bill, you look better in person than you do on paper."

It is important, however, not to mix up proper antonym combinations. The antonym of *born* is *died* and the opposite of *started* is *finished*. You shouldn't combine *born* with *finished* or *started* with *died*.

**ACCEPTABLE**

In this nightclub, a number of famous comics were born—and tonight, a number just died.

**ACCEPTABLE**

A number of famous comics started here—and tonight, a number just finished here.

**UNACCEPTABLE**

A number of famous comics started here—and tonight, a number just died here.

It is sometimes possible to include two or more antonyms in the same bit.

 Hard work pays off in the future. Laziness pays off now.

## Groupings

Another type of word play relies on the *grouping* of two or more words loosely associated with the same topic. These words don't have to be synonyms, antonyms, or homonyms.

 A political candidate must learn not only to stand on a platform, but also to sit on the fence and lie on the spot.

**—Frank Tyger**

I come from out west, where men are men and women are women, and you can't ask for a better setup than that.

**—Red Skelton**

I come from New York, where men are men—and women are men, too!

**—Robin Williams**

# SHOWTIME

Use a thesaurus to create a list of antonyms for the two most frequently used antonym pairs: *good* and *bad*, and *right* and *wrong*. Write

seven to ten reverses in which the antonyms are used as
paired words.

## PAIRED NUMBERS

Numbers and figures can also be paired to humorous effect. As with any
joke, save the surprise number or figure for the very end of the joke, just
as if it were a word.

 The sheriff said to the outlaw, "I'll give you a fair chance. We'll
step off ten paces and you fire at the count of three." The men
pace off, the sheriff shouts, "One, two"—and then he turns and
fires. The dying outlaw says, "I thought you said to fire on three."
The sheriff said, "That was your number. Mine was two."

Professional humor writers often use numbers in sequences. The
progression of a numerical sequence should be logical and rhythmic,
and sequences should always progress in one direction only: up
or down.

 **SON:** Dad, can I be your caddy?
**FATHER:** Son, a caddy has to be old enough to keep score.
**SON:** I can keep score.
**FATHER:** Okay, if I got six on the first hole, seven on the second
hole, eight on the third hole, and nine on the fourth hole, what
would my total score be?
**SON:** Eleven.
**FATHER:** Okay, son, you're my caddy.

### Numbers Progressing Up

 **MC AT OLD-AGE HOME:** "We're going to give a prize to the old-
est person here."
**FIRST VOICE:** I'm 63.
**SECOND VOICE:** I'm 73.

**THIRD VOICE:** I'm 83.

**FOURTH VOICE:** I'm dead!

There are still things you can get for a dollar—like nickels, dimes, and quarters.

—**Charles Lindner**

## Numbers Progressing Down

 Professor to class: Don't be afraid of rewrites. Just remember the first draft of Dickens' book was called *A Tale of Ten Cities*. The second draft was called *A Tale of Nine Cities*, then it was *Eight*, then it was *Seven*. ...

—**Kathy Leisering**

## Numbers Repeated

The following example not only repeats number pairs, it repeats phrases—with a reversal of the numbers in the second phrase of the pair.

 To have twenty lovers in one year is easy. To have one lover for twenty years is difficult.

—**Zsa Zsa Gabor**

The example below repeats the number five and establishes a pattern of phrases.

 The kind of humor I like makes me laugh hard for five seconds and think hard for five minutes.

—**William Davis**

## APHORISMS AND PAIRINGS:
## PLEASE WAIT TO BE SEEDED

Aphorisms are concise expressions of a bit of truth or wisdom. Following a misfortune, we have certain options. We can turn pessimistic and curse bad luck, or we can be optimistic and consider that fate has provided a valuable learning experience. (The comic writer is trained by necessity to see humor through woes-colored glasses.) These two options form the basis for one type of aphorism—a humorous contrast between the point of view of a pessimist and that of an optimist. This type of aphorism makes good use of paired elements. Let's imagine how you might go about creating such an aphorism. You can start with a built-in antonym pairing: optimist vs. pessimist. Your first effort might read something like this.

 A pessimist curses fate; an optimist looks for benefits from every decision.

There is some wisdom in that line, but nothing particularly marketable. So, you try again, using some repetitive adjectives and subjects.

 An optimist sees benefit in every disaster; a pessimist sees recurrence in every disaster.

The word *disaster* is repeated, and *benefit* has been contrasted with *recurrence*. Still nowhere, but certain possibilities are starting to appear. The contrast of *benefit* and *disaster* is stronger than the contrast of *benefit* and *recurrence*. This could make for good word-reversal opportunities. However, the word *disaster* seems too exaggerated for this problem. Perhaps *calamity*, one peg down, might be more appropriate.

 An optimist sees a benefit in every calamity; a pessimist sees a calamity in every benefit.

There's something wrong with the sound and connotation of *benefit*. *Opportunity* could work, but not every decision is an opportunity. You might try the word *test* before settling on challenge. That sounds better!

 An optimist sees a challenge in every calamity. A pessimist sees a calamity in every challenge.

The result is a set of paired phrases and a set of paired antonyms. It's good writing, and it's good advice, too!

## SHOWTIME

Paired elements are another example of how humor is written backwards—joke-first! And whichever medium is used for humor (printed word, spoken word, cartoons, etc.), writers find paired elements increase commercial value.

 The work will get funny, and the funny will get work.

Whether you're working with paired elements or any of the previously discussed techniques, humor writing requires daily practice. The following exercises will help fuel your comic imagination. (Additional exercises are included in chapter nineteen.)

Write a funny ...

- set of new malaprops and Tom Swifties
- list of new college degree programs
- neighborhood watch guide
- online personal ad
- etiquette guideline for using a cell phone
- list of new Starbucks coffee offerings
- review of a local restaurant, bar, or convenience store
- set of announcements for a K–12 PA system
- e-mail soliciting money for a bogus charity

# CHAPTER 9
## Bewitched, Bothered, and Bewildered: Triples

 I can't think of anything worse after a night of drinking than waking up next to someone and not being able to remember their name, or how you met, or why they're dead.

**—Laura Kightlinger**

Every joke structure has its devotees, but the triple is one format that all humorists use repeatedly. Featuring a grouping of three examples or a sequence of three actions, comments, or categories, the triple increases tension with its longer buildup.

 I celebrated Thanksgiving in an old-fashioned way. I invited everyone in my neighborhood to my house, we had an enormous feast, and then I killed them and took their land.

**—Jon Stewart**

Triples are one of the most common humor formulas. They have been used for so many years in the "There was a priest, a minister, and a rabbi ..." format that, when three such clergymen actually did walk into a bar, the bartender asked, "Is this some kind of a joke?"

The triple formula uses hostility, exaggeration, a buildup of tension, and a surprise ending that inflates the payoff. Most triples are short—two or three sentences—but longer triples can work if done correctly. The opening lines are logical setups and the final line is the most audacious.

 A woman recently had a baby from an embryo that had been frozen for seven years. She said, "I had no idea if I was having a little boy, a little girl, or fish sticks."

**—Conan O'Brien**

At eighty-eight, the king of popcorn, Orville Redenbacher, passed away. His family is mired in an ugly dispute over whether to cremate, microwave, or air-pop him.

—**Stephanie Miller**

If peanut oil comes from peanuts, and olive oil comes from olives, where does baby oil come from?

—**Lily Tomlin**

Neurotics build castles in the air, psychotics live in them. My mother cleans them.

—**Rita Rudner**

The only really good place to buy lumber is at a store where the lumber has already been cut and attached together in the form of furniture, finished, and put inside boxes.

—**Dave Barry**

## Reverse Construction: The Power of Threes

The mystical power of three has been known and used for centuries. The Bible is filled with triple designations: three wise men, the Trinity, and the Hebrew forefathers: Abraham, Isaac, and Jacob. Triple elements occur in our most powerful historical literature: Thomas Jefferson wrote "Life, liberty, and the pursuit of happiness," and one of Abraham Lincoln's most-quoted phrases is "Of the people, for the people, by the people." Three may be an odd number in math, but its even da-da-Ta da-da-Ta da-da-Ta cadence makes it the most important number in comedy. It's not a coincidence that we treasure Goldilocks and the three bears, the three blind mice, the three little pigs, the three musketeers, and the Three Stooges. People in the theater are so superstitious about numbers that actors will knock on stage doors three times and only three times. And that's the truth, the whole truth, and nothing but the truth.

Bart, a woman is like a beer. They look good, they smell good, and you'd step over your own mother just to get one!

**—Homer Simpson**

According to a comedic theory developed by author William Lang, there are only three parts to most comedic bits. We call these three elements humor's SAP test.

S = Setup (preparation)
A = Anticipation (triple)
P = Punchline (story payoff)

Notice how SAP fits these examples.

 **S** = We were Pentecostal.
**A** = When I was growing up we couldn't go to movies, we couldn't listen to rock music, we couldn't wear makeup.
**P** = That's just a lightbulb and a car away from being Amish.

**—René Hicks**

**S** = My wife and I don't get along.
**A** = I take my meals separately, I take a separate vacation, and I sleep in a separate bedroom.
**P** = I'm doing everything I can to keep this marriage together.

**—Milton Berle**

It's possible, of course, to abbreviate the SAP formula by combining two of the elements in one sentence. In the following example, the third part of the triple also includes the punchline.

 When you die there's a light at the end of the tunnel. When my father dies, he'll see the light, make his way toward it, and then flip it off to save electricity.

**—Harland Williams**

Notice how the triple sequence in the next example sets up the value of the last line.

 If you want to be seen—stand up!

If you want to be heard—speak up!

If you want to be appreciated—shut up!

The joke wouldn't be as effective as a series of two. When we leave off the first line, the triple reads:

 If you want to be heard—speak up!

If you want to be appreciated—shut up!

The humor is still there, but the punch is softer without the tension buildup of the triple. If you were to add more lines to this joke, you would overstretch the sequence and make the audience impatient to get to the punchline.

 If you want to be involved—show up!

If you want to be seen—stand up!

If you want to be heard—speak up!

If you want to be important—pay up!

If you want to be appreciated—shut up!

There's no reason to give five examples when three accomplishes all the preparation that's needed.

The final element of SAP humor can include a reverse to make it sound fresher.

 I was told to be accurate, be brief, and then be seated. So I promise I shall be brief as possible—no matter how long it takes me.

**—Willard Pearson**

The trilogy is not a commandment; it's a formula (which means it can be taught in schools). Although most series-based jokes are most effective when they contain three elements, the number of introductory setups in the series can be two, three, four, or as many as you wish—whatever it takes to build anticipation and a climax.

 A Washington, D.C., police chief once claimed he had broken down crime in the Capitol into four categories: murder, assault, robbery, and acts of Congress.

Comic Bill Dana once explained why a ranch with eleven names (Bar Nine, Circle Z, Rocking O, Flying W, Lazy R, Crazy Eight, Bar Seven, Happy Tow, Flying Nun, Lazy Six, and Bar Five) had no cattle: because none could make it through branding. Erma Bombeck preferred to use four, five, and sometimes six in a series. The length of a series is not what's critical—it's the anticipation created by the series.

 I called my friend Bernie in Miami and asked how he was feeling.

"Not well," he said. "I've got cataracts in both eyes, my hearing is almost totally gone, my memory is so bad I can't remember where I put anything, and my hands shake all the time."

"That's terrible," I said. "Any good news?"

"Yes," he said, "I still have my Florida driver's license."

It's no surprise that there are three rules specifically geared to the number three. Tension is important in humor structure, and a triple helps build tension, but be wary of too much of a good thing.

1. Never use more than three jokes about one subject in a monologue.
2. Three minutes is the ideal length for a skit.
3. Don't exceed three themes in an article.

## SHOWTIME

The punchline to the traditional lightbulb joke (*How many_____s does it take to change a lightbulb?*) often consists of a triple. Again, the first and second answers are only setups for the third. Here are some examples based on state stereotypes.

 How many Louisianans does it take to change a lightbulb?

Three: one to hold the ladder, one to screw in the bulb, and one to bribe officials for the permit.

How many Virginians?

Three: one to hold the ladder, one to screw in the bulb, and

one highly refined lady to remark how much lovelier the
old bulb was.

How many Oregonians?
Forty-two: one to hold the ladder, one to screw in the bulb,
and forty to draft the environmental impact statement.

Use a triple to write a lightbulb joke for each of the following professions.
Compare your punch lines to the ones listed at the end of the chapter.

 How many politicians does it take to change a lightbulb?
How many lawyers?
How many doctors?
How many L.A. cops?
How many auto mechanics?

## THE ANECDOTAL TRIPLE

An anecdote, as you know from chapter seven, is a short story told in the
fewest possible words. That's why, even in a long triple, you need to give
just enough information to set up the payoff line.

 A minister comes home to his apartment early and finds his wife
nude in bed and the room filled with cigar smoke. He looks down
from his tenth-story window and sees a man smoking a big cigar
just leaving the building. Enraged, he picks up his refrigerator and
throws it out the window, killing the man instantly.
"Why did you do that?" someone yelled from the street. "
"You killed my priest."
The minister was so distraught that he threw himself
out of the window.
A few moments later, three men—a priest, a minister, and a
rabbi—approach heaven's gate and an angel asks each how he died.
"I don't know," says the priest, "except suddenly a refrigerator
smashed me into the ground."

The minister says, "I threw it. But I was so filled with remorse, I jumped out of the window and killed myself."

"What about you, rabbi?" asks the angel.

"You got me. All I know was I was minding my own business, sitting in a refrigerator ..."

Humor takes even more literary effort than the average editorial story because the climax must be powerful enough to cause an immediate physical reaction in the audience. Your goal is to tell an anecdote in the fewest possible words. But sometimes cutting words can lessen the effect of a joke. Consider the following example.

 Three sons, with their wives, were celebrating their parents' fiftieth anniversary. At the dinner, the first son stood up and said, "Dad. Mom. I'd have brought you a present, but Suzy and I spent the summer in Europe, so we're kinda broke, but we do wish you the very best."

The second son said, "My dear parents, I, too, would have brought a present, but I just bought Nancy a diamond necklace, and we're short right now."

And the third said, "Folks, we purchased a powerboat, which left us strapped, but good health and love for years to come."

"That's okay, sons," said the father. "I know how it feels to be broke. I never told you this, but when your mother and I decided to get married fifty years ago, we didn't even have the money for a license, so we never had a ceremony."

One of the sons burst out, "My god, Dad. You know what that makes us?"

"Yes, I do," said the father, "and cheap ones, too!"

You can tell the same story without a triple in half the words.

 A son attends a fiftieth anniversary dinner for his parents. He apologizes that, because of personal luxury expenses, he couldn't afford a present. The father sympathizes, "We know how it is. When Mother and I were courting, we were so poor we couldn't afford a license, so we never got married."

"My god," says the son, "do you know what that makes me?"

"Yes," says the dad, "and a cheap one, too!"

The elimination of the triple decreased the suspense and minimized the buildup of hostility that makes the father's retort so funny. It isn't that one example isn't funny; it's just that ridiculing three is more pleasurable.

The third element in a triple can also be customized to fit a specific event.

## PAINTING HUMOR

Some humorists are blessed with the ability to paint a picture with words, affording the listener or reader the chance to visualize the joke. For example, the success of Garrison Keillor's mythical Lake Wobegon adventures is in large part due to his colorful phrasing and vivid references. Here are the opening lines to Keillor's book *Wobegon Boy*.

 I am a cheerful man, even in the dark, and it's all thanks to a good Lutheran mother. When I was a boy, if I came around looking glum and mopey, she said, "What's the matter? Did the dog pee on your cinnamon toast?" And the thought of our old black mutt raising his hind leg in the pas de dog and peeing on my toast made me giggle.

Humor provides the writer with great latitude to embellish—even exaggerate—with imagery. Consider the following triple.

 Based on what you know about him, what do you think Abraham Lincoln would be doing if he were alive today? One: Writing his memoirs of the Civil War. Two: Advising the President. Or three: Desperately clawing at the inside of his coffin.

**—David Letterman**

The joke works only because of the imagery in the final line, "Desperately clawing at the inside of his coffin." If a general phrase were used, such as "Trying to get out of his coffin," the joke would be less effective. The colorful language encourages the audience to visualize the joke.

The lack of imagery in many play-on-word (POW) jokes explains why the response to them is often less than enthusiastic. Most POW humor depends entirely on language subtleties to produce surprise, and only half of the brain—the left hemisphere—experiences the joke. When imagery is incorporated into a joke, both hemispheres are stimulated, and the result is full-brain humor.

One of the ways to enhance the visual nature of humor is by specificity. For example, the term *candy bar* is less likely to conjure up a visual cue than a specific reference, such as a Snickers bar. The challenge for comedy writers is to avoid general, abstract phrases and use concrete descriptions that stimulate the senses.

## SHOWTIME

The following exercises will punch up the imagery in your writing.

1. Rewrite each of the following phrases using specificity.

   grab some food
   watch TV
   read a book
   drive a car

2. Replace general words or phrases in your previous jokes with specific, graphic descriptions.

3. When you record everyday events in your humor diary, use the most vivid, colorful, and graphic descriptions.

## TRIPLE VARIATIONS

A common variation on the SAP formula is to set up a joke with a triple—in other words, to include the triple not in the A (anticipation) part of the formula, but in the first P (preparation). The second element of the joke then refers to something unrelated to the triple. Finally, in the punchline, the answer to the question references the triple in the setup. Once you learn this formula, the variations multiply.

 **WAITRESS, IN HOARSE VOICE**: For dessert, we got ice cream—vanilla, chocolate, and strawberry.

**CUSTOMER**: You got laryngitis?

**WAITRESS**: No, just vanilla, chocolate, and strawberry.

Triples can easily be combined with other joke formats. For example, you can start with a triple and add a take-off.

 The thing about being a professor is that if you can make just one student successful, if you can make just one student see the light, if you can make just one ready for the outside world, then you're still stuck with nineteen failures.

**—Mel Helitzer**

The thing about being a humorist is that if you only get one laugh, if you only get one smile, if you can make only one person happy, then you know your act stinks!

**—Gene Perret**

Another very popular combination of techniques is to start with a triple, then switch to a reverse. The reverse can supplement or replace the third element in the triple.

 More than any time in history, mankind faces a crossroads. One path leads to despair and utter helplessness, the other to total extinction. Let us pray that we have the wisdom to choose correctly.

**—Woody Allen**

Younger men are all right! They also come too quick and go to sleep right after, but they can do it every goddamn night.

**—Roseanne Barr**

I'd like to introduce a man with a lot of charm, talent, and wit. Unfortunately, he couldn't be here tonight, so instead ...

Any of you see *Survivor* on TV last night? Talk about plot, drama, great acting—it had none of those things.

I had a nightmare I was trapped in an elevator with Yanni, Kenny G., and Michael Bolton ... and I had a gun with only one bullet.

**—Dave Attell**

My wife's family consisted of three brothers and a dog: Tom, Dick, Harry, and Rover. Harry was the dog.

You can also combine a triple with another triple.

 My rules for dating: I don't want to hear about your car, I don't want to hear about your ex-girlfriend, I don't want to hear about your boring-ass job. The most romantic thing you can do is relax, buy me drinks, and shut the hell up.

**—Wanda Sykes**

Triples can also be used to enhance a mild piece of humor. Topping the first bit of humor with two additional comments encourages the audience to laugh instead of thinking *Is that all there was to it?*

 There are three ways to be ruined in this world. First is by sex, the second is by gambling, and the third is by telling jokes. Sex is the most fun, gambling is the most exciting, and being a comedian is the surest.

**—Paul Roth**

Triples can also be used in physical humor. Bob Nelson does a visual triple during his monologue about college football players being interviewed on camera. He places two balloons under an oversized sweater to indicate shoulder pads. But as he is putting them under the sweater he fills the time with a visual triple. He first pushes the two balloons underneath from the bottom and leaves them momentarily side-by-side. "Wanna see my grandmother?" he asks while the balloons are in a low position. Then he moves the balloons midway up the sweater and says, "This is what my dream girl looks like." Then he moves the two balloons, one to each side of the sweater, and says, "My dream girl lying down." Finally, he puts them in the shoulder-pad position for his football segment.

This is called a joke on the way to a joke because the triple is used to enhance a dead moment while changing props. Except in intentional pauses, silence is a comic's deadly enemy.

## SHOWTIME

Like a joke in any other format, a triple must be concluded with an audacious and surprising climax. Write an unexpected conclusion for each of the following jokes. Compare your answers to the pros' versions on the next page.

 Someone did a study of the three most-often-heard phrases in New York City. One is "Hey, taxi." Two is "What train do I take to get to Bloomingdale's?" And three is …

I like Florida; everything is in the eighties: the temperature, the ages, and …

Men should be like Kleenex: soft, strong, and …

Making love to a woman is like buying real estate …

## THE ANSWER MAN

Here are some possible punchlines for the lightbulb jokes on page 155.

 How many politicians does it take to change a lightbulb?

Thirty-six: Two to sponsor the bill, thirty-three to constitute a quorum, and one to change it.

How many lawyers?

Three: One to change it, one to call the electrician who wired the house, and one to sue the power company for causing the surge that made the bulb burn out.

How many doctors?

Three: One to find a bulb specialist, one to find a bulb installation specialist, and one to bill Medicare.

How many L.A. cops?

Six: One to screw in a new bulb, four to beat the crap out of the old one, and one to videotape the scene.

How many auto mechanics?

Six: One to give you an estimate, one to force it with a hammer, and four to go out for more bulbs.

Here are the professionals' conclusions for the triples on page 161.

 Someone did a study of the three most-often-heard phrases in New York City. One is "Hey, taxi." Two is "What train do I take to get to Bloomingdale's?" And three is "Don't worry. It's only a flesh wound."

**—David Letterman**

I like Florida; everything is in the eighties: the temperature, the ages, and the IQs.

**—George Carlin**

Men should be like Kleenex: soft, strong and disposable.

**—Cher**

Making love to a woman is like buying real estate: location, location, location.

**—Carol Leifer**

# CHAPTER 10
## Realism, Exaggeration, and Understatement

 When a thing is funny, search it for a hidden truth.

**—George Bernard Shaw**

Humor only appears to be free-form. To the trained ear, it's predictable because it's structured. Nowhere is this structure more evident than in the interaction of realism and exaggeration, two of the six ingredients in the THREES formula (target, hostility, realism, exaggeration, emotion, surprise). In humor, they balance each other like equal weights on a scale. Sometimes one side of the scale may tip, but the variation is always small—and that's no exaggeration.

 My dad's pants kept creeping up on him. By sixty-five he was just a pair of pants and a head.

**—Jeff Altman**

In the preceding joke, the realistic element is the rising waistband of the father's pants. The exaggeration is the waistband reaching the father's head. Realism is essential in order for the audience share hostility toward a common target. On the other side of the scale, facts and conclusions are exaggerated to build tension and surprise. This is a standard theatrical device, a dramatic license that portrays objects and events as larger than life.

### MAKE IT REAL

Realism was a big reason for the success of such classic sitcoms as *All in the Family* and *The Cosby Show*. "My one rule is to be true, rather than funny," said Bill Cosby. The more realistic we make the humor piece seem, the more our audience identifies with it.

My way of joking is to tell the truth. It is the funniest joke in the world.

**—George Bernard Shaw**

Truth (realism) involves the audience. This is why people want to know the latest news. (The most influential words in advertising are *free, sale,* and *new.*) We all care more about current events when they affect us directly. The key is remembering that a premise must be true and interesting to *we*, the audience, not *you*, the writer. Remember how bored you get when people dwell at length on their recent business or domestic problems. The classic line is:

 He's the kind of bore who, when you meet him on the street and say, "How are you?" he stops and tells you.

Fifty percent of the time people don't care about your problems, and the other fifty percent of the time they're glad you're getting what you deserve. You want to avoid having the audience react this way to your jokes.

 A customer in a bar is talking to the man seated next to him. "Strange, isn't it? Normally, I'm a very caring person, but in your case, for some reason, I don't give a damn."

The importance of realism might seem to run counter to our understanding that humor is fictional. But humor must contain some element of truth if people are to care. If everyone knows from the beginning of a joke that "any resemblance to anyone living or dead is purely coincidental," they won't care, and they won't laugh.

 I know a man who teethed on a set of alphabet blocks when he was a baby. He finally tired of them when he was fifteen.

This story is simple enough. We have some realism: Babies do teethe on building blocks. We have exaggeration with the age fifteen. We smile at the insult, but there's no big laugh, because nobody cares about "a man."

Yet, if we could find someone whose public reputation indicates limited intellectual abilities, and that person is an authority figure or some celebrity who irritates us, then naming that person adds realism and gives the audience something that focuses their laughter. Remember that good humor includes a strong target for the audience's hostility.

 Sylvester Stallone's mother reported he learned to read by teething on a set of alphabet blocks, and he's been swallowing his letters ever since.

We are so influenced by the hyperbole of media, theater, and advertising, we fall into the habit of believing that certain special events and celebrities are extraordinary. This inflated posturing by publicity specialists is the balloon humorists aim to prick.

## EXAGGERATION CONSTRUCTION: THE STRETCH-BAND THEORY

The British believe that the underclass overstates and the upper class understates. Humor writers are classless; they use both understatement and overstatement. Exaggeration is the Silly Putty of humor writing. You start with a realistic scenario, then bend and distort it for comic effect. Exaggeration is one of the easiest and most effective comedic tools, and it is used in all types of humor: Cartoonists magnify physical features, impressionists exaggerate speech mannerism, and comedians embellish language.

Effective humor is truth-based, so the key to maximizing comedic potential is striking a balance between realism and exaggeration. There *can* be too much distortion. The audience must understand the connection between the truth and the exaggeration.

 If I've told you once, I've told you a thousand times: Don't exaggerate.

Humor comes out of the unexpected: no surprise, no laugh. In a triple, as discussed in chapter nine, the first two lines are frequently straight lines; this is the realistic element. The third line is the surprise twist—logically related to the first two lines, but unexpected and exaggerated. Realism is the setup, while exaggeration is the joke. "Get your facts first," wrote Mark Twain, "and then you can distort them as much as you please."

Humor is like a rubber band; the more it can be stretched, the more useful it is. The process of refining the relationship between exaggeration and realism in humor can be related to stretching a rubber band. Imagine that the unstretched band is the realism, and exaggeration stretches the band.

When the rubber band is stretched to capacity, several things happen at once.

1. Stretching alters the shape of the band; exaggeration alters the perception of reality.
2. The rubber band can be stretched a little (understatement) or a lot (overstatement).
3. Just as tension increases in a rubber band when it is stretched, exaggeration increases tension in the audience—up to the breaking point.
4. When you pluck a rubber band, it makes a sound. The pitch of this sound gets higher as you stretch the rubber band further. This sound can be compared to emotion in an audience. The more you stretch the rubber band, the higher the level of emotion in the audience.

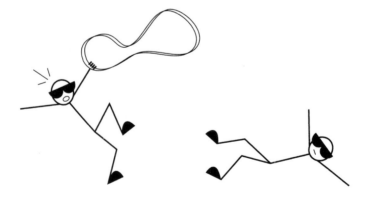

Finding the proper balance between realism and exaggeration is the ultimate test of a comedy writer's skill. Humor only comes when the exaggeration is logical. Simply being ludicrous or audacious is not a skill. It's amateur.

The humor writer starts with realism, then tries to determine how far in any direction the truth can be exaggerated without destroying credibility. One way to do this is to create possibilities under the headings *good*, *better*, and *best*. A story about a prisoner who calls his companion a *cell-mate* is good, but calling him a *roommate* is better, and calling him a *suite-mate* is the best of all.

Realism is frequently funniest when it's exaggerated to the most extreme possibility. In math, $1 + 1 = 2$. In humor, $1 + 1 = 11$. Exaggeration can work by either overstatement (hyperbole) or understatement. Here are examples of both.

 **OVERSTATEMENT**

CEO to members of the board: There you have it, gentlemen. The upside potential is tremendous, but the downside risk is jail.

**—Robert Mankoff**

The scarecrow scared the crows so badly that they brought back the corn they had stolen two years before.

**—Fred Allen**

**UNDERSTATEMENT**

I have my standards. They may be low, but I have them.

**—Bette Midler**

I have low self-esteem. When I'm in bed with someone, I fantasize that I'm someone else.

**—Richard Lewis**

How far can you go with exaggeration? Generally, the more your punchline exaggerates the introductory realism, the better the result.

 I drink to make other people interest me.

**—George Jean Nathan**

I'm Jewish. I don't work out. If God had wanted us to bend over, He would have put diamonds on the floor.

**—Joan Rivers**

There's nothing random about the random search at the airport. You go to the gate and they're standing there with a Sherwin-Williams paint chart. If your ass is darker than khaki, you're getting searched.

**—Wanda Sykes**

Exaggeration seems obvious, but it isn't easy. Many of today's novice stand-up comedians have trouble with it. They'll start with some realistic premise like the way women dress, picking up men in a singles bar, outsmarting the police, or advertising slogans, but then they'll shift into fifth gear in a wild display of ludicrous fantasy that's not well connected to the initial premise. Their material has a success rate of only about 20 or 25 percent because they make the same mistake repeatedly: They disrupt the equal balance of realism and exaggeration.

## THE PERFECT PUNCH

Three criteria determine whether a premise properly sets up the punchline: truth, emotion, and explicitness. The three factors form a memorable acronym, TEE. A solid premise will TEE-up a joke by containing the following elements.

- **T = TRUTH:** The most effective humor is reality-based, genuine, and true. If a setup is exaggerated, insincere, or untrue, then you lose the ability to bend reality to produce the surprise punchline.
- **E = EMOTION:** A solid setup includes a factual statement, opinion, or observation with a stated or implied emotion. The emotion is usually anger or hostility driven by the stupidity, absurdity, or weirdness of the premise.
- **E = EXPLICITNESS:** An effective premise is specific and readily understood by others.

The following exercises will help you identify targets with broad appeal, and premises that TEE-up the punchline.

- Previously, you identified the ways in which each of your targets causes anger, frustration, or irritation. Review each statement to determine if it is reality-based, genuine, and true. If a statement is exaggerated, insincere, or untrue, then either rewrite the premise or discard it.
- For each statement that passed the truth test, determine whether the premise is specific and clear. Also, consider whether the premise will appeal to others. Rewrite as needed.
- At this point, you'll have a list of premises that can TEE-up jokes. In the upcoming chapters, we'll explain how to fit your premises into various joke formulas.

## UNREALISTIC VS. REALISTIC HUMOR

If there's anything instinctive about humor writing, it's being able to determine the right balance of reality and distortion. It's the same instinct news editors use daily to determine what is newsworthy. You have to know it when you see it.

 In show business, the key word is honesty. And once you've learned to fake that, you're in.

**—George Burns**

Many believe that failed humor is most often the result of too much exaggeration. That isn't true. Most often, it results from too little realism.

Here's an example of humor that's unrealistic. It doesn't mean it's not funny. It does mean the performer has to work harder than if she had used more realism.

 Tommy came home from school very dejected. "I had an awful day," he told his mother. "I couldn't remember an answer and it was embarrassing."

"Forgetting one answer is nothing to be embarrassed about,"
soothed his mother.

And the boy said, "During roll call?"

**—Dick Shebelski**

The following examples are more realistic.

 "They threw me out of my hotel in Fort Lauderdale this spring
break for pissing in the pool."

"How could they do that? Lots of kids piss in the pool."

"From the fourteenth floor?"

The bushman remarked, "I'd like to get a new boomerang, but I
can't get rid of the old one."

You are not drunk if you lie on the floor without holding on.

**—Dean Martin**

Even my daughter doesn't give me any respect. I put her to bed
and tried to kiss her and she said, "Not tonight, Daddy, I've got a
terrible headache."

**—Rodney Dangerfield**

## Turning Sense Into Nonsense

Turning realism into exaggeration is easier to understand if we think of it
as a transition from sense to nonsense. Exaggeration is embellishing that
which you've seen or heard. It's almost instinctive. We learned as children that we could get attention by exaggerating. We also learned we
could get in a lot of trouble. But if we told stories in the form of jokes,
we not only got away with it, we got appreciative laughter.

 In grade school, I was such a hit with my exaggerated mimicking
and clowning that the teacher was charging a four-dollar cover
and a two-drink minimum.

**—Billy Crystal**

Every installment of *I Love Lucy* began with a logical premise, such as
Lucy's desire to be a singer in Ricky's band, or her suspicions he might be

philandering. Only after a plausible foundation had been established was the element of absurdity introduced. Then exaggeration continued to inflate the plot until the inevitable slapstick climax.

Since comedy encourages the audience to suspend disbelief, humorists can take advantage of every opportunity to stretch the truth. In other circumstances, unmitigated exaggeration would be castigated as lying. In humor, clever exaggeration guarantees laughter.

## SHOWTIME

Jeff Foxworthy's signature line, *You might be a redneck if ...* is always followed by an exaggerated punchline.

 You might be a redneck if your front porch collapses and four dogs get killed.

You might be a redneck if you think the last words to *The Star-Spangled Banner* are "Gentlemen, start your engines."

You should be able to provide the exaggerated last words of the following possible conclusions to the setup *You might be a redneck if ...* Compare your efforts with Foxworthy's at the end of the chapter.

 You might be a redneck if ...

... you think watching professional wrestling is ...

... you go to your family reunions looking for ...

... on Thanksgiving Day you have to decide ...

... your child's first words were ...

... you've ever paid for a six-pack of beer with ...

... the most common phrase you hear at your family reunion is ...

... you can't marry your sweetheart because ...

### Exaggerated Numbers

Math is usually logical. But when there's a lapse in the logic surrounding or involving numbers, it's hilarious.

 I want to live to be a hundred, because you rarely read any obituaries about people who are more than a hundred years old.

**—George Burns**

Exaggerated numbers are an accepted part of humor writing, They signal to the audience that they are listening to something fictional, that the ludicrousness of the plot is intended to make a point by shock as well as surprise.

 A graduating senior went to the board of health and asked for two thousand cockroaches. He said he promised his landlord he would leave his apartment exactly the way he found it.

The exaggeration is obvious. Would fifty cockroaches have been an acceptable number? Although that number might be more realistic, the mental image of two thousand roaches is more graphic. On the other hand, what about fifty thousand cockroaches? It could be argued that such an overwhelming number creates an image straight out of Hollywood's chamber of horrors and would be more distracting than effective. The number two thousand is easy to say (compared to two thousand five hundred) and easy to remember. It sounds right.

For some reason, fifty-nine sounds larger than sixty, sixty-nine sounds larger than seventy, and seventy-nine sounds larger than eighty—perhaps because the number nine is the highest number you can reach in the decimal system (before resetting to zero) and it can be emphasized during a performance. When including an old age number in a joke, choose seventy-nine over eighty.

 An elderly man, seated in a doctor's waiting room, picks up a copy of *JAMA*—the *Journal of the American Medical Association*. He reads that research indicates that young men who masturbate frequently in their youth have fewer prostrate problems in their senior years. The man slams the magazine down on the table and shouts, "Great! I'm seventy-nine and now they tell me."

## SHOWTIME

The selection of the best number for a particular bit is a basic skill. Test yours. Each of the following jokes uses a number as the surprise element. After you read each one, select a wide variety of numbers—from the highest conceivable to the lowest. Ask yourself if the humor can be strengthened by altering the number in any way.

The average man speaks twenty-five thousand words a day. The average woman says thirty thousand words a day. Unfortunately, when I get home at night, I've spoken my twenty-five thousand, but my wife doesn't start hers until we get into bed.

**—Michael Collins**

One evening a Washington street vendor came home with over a thousand dollars. "Where'd you get all that money?" asked his wife.

"Selling hot dogs for fifty times their regular price."

"Who'd pay that?" asked the wife.

"Lots of people. They all work in the Pentagon."

**—National Enquirer**

A newspaper editor was honored as one of the great leaders of his community by the governor at a testimonial dinner. Flushed with pride, he asked his wife on the way home, "I wonder just how many great leaders our city has?"

The wife said, "One less than you think."

## UNDERSTATEMENT

Subtle humor isn't underrated, it's just understated. Understatement is an effective humor device because it encourages the audience to participate. One of understatement's most famous practitioners is Woody Allen, whose own humor was influenced by S.J. Perelman, a master of the art. Allen's understatements start out very realistically, and are frequently non sequiturs.

 If there's a God, why are there such things as famine and daytime TV?

I don't really believe in the afterlife, but I am taking a change of underwear.

Understatement is an excellent technique in self-deprecating humor. The audience feels more comfortable with people who have a modest attitude toward their own accomplishments.

 People always ask me if I get stage fright. Believe me, it's not the stage that frightens me; it's the audience that scares the hell out of me.

**—Robert Orben**

A few years after my father died, my lonely mother moved to Florida to find Mr. Right. In Miami, the description of Mr. Right is a man who has money in two banks and is ambulatory.

Wilted father to wife and five children at front door: I've had a rough day, honey. Tell me everybody's name again.

**EDITOR TO WRITER:** That article wasn't bad.
**WRITER:** It wasn't meant to be.

**—Fred Allen**

I'm not shooting for a successful relationship at this point. I am just looking for something that will prevent me from throwing myself in front of a bus. I'm keeping my expectations very, very low. Basically, I'm looking for a mammal.

**—Janeane Garofalo**

## Understated Numbers
Understated numbers are as equally effective as exaggerated numbers.

When *New Yorker* editor Harold Ross was asked why he printed the cartoons of James Thurber, a fourth-class illustrator, Ross said, "I don't think he's fourth-class—maybe second-class!"

As in most humor, the pause before the surprise word effectively builds tension. When a reporter asked comedian David Brenner what he thought of the remodeling of a nightclub, he said, "It's beautiful, impressive. Must have poured three hundred and fifty ... dollars into this place."

 TV quizmaster to dull contestant: Well, I could go on talking to you for seconds!

## OVERSTATEMENTS AND UNDERSTATEMENTS ON STAGE

Jerry Seinfeld and Ellen DeGeneres each combine observational humor with understatement and hyperbole. Here are some of DeGeneres's under- and overexaggerations.

 The sixties were when hallucinogenic drugs were really, really big. And I don't think it's a coincidence that we had the type of shows we had then, like *The Flying Nun.*

You always know when the relationship is over. Little things start grating on your nerves: "Would you please stop that? That breathing in and out, it's so repetitious!"

I have just learned that penguins are monogamous for life, which doesn't really surprise me all that much because they all look exactly alike. It's not like they're going to meet a better-looking penguin someday.

When going to a restaurant, "party of one" is rarely cause for celebration.

When I was growing up, we had a petting zoo, and well, we had two sections. We had a petting zoo, and then we had a *heavy* petting zoo. For people who really like the animals a lot.

Here are some of Seinfeld's exaggerations.

 What is a date really, but a job interview that lasts all night? The only difference is that in not many job interviews is there a chance you'll wind up naked.

Now they show you how detergents take out bloodstains, a pretty violent image there. I think if you've got a T-shirt with a bloodstain all over it, maybe laundry isn't your biggest problem. Maybe you should get rid of the body before you do the wash.

I was the best man at the wedding. If I'm the best man, why is she marrying him?

## SHOWTIME

Exaggeration and understatement both distort personal attributes, behaviors, or experiences. Write an overstated or understated conclusion for the following setups and compare your response to the pros' versions at the end of the chapter.

 My father was so cheap. For Easter ...

My town was so little ...

My childhood was so bleak ...

I dye my hair so much ...

I have so much cybersex ...

I've been on so many blind dates ...

## WALK THIS WAY: BALANCING REALISM AND EXAGGERATION

As an exercise in balancing realism and exaggeration, start with an incident that really happened and make it bigger than life. But be careful. *Outrageous* doesn't mean *creative*.

Consider this description by critic Laurence Shames of a Monty Python "silly walk" sketch, in which John Cleese portrays a very ordinary Englishman on his way to work at a government office.

 Suited, hatted, carrying briefcase and cane, the Silly Walker faultlessly conforms to the type of the proper civil servant. Except that something is very wrong with the way he moves. He suddenly swoops down from his enormous height like some primeval, featherless bird; now he dodges, his spine contorts, his feet perform a going-nowhere shuffle; now his knees buckle so that, apelike, his hands are nearly dragging on the ground. So far, so good—in terms of sheer physical funniness, the sketch is virtuosic; it can have you rolling on the floor. But the kicker is the Silly Walker's face. It is expressionless, implacable, and smug. The fellow is a self-respecting Briton on his way to his perfectly acceptable job, and never in a zillion years would it occur to him that he's ridiculous.

The following examples contain an equal balance of realism and exaggeration to reinforce the surprise. Carefully examine them and note the formula: A realistic statement is followed by an exaggerated take-off reply. But when using this formula, be on guard not to overload both elements.

 Prof to class: Good morning students. And to those of you on speed, good afternoon!

**—Mel Helitzer**

At my age, sex is sensational. Especially the one in the winter.

**—Milton Berle**

In the following example, the exaggeration occurs in the setup.

 A waiter, his uniform badly torn, his hands scratched and bleeding, walks up to seated guests: I hate to inconvenience you, sir, but would you kindly pick out a different lobster from the tank?

**—Arnie Levin**

Many adults are ambivalent about taking their elderly parents into their homes for care. Their guilt, when personal comfort gets in the way of tender loving care, contains all the elements for realistic humor.

 Wife: Your father is playing basketball again. He's dribbling all over the house.

Son to aged father: Hey, pop, we're having company tonight. Do you mind staying out in the garage?

One of the writing modes that maintains realism along with exaggerated humor is the movie or play review. Critics feel compelled to use their own rapier wit to slice up the work of others, and excerpts from reviews are in every comedic library.

 When Mr. Wilbur calls his play *Halfway to Hell* he underestimates the distance.

**—Brooks Atkinson**

In *King Lear* last night, the lead played the king as though under a momentary apprehension that someone else was about to play the ace.

**—Eugene Field**

In a review of Cecil B. DeMille's movie *Samson and Delilah*: Saw the movie. Loved the book.

**—John Steinbeck**

# SHOWTIME

Write an overstated or understated description of someone you know. Focus on the person's salient features and distort each characteristic to the point of absurdity.

Rewrite a favorite anecdote using exaggeration. As you write, try to enter a dreamlike state in which reality blurs with fantasy. The resulting story will be far-fetched, but the idea is to tap the full potential of your comic imagination.

*Whose Line Is It Anyway?* is a TV program that showcases the improvisational skills of four comedians. A regular feature requires the performers to create new uses for miscellaneous everyday items. You can do the same by imagining creative and inventive uses for various items around your house. As you do this, maintain a childlike, playful mood that encourages exaggerated imagination.

Select someone you know and write a series of overstated and understated punchlines about that person using the following antonym pairs: *fat* and *skinny, organized* and *sloppy, conservative* and *liberal, poor* and *rich,* and *dumb* and *intelligent.* For example, *My father is so organized that ...* and *My father is so sloppy that ...*

## THE ANSWER MAN

Here are the conclusions for the redneck jokes on page 171.

 You might be a redneck if ...

    ... you think watching professional wrestling is foreplay.

    ... you go to your family reunions looking for a date.

    ... on Thanksgiving Day you have to decide which pet to eat.

    ... your child's first words were "Attention Kmart shoppers!"

    ... you've ever paid for a six-pack of beer with pennies.

    ... the most common phrase you hear at your family
        reunion is "What the hell are you lookin' at, Diphead?"

    ... you can't marry your sweetheart because there is a
        law against it.

Here are the pros' exaggeration jokes from page 176.

 My father was so cheap. For Easter, we'd wear the same clothes, but he'd take us to a different church.

                                    **—A.J. Jamal**

My town was so little, when I was a kid we used to play Monopoly on it.

—**Jean Young**

My childhood was so bleak, I wanted to stick my head in my Easy Bake oven.

—**Mary O'Halloran**

I dye my hair so much, my driver's license has a color wheel.

—**Nancy Mura**

I have so much cybersex, my baby's first words will be "You've got mail!"

—**Paulara Hawkins**

I've been on so many blind dates, I should get a free seeing-eye dog.

—**Wendy Liebman**

# CHAPTER 11
## Funny Words and Foul Language

In his play *The Sunshine Boys*, Neil Simon wrote about funny words. One of the main characters, Willy, says to his nephew:

 Fifty-seven years in this business, you learn a few things. You know what makes an audience laugh. You know what words are funny and which words are not funny. Alka Seltzer is funny. You say "Alka Seltzer" you get a laugh. ... Words with "K" in them are funny. Casey Stengel, that's a funny name. Robert Taylor is not funny. Cupcake is funny. Tomato is not funny. Cookie is funny. Cucumber is funny. Car keys. Cleveland. ... Cleveland is funny. Maryland is not funny. Then, there's chicken. Chicken is funny. Pickle is funny.

Mel Brooks agrees. There are phonetic values in certain words that almost guarantee a laugh. "Instead of saying salmon, turkey is a funnier sound. It just helps."

Why is the *k* sound funny? Research indicates that babies associate the sound with comfort and joy. Think of many of the words we coo to babies, and you'll notice they have a *k* sound, even though most of them begin with the letter *c*. Just a few are *cutie, cookie, kitten, cuddle, car, come, count, kiddie, clean,* and *cupcake.* No other sound has such a universal humor kick. As you say *kiss,* for example, your mouth smiles, it doesn't pucker up.

There are thousands of funny words that kick over the laugh motor. While, in humor, most key words come at the end of a sentence, funny-sounding words work best in the middle of a joke and are frequently used in groups—for example, as lists of names, foods, or physical activities.

All writers have their own favorite buzzwords, and they're jealous of them, even to the point of anger when someone else uses them. Fortunately, these words are not private property.

 Every time I look at what I have to pay in taxes, it scares me shirtless.

**—Robert Orben**

## THE SPARK PLUGS OF HUMOR

To be categorized as funny, a word has to have at least one of the following three characteristics: a funny sound, a double entendre, or an association with a famous person. The same is true of funny names.

**1. IT MUST HAVE A FUNNY SOUND.** Jonathan Winters's characters have names like Granny Frickert, Melvin Gohard, Lamargene Gumbody, and Elwood P. Suggins. Other funny names are Faith Popcorn, Hortense Powdermarker, and Daphne Kugelmass.

S.J. Perelman, the master of humorous appellations, invented Professor Motley Throng, Ernest Void, Irma Voltaire, the Flagellation Trust Company, and the Cutlass and Blintzes Pub. His version of *Sleeping Beauty* starts off with "Once upon a time, there was a king and queen named Morton Steinberg and his wife, Fanny. ... They made up their minds that if they ever had a child they would name it Shirley, even if it was a boy." In this case, the names themselves aren't funny, but their association with fairy-tale royalty is.

Was it only a coincidence that Jacob Cohen first started with a stage name of Jack Roy, but gained fame and respect only after changing his name to Rodney Dangerfield? Or that the Marx Brothers' act went into high gear when Julius became Groucho and his brothers Leonard and Adolph became Chico and Harpo?

Zero Mostel's real name was Sam. He said he changed it to Zero so he could make something out of nothing.

**2. IT MUST HAVE A DOUBLE ENTENDRE.** It's hard to forget a name like John Dough. And it's easy to understand a characterization when a character has a name like Lionel Bedwetter or Sandor Needleman.

As children, our first exercises in homonym humor consisted of fabricating book titles to match off-color author names.

*The Yellow Stream* by I.P. Standing
*The Open Kimono* by Seymour Hare
*The Hawaiian Prostitute* by Wanna Layahora
*My Shotgun Wedding* by Himalaya Last
*The Russian Rabbi* by Ikan Kutchadikoff

**3. IT MUST BE A NAME OF A FAMOUS—OR INFAMOUS—PERSON.**
The person's activities should be well known and should encourage our ridicule, hostility, or derision (even if we're really not justified in feeling these emotions). As soon as these names hit the headlines (Monica, Saddam, Osama), they also hit the top of the humor charts. Old jokes—new names!

At least one of these same three qualifications must apply to all funny words. Here are just a few examples, listed by the most popular categories.

## Names

Every ethnic group has names that encourage a smile. One of the best recent examples is Tony Soprano. Here are few examples for various ethnic groups.

| AMERICAN | ENGLISH | ITALIAN |
|---|---|---|
| Dick | Percy | Guido |
| Chuck | Humphrey | Tony |
| Spike | Reginald | Giuseppe |
| Trixy | Victor | |

| JEWISH | FRENCH | CHICANO |
|---|---|---|
| Mendel | Pierre | Margarita |
| Sadie | Francois | Jose |
| Irving | Henri | Pablo |
| Sam | Pepe | Manuel |
| Morris | Suzette | |
| Lena | | |

Most male comedians purposely take short names, more often than not a nickname: Woody, Soupy, Adam, Chris, Dave, Jay, Tim, Billy, Eddie, and Sinbad. Female humorists names are just as short: Goldie, Lily, Lucy, Whoopi, Rita, and Tina.

 Donald Trump said he named his daughter Tiffany after his favorite store: Tiffany's. How ridiculous is that? In fact, I was just talking about that with my two sons, Crate and Barrel.

**—Shawn Dion**

### Cities and Places

There seems to be no limit to the names of cities, small towns, streets, restaurants, bars, hotels, colleges, and department stores that can be used as humor fuses. The more localized they are, the better.

Years ago, funny names for hick towns (Oshkosh, Paducah) frequently appeared in jokes. Today, because a large portion of comedy is played to New York audiences, no locale seems to be a target of humor more often than New Jersey. (*Isn't it a shame that the light at the end of the tunnel is New Jersey?*) Within New York, no borough gets kidded more often than Brooklyn. Sheboygan is a funny name, and no city is the butt of more jokes than Cleveland (either because of the *k* sound, or because Cleveland is proof that God had a quality control problem).

### Foods

Many generic and brand-name food products just sound funny. There's probably no more guaranteed laugh in comedy than the word *Twinkie*. Use it at the end of a list of foods you ate last night, and involuntary smiles come to the lips of your audience. Archie Bunker used this word ad nauseam, but not so much to refer to the snack food. Here are some other funny generic and brand-name foods.

| GENERIC | BRAND NAMES |
|---|---|
| frankfurter | Jell-O |
| salami | Fig Newtons |
| tutti-frutti | Whopper |
| fruitcake | Ex-Lax |

| | |
|---|---|
| hot dog | Kotex |
| coconut | McNuggets |
| kumquats | Chock Full o' Nuts |
| meatball | Spam |

## Ethnic Expressions

While ethnic jokes are a major category in contemporary humor, the utilization of ethnic expressions in a joke requires precise knowledge of their meaning and cadence. For example, many comedians use the Yiddish word *schmuck* to describe a loser, not realizing that the word's literal meaning is "penis."

When Jewish comedians dominated mainstream American comedy, Yiddish expressions achieved a certain humor value because Yiddish words sound funnier than their English counterparts. For example, *bar mitzvah* sounded funnier than *confirmation*, and *rabbi*—because of stereotyping—conjured up more humorous possibilities than the title of *minister*. The following are common Yiddish words: *putz, klutz, schlemiel, shtick, chutzpah, goyim, schlep, kvetch,* and *meshuggener.*

Closely allied in humor with Yiddish expressions are German names and foods (a good deal of Yiddish originated from German). When the monster makes love to Madeline Kahn in Mel Brooks's film *Young Frankenstein,* he thrills her with his enormous *shvantzenstucker.* Sid Caesar's stupid German professors had names like Kurt von Stuffer, Siegfried von Sedative, and Rudolf von Rudder. And *Meet the Fockers* was a multimillion-dollar movie.

## Animals

The names of certain pets and animals also convey funny images. Puppies, cats, mice, and rabbits all have double entendre associations. And even insects—like bees and cockroaches—are funny humor sources.

 A German professor was addressing a Westchester ladies club on the life of the porcupine. "And would you believe it, ladies," he said, "that the porcupine has a prick that is ten inches long?" There were gasps all over the room, and the MC hastily whispered in the professor's ear. "Oh, my dear ladies," the professor said, "I have made a terrible mistake in English. What I should have said is that the quill of the porcupine is ten inches long. Obviously, the prick is only one inch long."

## Numbers

Even some numbers are funnier than others, and we're not just talking about sixty-nine. In humor, the economy of words is almost fanatical. There is one exception, and that is when numbers are used. If they're essential in the joke, when we want to give them extra power, they must sound or look important. The number *1,500* should be pronounced (or written) as *one thousand, five hundred*. The time of *8:15* should be pronounced (or written) as *a quarter after eight*. The height of *6'2"* should be pronounced (or written) as *six foot, two inches tall*. Every syllable must be an atom of meaning as well as information.

## SHOWTIME

From now on, every time you hear a name, place, product, or ethnic expression that tickles your funny bone, write it down. Create a funny-word catalog that can be referenced when you need to embellish the setup.

## FOUL LANGUAGE: THE MUCK STOPS HERE

The punchline of this story is a classic combination of surprise and shock. The vulgarity—so unexpected—is like watching a friend take a banana-peel fall. We laugh, and then look around to see who else is laughing. If no one is, we realize that perhaps we shouldn't have either.

 A walking path bordered the golf course. One afternoon a tee shot nearly smashed into a little old lady.

She screamed, "Why didn't you yell fore?"

"I didn't have time," said the golfer.

"Oh, no?" said the little old lady, "Then how come you had time to yell 'Oh, shit!'"

But vulgarity sometimes works. In fact, the writer could not have used any other word to end this story. It just wouldn't be as funny if the woman had said, "You had time to yell 'Oh, darn!'" There would still be an element of surprise, but not the double surprise triggered by the expletive. "Humor is like guerrilla warfare," wrote author Dwight MacDonald. "Success (and survival) depends on traveling light, striking unexpectedly, and getting away fast." The original sin may have been nothing more than a bad pun Eve made about Adam's apple.

Both Lenny Bruce and George Carlin used the most shocking language possible to enliven their material—and call attention to themselves. (Lenny Bruce once called George Carlin his comedic heir.) Obscenity is partly in the eye (or ear) of the beholder, and Carlin believes that "if a word shocks you, it's your problem." The fact is, there are no strong words left anymore. Carlin's list of "unmentionables on TV" is down to seven, and some of them are acceptable when used in a certain way.

 On TV today, you can say I pricked my finger, but you can't say it the other way around.

**—George Carlin**

There also are times when obscenity enhances a joke. Consider the following joke. If any other phrase replaces the final words, the joke loses its punch.

 I had an interesting morning; I got into an argument with my Rice Krispies. I distinctly heard "Snap, crackle, fuck you!"

**—George Carlin**

Body functions and malfunctions are another favorite source of humor because they are generally taboo table conversation and therefore lend themselves to shock appeal. There's a lot of genuine fun in bedpan humor—however, there is a proper time and place to use hard-core language, as we'll discuss shortly.

I'm in a restaurant and I'm eating and someone says, "Mind if I smoke?" and I say, "Uh, no. Mind if I fart?"
—**Steve Martin**

## Rock the Boat

According to Professor William Chisholm of Cleveland State University, obscene language is now so prevalent and commonplace in our society that nobody is really shocked or disgusted by it anymore. Since humor is disguised hostility, violent language can be a device to communicate true feelings.

 People tell me that they're disgusted with my kind of language. So, I ask if I can take 'em out to the parking lot and slam a car door on their hand. Then, they'll say both "shit" and "motherfucker."
—**Redd Foxx**

To get mass attention in public concerts, Chris Rock deliberately uses material guaranteed to offend everybody by challenging the established order, yet Rock's language and persona reflect everyday inner-city street conversation.

 Black people dominate sports in the United States. We're 20 percent of the population, but 90 percent of the final four. We own basketball, baseball, football, golf, tennis, and as soon as they make a heated hockey rink, we'll take that shit, too.
—**Chris Rock**

Nothing is more pestiferous in contemporary comedy than the growing use of unexpurgated language and the emphasis on bed-to-bidet humor. Many may not like it, but the widespread use of obscene words is closely braided into the fabric of contemporary comic material.

 I think pot should be legal, I do. I also think if your cousin is really hot, you should be able to fuck one time.
—**Dave Attell**

There's straightforward logic for using appropriate obscenities. Humor doesn't lead society—it follows. Humor pokes fun at human antics, and that includes our language. In everyday life, we use shock words to get attention, so while obscenity isn't synonymous with humor, it's certainly an important ingredient.

A lot of humor serves as communion among members of a specific social, political, or ethnic group. It reinforces group solidarity. If the audience is prejudiced, so is the performer's humor.

## SHOCK THERAPY

Irreverence is a salable commodity. Comedy questions everything that's said and done. Nothing is off-limits, nothing is so sacrosanct as to be beyond criticism—the pope, God, the president, the flag, handicapped children, debilitating social diseases, and not just mother-in-law, but mother.

 We spend so much money on the military, yet we're slashing education budgets throughout the country. No wonder we've got smart bombs and stupid fucking children.
**—Jon Stewart**

On the other hand, many question whether shock language is humorous or just adolescent exhibitionism. Successful writers are more often lauded for the hard work that goes into creative art than for outrageous acts. Too often, it is claimed that blue humor doesn't make us laugh, it makes us blush.

 I have one pick-up line which never works. If I'm at a club and I see a guy I like, I smile. And if he smiles back and I feel really comfortable, I'll walk over and say, "Stick it in!"
**—Margaret Cho**

And why, critics ask, must humor concentrate on the negative aspects of life: drug- and alcohol-related problems, sexual inadequacy, perversion, and communicable diseases? The answer is simple—shock humor gets laughs.

Permissive language has grown rapidly. More than sixty years ago, Clark Gable shocked the nation with his closing line in *Gone With the Wind*: "Frankly, my dear, I don't give a damn!" Today, depending on a film's rating, there are no longer any unmentionables. Meryl Streep wins awards for movies in which she says words that once got Lenny Bruce arrested.

## "Mor-Ass" in the Future

While there's a difference between being rude and being funny, obscenities are sometimes the perfect words. And when they are, they should be used. A word is not just a sound or a random combination of printed letters. Each word in humor is a carefully designed missile calculated to penetrate the mind and create a very specific impact. The perfect word is not easily interchangeable, even if you have access to an unabridged thesaurus. Consider this story.

 A few days before Christmas, a postman is greeted at the door of a suburban house by a beautiful, curvaceous wife in a see-through negligee. "I've got your Christmas present upstairs," she says, grabs the man's hand and leads him to the bedroom. In seconds she is making passionate love to him.

Finished, she takes him back to the kitchen for a cup of coffee.

"I gotta tell you, Mrs. Martin," says the postman, "I've fantasized about this moment since you moved into the neighborhood a few months ago. That was quite a present."

"Oh, and that's not all," says the woman. "Here's five dollars."

"What the hell is this for?" asks the mailman.

"Well, if you must know," said the wife, "I asked my husband last night what we should give you for Christmas, and he said, "Screw him. Give him five dollars.""

The following two examples are the same joke told with and without profanity. Which do you think is more powerful?

 **WITHOUT PROFANITY**

Two chickens are talking. One says, "My farmer gets sixty cents a dozen for my eggs. Laying eggs is easy." The other hen says, "Not for me, it isn't. I grunt and groan, so my eggs are bigger and my farmer gets sixty-five cents a dozen." The first hen replied, "For five cents a dozen, it doesn't pay to strain yourself."

**WITH PROFANITY**

Two chickens are talking. One says, "My farmer gets sixty cents a dozen for my eggs. Laying eggs is easy." The other hen says, "Not for me, it isn't. I grunt and groan, so my eggs are bigger and my farmer gets sixty-five cents a dozen." The first hen says to her companion, "What! I should bust my ass for a nickel?"

Audiences appreciate clever word play with off-color words even without regard for a statement's logic.

 Toastmaster: Please be patient with Sam. He's having trouble with his pacemaker. Every time he farts, his garage door goes up.

Why do we laugh? The joke doesn't even make sense. And that's the point. It wasn't the joke, it was the language.

Writers search for the perfect word just as composers search for the perfect note; both are searching for the perfect sound. And when it's found, it shouldn't be cast aside because of fear or priggish morality. Humor must use the colloquial language of its subject and the audience—and be appropriate to the persona of the performer.

 A visitor to Harvard asks a professor, "Excuse me, but would you be good enough to tell me where the Harvard Library is at?"

"Sir," came the sneering reply, "at Harvard we do not end a sentence with a preposition."

"Well, in that case, forgive me," said the visitor. "Permit me to rephrase my question. Would you be good enough to tell me where the Harvard Library is at, jackass?"

**—Charles Osgood**

Humor writers who fail to shrink from carefully selected risqué language and situations may incur severe criticism from Bible-thumpers and English purists. Fortunately, humor is as constitutionally guaranteed as any free speech—in fact, courts have held that satire is the freest of free speech—and shouldn't be censored, especially by its own writers.

The following story is a test case in the acceptable use of obscene language. Without profanity, there's no point to the joke.

A young man walked into a bank and said to the teller, "I want to open a fuckin' checkin' account."

The young lady gasped. "I beg your pardon, but we don't tolerate that language in this bank."

"Get your fuckin' supervisor!" the man said.

In a few moments the supervisor came up. "What's the problem?"

"I just won ten million in the lottery, and I want to open a fuckin' checkin' account!"

The manager said, "I see. And this bitch is giving you a hard time."

**—Playboy**

People who rail the loudest against tastelessness are often the most hypocritical. What magazine in the country could be more conservative and apple-pie than *Reader's Digest*? Yet, 50 percent of the humor in *Reader's Digest* is jokes on brassieres, girdles, toilets, breasts, and sex (although there is no profanity in these jokes). In fact, the following anecdote by gossip columnist Hy Gardner was reprinted in the *Digest*:

 Advertising director Mel Helitzer flew to the coast to discuss a TV show starring José Ferrer. The actor apologized for the absence of his wife, Rosemary Clooney, explaining that she was upstairs caring for their five children. "What ages?" asked Helitzer. "Five, four, three, two, and one," smiled Ferrer. "Say," commented the advertising executive, "I hope I'm not keeping you from anything!"

## SHOCK HUMOR ON STAGE

Today's comedians take a no-holds-barred attitude toward obscene language and taboo subjects.

 Religion to me is like a sanitary napkin—if it fits, wear it.
**—Whoopi Goldberg**

A man's not a man until he can find his way to Sears blindfolded, and the Craftsman tool department makes his nipples rock hard.
**—Tim Allen**

At my age, I'm lucky to get an erection. I'd be happy if a flag came out with a sign that said, "Hey, thanks for the opportunity."

**—Richard Lewis**

The Web brings people together because no matter what kind of a twisted sexual mutant you happen to be, you've got millions of pals out there. Type in "Find people that have sex with goats that are on fire" and the computer will say, "Specify type of goat."

**—Richard Jeni**

I spent five years in the air force, and if it weren't for sexual harassment, no one would have talked to me at all. An officer accused me of being a lesbian. I would have denied it, but I was lying naked on top of her at the time.

**—Lynda Montgomery**

How much roadkill do you think is actually suicide? Come on, some of those bastards are stepping out on purpose.

**—Kathleen Kanz**

I know more about Bill Clinton's penis now than I do my own, which says something about the media or just something really sad about me.

**—Jon Stewart**

Read the condom boxes, they're pretty funny. Trojans says, "new shape." I didn't know this was necessary. Another box said, "reservoir." I said, "You mean these things can actually generate hydroelectric power?"

**—Elayne Boosler**

I thought about being a nun for a while and believed I'd make a god-darned good nun. Then I had sex and thought, "Well, fuck that."

**—Diane Ford**

## TO SHOCK OR NOT TO SHOCK

It's easy to be prudish and claim that hard-core expressions are just intended to shock, and whether the expressions are funny or not, hard-core language—in fact almost anything taboo—shocks young people into laughter. That's why second-rate comics use it as fallback shtick when their first-string jokes fail. Your decision to use profane or obscene language—and at what level to use it—should be guided by the MAP theory—your act should match your character as a performer and the character of the audience. Hard-core language and situations, even when overused by shock comics like Andrew Dice Clay and Sam Kinison, are likely to be successful, which makes them hard to disparage.

The question then is not whether shock words should be used, but when and to what extent. Experienced performers test the limits of their racier subjects by purposely inserting trial material in their act up front. If the reaction is negative, they respect the signals immediately, because humor can never be forced.

 You ever wake up with an erection, roll over, and think you broke your dick?

**—Dave Attell**

Opinions about what constitutes good taste in humor are as varied as sex acts between consenting adults. However, humor has so many forms, it's easy to avoid words that might offend the audience. X-rated material only works in venues such as comedy clubs, movies, and cable shows. There are just as many "clean" synonyms for hard-core words as there are for a man's penis. A humorist's language should be appropriate to the specific audience. There is a comedic axiom: Insult only ugly people and ignoramuses. Who's going to come up and complain, "Hey, man, I'm an ignoramus"?

There are three instances when professional writers should work very hard to avoid hard-core words.

1. When it is the definition rather than the shock of the word that sparks the humor, the soft-core word can be just as funny.

Young man to drug store clerk: "Do you handle condoms?"

"Yes, I do."

"Well, wash your hands, I want a ham sandwich."

2. The soft-core word is acceptable to a wider range of audiences. Therefore, it's more commercial—if earning money is an important consideration.

 My husband's idea of oral sex is talking about himself.

3. Soft-core may suggest the act and encourage the audience to fill in the blanks. Then, who can complain about the language?

 When doctors tell us that our teens were our peak sexual period, we feel bad that we let so many good years slip between our fingers.

Another issue to consider is political correctness, particularly in broadcast. The FCC constantly patrols the marketplace of humor, and unfortunately, many humorists have been fined or busted for politically incorrect speech.

Shock humor has its place, but it's often the easy way out or is simply unnecessary. More importantly, shock humor has limited marketability. If you plan to sell your writing, you should recognize that most markets require PG—or at most PG-13—material. You might have a gift for using obscenities, but that skill will not translate into profitability. If you don't believe us, then we don't give a doo-doo.

## UNDERSTATEMENT:
## EAT, DRINK, AND BE MARY

Understatement is an admirable alternative to obscene language and one of the higher techniques of humor writing, because it's so difficult to carry off effectively. Both understated realism and understated shock material cater to the audience's imagination and intelligence, encouraging them to complete the script using their own words. Then, who can complain?

Saw this commercial on TV for Ex-Lax, it says, "Works while you sleep." That scares me.

**—Steve Mendoza**

"Doc, my girlfriend has a problem. She thinks she's a rabbit."

"Okay, bring her in. I'll examine her."

"Thanks, doc, but whatever you do, don't cure her!"

Understating is a sign of confidence as well as maturity. Just as in real life, the rich and the very successful understate. The insecure or nouveau riche overstate.

 Soon after I arrived in Athens, our gardener invited me to go fishing. At the end of the day, I said, "I don't understand it. I've got better gear than you. I use better bait. I'm in the same boat. And I haven't caught a thing and you've caught the whole lake."

The man said, "I fish by hunches. When I get up in the morning to go fishing, if my wife is sleeping on her right side, then I fish off the right side of the boat. If she's sleeping on her left side, then I fish off the left side of the boat."

"And if she's on her back?" I asked.

"Then, I don't go fishing."

James Thurber's most famous cartoon shows two dueling men. One of them slashes his foil across the neck of his opponent, decapitating him, and shouts, "Touché!" That's shocking, but it has lived for sixty years as a classic example of understatement.

 I knew psychology as a child. I had a lemonade stand and I gave the first glass of lemonade away free. On the second glass I charged five dollars—it had the antidote.

**—Emo Philips**

One of George S. Kaufman's most famous quotes came from a letter to his daughter.

 Try everything in life except incest and square dancing.

That's shocking enough, but a biographer added a reverse that really throws your imagination into high gear.

 … so you can see that Kaufman's humor comes from the fact that he is ridiculing something increasingly popular, lots of fun, and American as farm apple pie. Now, as for square dancing …

## Outrageous Humor: Disguise the Limit

Reforming words is an easy way to be shocking. It takes no great talent. The talent comes from suggesting hard-core humor but never actually stating it.

 A sexually frustrated young girl sat on Pinocchio's nose and said, "Now lie to me. Now tell me the truth. Now lie to me. Now tell me the truth."

**—Paul Krassner**

When Ron Nessen, a former presidential assistant, guest hosted *Saturday Night Live*, writer Alan Zeibel created a skit that reformed *presidential elections* to *presidential erections*. That could have been a cheap laugh—and probably wouldn't have been acceptable to NBC censors—but Zeibel finessed that by referring to buildings and monuments. The audience got the point immediately, and the laughter was even louder because the implicitness of the joke made them feel more comfortable.

# PART THREE

## Writing Humor for
## Specific Markets

# CHAPTER 12
## Testing, Testing, One, Two, Three: Writing Humor for Speeches

 Once you get people laughing, they're listening and you can sell them almost anything.

**—Herbert Gardner**

The first humor performance for most young people is when they're called upon to deliver a speech. Newscaster David Brinkley once commented that we are reaching the point where there are more people willing to give luncheon speeches than are willing to listen to them.

 A recent survey stated that the average person's greatest fear is having to give a speech in public. Somehow, this ranked even higher than death, which was third on the list. So, you're telling me that at a funeral, most people would rather be the guy in the coffin than have to stand up and give a eulogy.

**—Jerry Seinfeld**

But the fact is that speechmaking continues to be more popular than ever. In this electronic society, in which so much information comes to us via the Internet, television, PDAs, radio, e-mail, and mobile phones, there still seems to be a need to get out from behind our desks and communicate in person with groups of other people.

We make the time for it. The number of luncheon clubs, service clubs, and social, political, and religious organizations—all looking for entertaining speakers—continues to grow. Event planners still think of speeches first when they're assigned to schedule programs for organizations.

 I feel very much more at ease speaking here than I did at the last luncheon. They had a sign there that read: "Do not photograph speakers while they are speaking. Shoot them as they approach the platform."

According to the old saying, all of us are ignorant—just about different subjects. The corollary is that each of us can be an expert at something—or at least know more than the other people in the room—so we're qualified to talk about it. But that's only half the story. Speakers are selected just as much for their ability to know *how* to say things. This hasn't changed in a hundred and fifty years. In the late nineteenth century, British politician John Morley wrote: "Three things matter in a speech. Who says it, how he says it, and what he says. And of the three, the last matters the least."

Speeches provide a good opportunity to test comedy material, and humor writers will often accept small speaking engagements just to test public reaction. If George Carlin had not plunged into stand-up comedy, he could have made his fame as a great speechwriter. After his wife died, he wrote a 1,500-word homily on the need for people to cherish their moments together. In this essay, he used several formulas and techniques—such as pairing, triples, and association—that are effective in both serious and humorous speeches. Here is a small part.

 We've learned how to make a living, but not a life. These are the days of quick trips, disposable diapers, throwaway morality, one-night stands, overweight bodies, and pills that do everything. It is a time when there is much in the showroom window and nothing in the stockroom. Remember, spend some time with your loved ones, because they are not going to be around forever. Give time to love, give time to speak, and give time to share the precious moment. Life is not measured by the number of breaths we take, but by the moments that take our breath away.

Whether you are writing a speech for yourself or for a client, there are five areas in the speech in which humor can be important.

1. the title
2. the introduction of the speaker
3. the introductory remarks

4. the body of the speech

5. the closing remarks

## THE TITLE: GETTING 'EM INTO THE HALL

The title of a speech is far more important than most writers believe. The title not only indicates the subject, but also attracts attention when listed in advance publicity; sometimes it can prompt press coverage. Then, when it is announced by the MC during the event, the title sets the mood for the audience. The audience is ever hopeful that the next speech they hear will be far better than the last one. That's why experienced MCs often thank the previous speaker and then add, "And now, we've got a special treat for you. Our next speaker ..." (After all, you wouldn't want the MC to say, "Well, folks, you've heard the best, now on to the rest.")

 The last time I made a speech, the program chairman asked me to talk about the serious problems resulting from sex between faculty and students. But my wife doesn't like the subject, so I told her I was going to talk about the problems with too much air travel. Well, the sex speech got a good reception. And the next day, the wife of a member of the audience met my wife in the supermarket and she said, "I heard Bill made a very good speech last night. He must be an expert on the subject." And my wife said, "Oh, no. He's only tried it twice. The first time, he lost his bag, and the second time he got sick to his stomach."

Even if the speech is on a serious topic—politics, the economy, business, or education—a humorous twist in the title will increase interest and attendance. For example, there's nothing more important than sales training speeches, but astute sales managers have learned to avoid making them deadly with titles like these.

 Yogi Berra Was Right—It Ain't Over 'til It's Over
As Alexander Bell Said: "What D'ya Mean My Three Minutes Are Up?"
Caterpillars and Other Special People
What They Never Dared Tell You About ...

## SHOWTIME

List topics that you are qualified to speak about, and for each topic, write three to five titles with a humorous twist. Remember, the title must identify the content of the speech while being funny.

## THE SPEAKER'S INTRODUCTION: HOLD ON TO YOUR SEATS

If done correctly, a humorous introduction can humanize the speaker and put the audience at ease. Don't let some inept MC start the speech off on the wrong footnotes. (Who remembers any facts from a detailed bio lifted from *Who's Who?*)

To give an introduction true character and spark, write it yourself. Several days in advance, ask the MC if there's one already written. Even if there is, suggest that yours contains some humor that may help make the introduction more fun. MCs always respond positively to that suggestion, since they'd like to use a few funny lines, too. Don't be timid. You and the MC will be the only ones who'll know who wrote your introduction.

 Nothing helps you to be a better listener than knowing you're going to be the next one called to the podium.

## SHOWTIME

Write a one-paragraph introduction that summarizes your professional experience. The introduction should connect to the speech title, prepare the audience for the content of the speech, and explain why you are qualified to give the speech. Humor should be included in the introduction, but not at the expense of minimizing your qualifications. Take a look at how Mark Twain chose to introduce himself before a public speech.

 Ladies and gentlemen: The next lecture in this course will be delivered this evening by Samuel L. Clemens, a gentlemen whose high character and unimpeachable integrity are only equaled by his comeliness of person and grace of manner.

And I am the man!

I was obliged to excuse the chairman from introducing me, because he never compliments anybody and I knew I could do it just as well.

## INTRODUCTORY REMARKS

After the flattering introduction, you can take the stage and charm the audience with acknowledgments like this pairing.

 I'm sorry my father and mother aren't here. My father would have loved it, and my mother would have believed it.

A little self-deprecating humor always helps.

 I was flattered by our toastmaster's introduction. The hardest thing for a speaker to remember is to not nod his head in agreement when the toastmaster praises him.

Although you want to display a little humility, it's important not to go overboard. The audience gets suspicious of those too pious. Former Israeli Prime Minister Golda Meir once said to a colleague after an introduction: "Don't be so humble. You're not that great."

Even for an accomplished professional, a certain amount of anxiety is natural (and even desirable). Anxiety pumps adrenalin into the system and primes performers—including speakers—to do their best. A few humorous lines can overcome skepticism from the audience and make the audience members receptive to the speech.

I must admit I am more comfortable behind a desk than I am behind a podium lectern. Let me give you an example. As I was coming into the building today, I decided to go to the washroom and freshen up. I heard a voice behind me ask, "Mr. Wells? Do you always get nervous before a speech?" "Why, no," I said, "not really. Why do you ask?" And the voice said, "I was just wondering what you were doing in the ladies' room!"

Here's a line so overused as a dinner speech opening that it's become a cliché—and was even the basis for the title of the Broadway musical *A Funny Thing Happened on the Way to the Forum.* It would be easy to recommend that it never be used again, yet—as with so many other rules—there are exceptions.

 I had a terrible day. This morning my collar button fell off. On my way here, the handle of my briefcase fell off. You know, I'm afraid to go to the men's room!

**—Larry Wilde**

A speaker should never use more than three pieces of humorous material during the introductory remarks. (Remember the rules of three from chapter nine: Never use more than three jokes about one subject in a monologue; three minutes is the ideal length for a skit; don't exceed three themes in an article. These rules of three often apply to other activities and situations.) And a speaker should never try to act like a pro comic or brag like David Letterman, who gets away with it because that is his character.

The following opener puts a small smile on the lips and a large pain in the stomach.

 One thing I can guarantee you. You may not be a great deal wiser from my talk today, but you will be a great deal older.

## SPEECH CONTENT: EVERYBODY'S ENTITLED TO MY OPINION

Usually, the easier something reads, the harder it was to write. Public speaking is like writing. But it does come more easily if you have something to say, so it's important that you never forget why you're making a speech in the first place.

 Public speaking is the art of diluting a two-minute idea with a two-hour vocabulary.

**—Evan Esar**

Don't sacrifice the message for the sake of the humor. Speechwriters who spend all their time writing funny words would be better off if they put in a few important ideas. Wit is the salt of conversation, not the meat.

 The recipe for being a successful after-dinner speaker includes using plenty of shortening.

A good speaker is one who rises to the occasion and then promptly sits down.

A speech, including introductory material, should never take more than twenty minutes. The normal speaking rate is two and a half words per second, and that means a speech should be a maximum of 3,000 words long. That was Ronald Reagan's favorite time frame, and his motto was that an immortal speech should not be eternal.

 If you can't write your message in a sentence, you can't say it in an hour.

**—Dianna Booher**

Sentences in speeches must be shorter than sentences meant for reading, because the audience members have no chance to reread something they haven't comprehended. The best length for a sentence in a speech is approximately fourteen words. This is a good guideline to remember, but you should of course vary your sentence length to avoid monotony.

## Making a Speech Funny

For a humorous speech to be successful in delivering its message in a memorable way, all three of the following ingredients are necessary.

1. It must be funny.
2. It must be comfortable for the speaker.
3. It must be comfortable for the audience.

As required by the MAP theory, all three of these items are of equal importance, and each depends upon the others in order for the speech to work. After all, if the speaker's uncomfortable, then the audience is going to be uncomfortable, and the material is going to come off as stiff and awkward.

 During an election campaign in the backwoods of Kentucky, a Huey Long–type state senator was running against the president of a small college. He would begin his speeches with "Now, you all know me. But what do you know about my opponent? Did you know his college is a den of iniquity? Why, in his college, male and female students use the same curriculum. Not only that, but they sometimes secretly show each other their theses. And if that isn't bad enough, folks, he even lets these young people matriculate together."

### Make It Funny

The humor must be funny, and not just funny on paper but *performable*. Some humor takes a long buildup (that's out), some requires a dialect (that's out), and some reformed clichés (puns) contain homonyms that work only on paper (those are out, too). The following puns would be next to impossible to pull off aloud.

 Once a knight, always a knight. But once a night is usually enough.

In my day, the little red schoolhouse was all too common. Today, however, it's the little-read schoolboy who's all too common.

Jokes and anecdotes should not be read, but told looking out at the audience. If there's anything a speaker needs to memorize, it's the humor. It must be delivered confidently, and memorizing it encourages a more accurate rendition.

Personalize and localize the humor whenever possible, even though many in the audience will know it's fabricated. Humor, as we've already noted, permits the audience to set aside disbelief. No one will stand up and challenge you. Use words like "I" and "last week," and mention local names and places.

President Ronald Reagan usually began each speech—particularly the less formal ones—with self-deprecating humor. For example, when hundreds of school principals and teachers gathered on the South Lawn of the White House for a recognition ceremony, the president's gag writer gave him a typical Reagan charmer.

 Y'know, I've been out of school for some time now, but I still get nervous around so many principals.

This opener is also a perfect example of using the right joke for the right audience. This rule should not be a law—it should be a commandment. It's the apex of the MAP triangle. Reagan would never use the following line in a speech to members of Congress, but it always hit the nail on the head when he used it in speeches to voters.

 Politics is supposed to be the second-oldest profession. I've come to realize that it bears a very close resemblance to the first.

By letting the voice rise on the last word or two of a joke, the speaker can punch up the punchline. It's the last few words that gives the joke life.

 I thought I was a good drinker, but I'm nothing compared to Mike. He doesn't drink when he's driving, not only because it's dangerous, but because he might spill some.

Just before lunch, he went up to the bartender and said, "A martini, very dry. In fact, make it about twenty to one."

The bartender asked, "Shall I put in a twist of lemon?"

And Mike said, "Listen, when I want lemonade, I'll order lemonade."

Never apologize. Saying "Here's something I just dashed off" or "This may not be very funny, but ..." sets an expectation that the humor is weak. Also, don't explain. "See, the guy was an atheist, and ..." If you have to explain a joke, don't use it. And avoid words that are hard to say or that don't sound good when spoken. The words *dejected, appraisingly,* and *sarcastically* read better than they sound, and should be deleted from your speech.

Don't hesitate to give credit to other professional humorists when using their material. Not only is it courteous, it shows you're well-read and aren't afraid to surround yourself with brilliance. And don't be afraid to use a story you've used before. You can never satisfy 100 percent of an audience with any material, so if you've got surefire material that a few audience members may have heard before, don't hesitate to reuse it. Humorist Robert Orben states that the only old joke he knows is the one told by the previous speaker.

 One day I went to a trial of a guy accused of trying to rob a warehouse, but the police grabbed him when his getaway car stalled. I was seated next to a little old lady in the back of the room who was weeping and repeating, "They never listen. They never listen."

Being a parent, I tried to comfort her. She turned and said, "If he had only listened to his mother. How I begged him. How I pleaded with him. 'Get the points checked, get the car overhauled.'"

## QUESTION & ANSWER

### HOW DO YOU LOCALIZE HUMOR?

Localizing—tailoring material for specific audiences—is an important and common practice for professionals who play on the road or make frequent personal appearances at banquets. The audience wants to know that you care enough to use material personalized for them. Bob Hope was famous for inside material. He would send a  writer to a site a few days before his appearance to write dozens of opening lines about local people, places, and controversial activities.

You can customize material with the name of a local hotel this way.

 A guest at [name of a posh local hotel] called room service. "I want three overdone fried eggs, hard as a rock, some burnt toast that crumbles at first touch, and a cup of black coffee that tastes like mud."

"I'm sorry, sir, but we don't serve a breakfast like that."

"No? Well, you did yesterday!"

You can use a similar technique for a local airport.

 Passenger to [name of airline] ticket agent: "Ship this bag to New York. This second one to Kansas City, and this third one on your overseas flight to Calcutta."

"We can't do that."

"Well, you did when I was here last time!"

It's a good idea to keep a file of open-ended jokes that can be completed by inserting the names of local targets.

## Make the Humor Fit the Speaker

The humor must be comfortable for the speaker (who may be yourself or, if you're a speechwriter, someone else). Here are just a few do's and don'ts for making sure the material fits the speaker.

You must believe in the importance of the material, because the audience will be able to tell if you don't. If you don't care about what you're saying, why should the audience? Go slowly, but not too slowly, and take pauses so that the speech will sound less rehearsed.

Use self-deprecating humor. The audience appreciates it when—despite a speaker's title, age, or reputation—the speaker is human. When people comment that someone has a good sense of humor, they mean they can relate to that person.

Tell funny anecdotes in addition to one-liners. This is important, because unlike one-liners, anecdotes add a personalized feel to the material.

Never use multimedia software, such as *PowerPoint*, for humor. If you are making a multimedia presentation, make sure the humor is not on screen but spoken over the slide so it appears that the humor was spontaneous and not programmed.

## SHOWTIME

By now you're probably tired of hearing about the importance of matching the material with the right audience. You probably think you've got it down. Fair enough, then answer this quiz. What audience would be the most receptive to this joke?

 A lawyer dies and goes to Heaven. "There must be some mistake," the lawyer argues. "I'm too young to die. I'm only fifty-five."

"No," says St. Peter, "by our calculations, you're eighty-two."

"Impossible," retorts the lawyer. "How did you calculate that?"

"It's all here in black and white," answers St. Peter. "We added up your time sheets."

There are four audience choices: (a) consumers, (b) lawyers, (c) corporate executives, or (d) religious leaders. Pick one.

Lawyers would be irritated for being ridiculed, consumers don't know a great deal about time sheets, and religious leaders have heard this joke a score of times before. The correct answer is corporate executives, who are always suspicious about professional time sheets and overcharges, making them the right audience for this hostile material.

### Make the Audience Comfortable
The speech and the humor in the speech must be comfortable for the audience. According to columnist Ed Hercer, audiences want each speaker to succeed. They spent time and money to hear you and they

want their just desserts. If the speaker is enthusiastic, they'll be supportive. But here are a few warnings.

E.B. White once wrote, "Nothing becomes funny by being labeled so." Therefore, don't predict humor or give it a preliminary fanfare: "Hey, here's something funny!" The audience will be thinking, "Just tell us the joke. We'll decide."

When you do humor, hecklers seem to feel encouraged to join in. For instance, hecklers might respond to a line like "to make a long story short" with the reply "Toooo late!" And don't ever say, "I just threw that in," because some heckler will shout, "Well, you should have thrown it out."

Technical difficulties are a constant hazard, so you should be prepared for what can go wrong. And hecklers can take advantage of these types of situations, too. If the mike goes dead and the speaker yells, "Can you hear me in the back?" and someone says "No!" then the heckler will stand up and shout, "Well, I can hear him, and I'll change places with you."

If there is a question-and-answer period, don't reply to the loaded questions of hecklers. First of all, you'll be giving them the attention they want. More importantly, if you answer one, you may find there are fifty more, each with one good line. They will always outnumber you.

According to author Fred Ebel, humor in front of a small audience—ten or twenty people—is very hard to bring off because each individual is afraid to laugh for fear of being conspicuous. The speaker should try to find the one person who's got a booming laugh, look at him, and even wink at him once or twice. His laughter may be the catalyst that starts the audience laughing. Also, the speaker should get as friendly as possible with the senior officials of the group. People follow the leader. If the boss laughs heartily, it gives them permission to break out.

 Let me tell you how I got elected. I was campaigning against the former incumbent and we were asked to speak at a farm festival. My opponent went first, but just as he was really getting going the rain started. Most of us ran and stood under a tree. But not him. He just kept talking to a few die-hard supporters who were left. Finally, a farmer walked over to me and said, "You certainly proved you're the smartest. None of us are ever going to vote for anybody who's too dumb to come in out of the rain."

# GIVE YOUR SPEECH A PULSE

When writing a speech, you should know the reasons why speeches fall flat so you can prevent yourself from tripping in the first place.

**1. INADEQUATE BACKGROUND RESEARCH.** You need the following information to determine the proper style, tone, content, and humor for the speech.

- What is the occasion? (Is it a social event, seminar, conference?)
- What is the purpose of the speech? (To entertain, enlighten, persuade?)
- Who is the audience? (What will be their number, composition, background, expectations?)

If you are writing for a client, you'll also need to know the speaker's professional qualifications, personal experience, and speaking habits.

**2. BORING OPENINGS.** The audience is most attentive in the first few minutes and will quickly pass judgment on the speech and speaker. As George Jessel noted, "If you haven't struck oil in the first three minutes—stop boring!"

**3. INFORMATION OVERLOAD.** The ideal speech length is twenty minutes, but groups often request talks of forty-five to sixty minutes. Long speeches are usually too detailed, and quickly become monotonous, tedious, and boring. As Thomas Jefferson observed, "Speeches that are measured by the hour will die with the hour." Humorous personal anecdotes, good metaphors, and funny stories and jokes will keep the speech going. It's also a good idea to use the KISS (Keep It Simple, Stupid) approach and only focus on a few key points, and to use repetition to reinforce the critical concepts.

> **4. SOUNDS LIKE A SPEECH.** The language of speechwriting is different from that in other media. It should be written and performed in correct, colloquial, spoken English. If a sentence is longer than fourteen or so words, edit it down.

## CLOSING REMARKS: GETTING OFF STAGE WITH A STANDING OVATION

Any speaker can rise to the occasion, but few know when to sit down. The best speeches seem to have a good beginning and a good ending—close together!

 During my last speech, I noticed a little old man in a wheelchair. After I stepped down from the podium, I went over to him and thanked him for coming. I said, "And I hope you get better real soon." And he said, "After listening to you, I hope you get better, too!"

If possible, never be the last speaker at a conference; if you can't avoid it, then never speak at length. And end with lines like this one.

 It has been my responsibility to speak and yours to listen. I am delighted that we've fulfilled our responsibilities at the same time.

Always thank the audience. There is no better exit line.

 If I've held your interest, this is a good place to stop. And if it's been a bad speech, then this is a very good place to stop. Thank you.

In conclusion, say "In conclusion." Next to "I'll take the check," this is a dinner audience's favorite phrase.

 In conclusion, I have had a very difficult task. The food has been good, the drinks plentiful, and you have been a wonderful audience. I feel like the preacher who noticed a small boy sitting in the front pew alongside his father, who was nodding off.

"Billy," he said, "wake up your father."

And the boy said, "Wake him up yourself. You put him to sleep."

A good salesperson always ends a pitch by asking for the order, and that's not a bad idea for speakers. Tell the audience what you want them to do: buy a product, donate to a cause, or vote for a person or issue. You can do it with humor, too.

 Young boy to family: I'm going up to say my prayers. Anybody want anything?

## SHOWTIME

Compose a five-minute speech following the guidelines described in the previous sections. Include humorous remarks in the opening, make just three key points, and conclude with a humorous ending.

## SPEECHES FOR CLIENTS

Whatever the reasons, humor speechwriters for politicians, businessmen, newspaper editors, and entertainers are in such tremendous demand that there are not enough qualified writers to fill the demand. A ghostwriter with humor material has become a businessman's status symbol, like a chauffeur. For full-time business employment as a speechwriter, the salary runs high.

### Preparing the Speaker and the Speakeasy

It's critical that the speechwriter work directly with the presenter and not get the assignment from a third party. Writing and thinking are interwoven. You can't have one without the other. Writers must know the client's philosophy intimately in order to clarify "executive thinking."

I asked my secretary to find some good "quotable quotes" that packed some solid advice in them for today's speech, and she came back with this little memo: "Dear Boss: The only good quotes I could find are these few from Socrates, who also went around giving people advice, and—in case you've forgotten—they poisoned him."

A good speechwriter is aurally oriented. There is a major difference between language for the ear and language for the eye; the way a speaker phrases humor is as important as what's written. "Write a speech with your mouth," recommends Ed McMahon. So, speechwriters must practice with the client, because only you know the *sound*, the appropriate phrasing, of the words you wrote.

Speakers should rehearse their speech at least twice. The second rehearsal should be recorded, and the recording should be played back over and over. Many speakers sincerely believe that one run-through is sufficient before going onstage. But once is not enough in any area. And it's particularly not easy with humor, in which timing is so critical. The pros just make it look easy.

 Nobody realizes that I work eighteen hours a day for a solid month to make that TV hour look like it's never been rehearsed.
**—Jimmy Durante**

Speakers are in show business, whether they want to admit it or not (and because they like the sound of it, they admit it). Even seated at the head table, they're on stage. When they look bored, talk to their neighbors when others are speaking, or make last-second changes in the speech, they may think they're invisible—but not to a critical audience.

All speechwriters must develop tolerance—that's the ability to listen to a client louse up one of your best jokes. Instruct your client not to try to finish a joke that's been stumbled over. The joke has been killed, so take the loss right away. Write savers, those little disclaimer lines that help save face when a joke gets messed up or bombs.

 Now you know why my wife says, "Unaccustomed as you are to public speaking, you still do it!"

My husband says I have a wonderful way of making a long story short. I forget the punchline.

The speechwriter is also a director, a detail person, and a publicist. Here are just a few tricks of the trade.

## Early Birds

You and your client should get to the hall early. You must check the mikes, the podium height, and whether the AV and multimedia systems are cued up and the lighting system is organized. While you're doing all that, the client should be shaking hands with as many members of the audience as possible, reading their name tags and calling them by their first names as soon as they're introduced. The speaker should circulate quickly and not stay in any one place for too long. The object is to make friends, since we laugh more easily with friends.

 Theater critic John Mason Brown was a famous lecturer, particularly with women's clubs. As he was circulating around the room before a speech, a little white-haired lady holding a cane approached him and said, "I'm so looking forward to your speech, sir, because I've heard that you just love old ladies." Quick as a flash, Brown said, "I certainly do, but I also love them your age, too."

## The More the Merrier

Laughter is contagious. Everyone wants to know, while they're laughing, that this is a shared experience—so they can enjoy even taboo material without being ridiculed. Try to jam-pack the hall. Better fifty standers than fifty empty seats. Also, the smaller the room, the better laughter sounds.

There is something else unique about laughing out loud. We rarely laugh out loud when we're alone. To encourage the home TV viewer to laugh out loud, sitcom producers refined the electronic laugh track. Even when action takes place in a combat zone operating room (as in *M\*A\*S\*H*), the home audience enjoys the show more when an amplified laugh track is added. It gives them permission to laugh.

### Can You Hear Me Now?

Goose the sound system slightly above normal. At best, the client is competing with normal crowd movement, whispers, paper rustling, and plates clinking. At worst, a speaker may need to overcome competition from those who are telling their companions how the joke ends two seconds before you deliver the punchline. And avoid attempting humor outdoors. The vastness of any outdoor arena dissipates even enthusiastic laughter.

## POLITICAL SPEECHWRITING: INHALE TO THE CHIEF

Every public servant from the president of the United States to the mayor of your local town has to speak regularly to fellow lawmakers, organizations, and the voting public—and for the most part, they hate it. So they look for writers who can make them sound erudite. While hard to break into, political humor is one of the most profitable areas for professionals who know how to write a speech.

 Today's public figures can no longer write their own speeches or books, and there is some evidence that they can't read them either.

**—Gore Vidal**

Months before every major election, candidates duke it out with the witty gibes that have become standard in the dog-eat-dog world of politics. Aneurin Bevan, a British prime minister, once called politics a blood sport.

Every U.S. president since Franklin D. Roosevelt has had a gag writer on his speechwriting team. Their humor has two objectives—to destroy the opponent or to humanize the speaker, especially with self-deprecation. President George W. Bush used such humor very successfully in 2004. (His opponents said this was because he had so much material to work with.) Humor is the most acceptable method to characterize your opponent as a wimp, or a menace, or a fool, or a puppet, or a crook (or all of the above). Years ago political humor was gentle and mean. Today it is harsh and mean.

If a committee had written the Gettysburg address, "four score and seven years ago" would have to be written as eighty-seven or rounded off to ninety for fear the less sophisticated would think that scoring has something to do with sexual prowess. And "our fathers brought forth on this continent a new nation" would have had to be reworded because it left out women.

**—Mike Royko**

Mark Katz was President Bill Clinton's official humor writer. Several times a year, Katz prepared Clinton's humorous speeches for various off-the-record events, such as the White House Correspondents' Dinner. Tidbits from those speeches always made a column in the next day's news.

 Political speeches are like steer horns. A point here, a point there, and a lot of bull in between.

**—Alfred E. Neuman**

Humor may be just a small part of any speech, but most often it ends up being the most memorable and most effective part. Franklin Roosevelt once described his opponent, Tom Dewey, as looking like "a little man on a wedding cake." Dewey lost big. And when Bill Clinton was running against George H.W. Bush, former Texas governor Ann Richards described Bush as having been "born with a silver foot in his mouth." Richards's oft-quoted remark opened the humor floodgates, and Bush was stigmatized as a mixed-up, double-talking politician for his entire losing campaign. John F. Kennedy lambasted Richard Nixon's dark facial make-up by claiming, "Nixon was offered two million dollars by Schick to do a TV commercial for Gillette."

Unquestionably, former president Ronald Reagan was the most expert at delivering great lines. Like this triple:

 Recession is when your neighbor loses his job. Depression is when you lose yours. And recovery is when President Carter loses his.

During his campaign against Walter Mondale in 1984, Reagan's humor completely spiked the Democrats' best personal attack—the age issue

(Reagan was seventy-two years old). Everyone knew this concern would come up during the election debates. It did, in a question from a reporter. Reagan's humorous reverse will be a textbook classic for generations, for it deflated the press and even had Mondale laughing.

 I will not make age an issue of this campaign. I am not going to exploit, for political purposes, my opponent's youth and inexperience.

According to *Newsweek*, Reagan's joke sealed his reelection.

Here's how an important political joke, using a paired antonym, was actually written. When Adlai Stevenson was running for president in 1956, he was accused of having homosexual affiliations. If the public believed these stories, Stevenson would have no chance in the election. Governor Stevenson had few choices. To defend the charges in public would only give them wider currency. To sue would take too long. The Democrats decided to use humor to get the voters on Stevenson's side and began working on a joke he could use in an upcoming speech. The bottom line was to get President Eisenhower, or his associates, to stop telling lies. The first time the joke was drafted it went like this.

 Eisenhower must be worried. Just as soon as I started telling stories about him, he started telling lies about me.

That was the thrust they wanted, but the last line was not what Stevenson wanted the people to remember. So, they tried a number of other variations until they found a paired antonym that worked. This is still heralded as one of Stevenson's great lines.

 President Eisenhower and I have a pact. If he'll stop telling lies about me, I'll stop telling the truth about him.

Breaking into the field of political speechwriting without the proper background training and experience is difficult. And while the pay can be excellent, humor writers are only temporary employees unless their candidate wins. Even after they are hired, the identities of joke writers is kept as secret as those of CIA operatives. Only the politician—never the public or even the press—knows who placed those pearls of humor in his campaign oratory. And only a few comedy writers have ever become famous after leaving public life. They include Robert Orben, Al Franken and Peggy Noonan, who once quipped, "The battle for the mind of Ronald Reagan is like trench warfare in World War I; never have so many fought so hard for such barren terrain."

Disseminating political humor via the Internet increases its impact a hundred fold. The Internet is uncensored by broadcast or publication codes, and a joke can be passed on through hundreds of independent sites to thousands of people with similar political leanings and tastes in humor. However, because political humor is so biased, political analyst David Cross believes the humor incites the faithful more than it convinces swing voters. "I'm mostly preaching to the choir, but at least the choir is laughing."

Speechwriter wannabes can practice with humor for local candidates, who make dozens of speeches and are constantly quoted in the city press. Offer them your personalized zingers. A few may make national wire service round-up stories.

## THE PROFESSIONAL SPEECHWRITER: THIS LIL' PIGGY WENT TO MARKET

Writing for public speakers is lucrative, with rates of five hundred dollars and more per speech. But the insatiable demand for humorous speeches means writers are even better compensated, with fees of a hundred dollars and up per page of text.

Before attempting speechwriting, explore the profession and its available markets. Professional organizations include the National Speakers Association (www.nsaspeaker.org), Toastmasters International (www.toastmasters.org), and The Executive Speaker Company (www.executive-speaker.com).

The most important factor for marketing a speech is the topic. Booking agents look for humorous motivational presentations—a speech that is informative, inspirational, and entertaining.

If you plan to deliver your own speeches, begin with freebies for community groups and local organizations. After you develop a "stock" speech, contact a local speakers bureau and request a listing in their catalog. The agencies will help with marketing and booking your speech. Each bureau has different guidelines for listing speakers, and commission rates vary (typically 25 to 35 percent), but most will require a videotape of one of your speeches.

# CHAPTER 13
## Stand-Up or Sit Down:
## Humor for Live Entertainers

 He was born with the gift of laughter and a sense that the
world was mad.

**—Raphael Sabatini**

Stand-up and sketch comedy are undergoing a renaissance.
Just consider the popularity of the Comedy Central
network (*Comedy Central Presents*), movies showcas-
ing stand-up comics (*The Original Kings of Comedy,
Blue Collar Comedy Tour: The Movie*), and even stand-
up comedy contests (*Last Comic Standing*).

The problems of stand-up and sketch comedy are
often attributed to the public's diminishing attention
span. Larry the Cable Guy, one of the *Blue Collar*
comics, explained the audience's preference of
sketch performances to sitcoms, saying, "It's boom-boom. In just two
minutes, there are thirty jokes. With a sitcom, if you're three or four minutes into it and you haven't laughed, you're turning the channel."

The need for humor writing is now nearly insatiable because of the
renewed interest in live comedy. Professional stand-ups need it to get
started, and they need it even more when they're on top, because that's
when they're the most fearful.

 Now that my ratings are good, I have a different kind of fear. It's
like a tap on the shoulder from an ominous unknown force. That's
the position you don't want to find yourself in, the one you can't
sustain. It's like a warning that I've got to do better, and keep
doing better, or the ratings will go down and I'll be left a lonely
broken shell of a human—like I am now.

**—David Letterman**

In today's comedy climate, there are many golden opportunities for humor writers. Because, next to drops of water on a hot frying pan, nothing evaporates faster than the value of a topical joke. If you can write funny fast, you can expect a seller's market for the foreseeable future.

Many resources, such as *The Comedy Bible* by Judy Carter and the *Zen and the Art of Stand-Up Comedy* by Jay Sankey, explain the art of stand-up and sketch comedy. But it's also a craft, with learnable characteristics and skills. The first—and most important—aspect of the comedy craft is the performer's character.

 Stand-up comedy hasn't changed. It's still the last refuge of the bitter alcoholic.

**—Bob Odenkirk**

## STAY IN CHARACTER:
## SPEAK SOFTLY BUT CARRY A BIG SHTICK

Just as you're obligated to know your audience before you write material, it's essential to know the character the performer is playing. Humor doesn't go into a character; it comes out of a character. This point is critical and merits repeating—each successful performer has a persona, and humor is written for the persona, not the performer.

 Your stage character is the magic glue. It makes sense of all your jokes, giving them a context to spring out of and a perspective to reflect. If your material is the what, then your delivery is the how, your timing is the when, and your character is the who.

**—Jay Sankey**

A character needs a trademark, a predictable point of view that does not change. If a performer doesn't have an individual style (sometimes called a hook or shtick), the writer (frequently a writer/director like Jane Wagner, who works with Lily Tomlin) shares the burden of finding one that fits. Without a shtick, the performer is just a reciter of jokes, an eyewitness to insignificant history. With it, a comic can get laughs even with mistakes— because, in a way, the character is part of the joke.

It's unusual for a famous performer to have more than one character—it's also dangerous, because audiences feel more comfortable with stereotyped humorists. It's also easier to write for just one character.

Stereotypes are a shortcut around thinking, and the audience may get confused if a performer changes characterization in mid-act. Rarely do comedians established in film or theater play characters that are opposite to their personas. The most successful movie comedians are those who play every part the same, such as Woody Allen, Billy Crystal, and Steve Martin.

When those same comedians attempted to alter their film characters, audiences were not always receptive. That said, it is possible for performers to successfully change their personas, as Robin Williams has proven.

 Audiences are really something else. When you're apprehensive and show a little fear and doubt because you're not getting any laughs, man, an audience will eat you alive. They sense fear, and it's like being in a confrontation with a wild animal that senses you're afraid. In both cases, you're doomed.

**—Richard Pryor**

Professional humor writers are known for two types of reliability: They can reliably produce material that is (a) of high quality and (b) on target. A rejection slip that reads "I don't do that kind of material" is damaging because it indicates that the humor writer didn't know the market. He not only wasted his time, but that of the performer as well. Sad sacks who get that kind of rejection had better hold on to their day jobs.

Pro writers involve themselves in serious performer research. Reading previously published material, attending live performances, and watching recorded performances takes time. The background research will help you identify the style and tone of the performer's character, as well as the performer's typical material. Humor written for one character will rarely work for another—even if it's written for a similar character.

Basically every joke's been done, so you get laughs out of looks, gestures, and catchphrases. The writer must instinctively hear a little voice inside that says, "This isn't right," or "Hey, this works!"
— **Eric Allen**

## SHOWTIME

As you watch performances of your favorite comedians, identify each performer's dominant characteristics (style, attitude, mannerisms) and the material used (topics, tone, catchphrases, form). Write a one-sentence description that summarizes each comic's character.

---

### QUESTION & ANSWER

**HOW DO I KNOW IF I'M REALLY FUNNY?**

Try your material out before a live audience, but remember that the audience must be your target audience. And that's where most beginners make a fatal mistake.

The MAP triangle (discussed in chapter three) identifies the audience with the letter A at its apex, because it is essential for a comedian to appear before or write for a specific audience. And the right audience is as different for each performer and writer as is the right spouse. The male student audience for Letterman is directly opposite the feminist audience for Ellen DeGeneres, and Jeff Foxworthy's redneck beer swillers would be out of their element shuffled into Rita Rudner's mature audience. The Academy Award audience is so grumpy that the awards show proved to be a deathtrap for MCs David Letterman and Chris

---

Rock, both of whom tested Hollywood's waters with their best laugh preservers, and drowned.

If any test produces a two-second laugh, you've hit pay dirt—or some kind of dirt. Getting a four-second laugh is known as going gold. Most jokes go vinyl.

Before Jay Leno delivers his five-minute monologue each evening on *The Tonight Show*, he tests his material the night before at a local Orange County comedy club, with an audience similar to his show's audience profile. His twelve writers provide him with twenty minutes of new jokes, and then the audience helps Leno throw out 75 percent of the test material and get down to the final five minutes he delivers the next evening to a national TV audience. That's a lot of rejection every day. Professionals are used to those odds. So should you be.

## THE MASKS OF COMEDY

Theater began in Greece with one actor in a variety of masks playing all parts. In humor, there are many distinctive character masks. But each comedian can have only one. The character can be anything from an erudite scholar to a simpleton, a suburban yuppie, a dope addict, a sexual deviate, a braggart, a tightwad, a drunk, or a coward (and that should take in every friend you've got).

 A comedian says funny things. A comic says things funny. Tonight, I will prove that I am a juggler!
**—Michael Davis**

Each of the masks has a number of variations; there is also a great deal of overlapping. The basic stock characters are categorized into three groups: the single, the team, and the artist (with props). In the majority of cases, the character fits the personality of the performer, complementing physical appearance and speech ability as well as talent. Paradoxically, the comedian must create a perfect characterization of an imperfect character.

Although humorists debate the appropriate label for each comedy mask, most agree that there are about twenty different comedic characters. The twenty masks of comedy are:

**THE SINGLE**

1. The Jester
2. The Aggressor
3. The Sad Sack
4. The Drug Rebel
5. The Intellectual
6. The Political Satirist
7. The Storyteller
8. The Rube
9. The Old Timer
10. The Ethnic Type
11. The Immigrant

**THE TEAM**

12. Partners
13. The Sketch Performer
14. The Ventriloquist

**THE ACTOR**

15. The Impersonator
16. The Clown
17. The Artist, Musician, and Cartoonist
18. The Vaudevillian
19. The Improviser
20. The Bumbler

As audience preferences change, characters may disappear from the stage. For example, there are few comedic partnerships today—with the exception of Penn and Teller, who are primarily magicians. Skits, the heart of burlesque and review comedy, have also become rare comedic meat. They appear in only a few TV formats: in take-offs on quiz shows and news broadcasts, and in interview shows on *Saturday Night Live, Whose Line*

*Is It Anyway?*, and *MADtv*. Many of the masks of comedy, such as The Vaudevillian, The Old Timer, and The Ventriloquist, have not been performed on a regular basis for years, and no one can explain why. It's also impossible to predict whether the retired masks of comedy will ever return.

 Stand-up comedy is transient. History shows that you can stand up for so long; after that, you're asked to sit down.

**—Steve Martin**

Comedic styles and audience preferences may change with time, but the basic building blocks of comedy remain the same—the humor-writing formulas that comprise an Ellen DeGeneres routine are the same as those used in a Jack Benny monologue. Most successful comics, if given truth serum, will admit that another performer influenced their style and delivery.

Here are the seven most common characters seen in today's stand-up and sketch comedy.

## The Jester

The most popular comedic character is the stand-up comedian—sometimes called a jester, a jokester, a wag, a wisecracker, or a quipster. The jester's material is a series of one-liners and short comments on the contemporary scene. Thousands of comedians could be listed in this category, including veterans such as Bob Hope, Milton Berle, and Henny Youngman.

 I love to go to Washington—if only to be near my money.

**—Bob Hope**

Any time a person goes into a delicatessen and orders pastrami on white bread, somewhere a Jew dies.

**—Milton Berle**

My doctor grabbed me by the wallet and said, "Cough!"

**—Henny Youngman**

Variations of the jester character can be heard today in the free-flowing material of such performers as Chris Rock, Laura Kightlinger, and Wanda Sykes.

You know the world is going crazy when the best rapper is a white guy, the best golfer is a black guy, the tallest guy in the NBA is Chinese, the Swiss hold the America's Cup, France is accusing the U.S. of arrogance, Germany doesn't want to go to war, and the three most powerful men in America are named "Bush," "Dick," and "Colin."

**—Chris Rock**

I hate the saying "Always a bridesmaid, never a bride." I like to put things into perspective by thinking, "Always a pallbearer, never a corpse."

**—Laura Kightlinger**

They say marriage is a contract. No, it's not. Contracts come with warrantees. When something goes wrong, you can take it back to the manufacturer. If your husband starts acting up, you can't take him back to his mama's house. "I don't know; he just stopped working. He's just laying around making a funny noise."

**—Wanda Sykes**

Today's stand-ups differ from past jesters in their joke-telling method. The old-school approach was a recitation of a series of one-liners. The "new-school" method places more emphasis on social commentary and extended rants on everyday life.

 Remember the crayon box with the flesh-colored crayon? Little white kids: "I'm going to draw my mother and father." Black kids: "I don't know nobody who looks like this." "Don't throw it out, I can use it to draw the police."

**—D.L. Hughley**

The most successful jesters match their delivery, content, and attitude to their character. The brash Joan Rivers inspired Roseanne Barr, the disgruntled housewife, and Rita Rudner and Wendy Liebman became the women's-lib icons.

My mother always said don't marry for money, divorce for money.

**—Wendy Liebman**

## The Sad Sack

The sad sack has been a comedy standard for centuries. The comic plays the insecure, timid Milquetoast, always seeking approval, confused by the opposite sex, unable to get dates or make any relationship work. Rodney Dangerfield played this character for decades.

 I went to my psychiatrist. I said, "Doc, I have this terrible feeling that everyone is trying to take advantage of me."

He said, "Relax. Everyone thinks somebody else is trying to take advantage of them."

"Gee, thanks, Doc. How much do I owe you?"

"How much have you got?"

The audience delights in laughing at the plight of others. The sad sack is one of the easiest characters to use when you're a neophyte performer trying to get your first laughs. The trick is to get the audience to like you; otherwise, they'll have no sympathy and will be happy to see you get what you deserve. Thus, the opening joke is far more important for this persona than for most others because it clearly defines the character.

Garry Shandling and Richard Lewis are two other practitioners of this style. Every joke is self-deprecating.

 I'm dating a girl now ... who's unaware of it, evidently.

**—Garry Shandling**

I quit therapy because my analyst was trying to help me behind my back.

**—Richard Lewis**

I have such poor vision, I can date anybody.

**—Garry Shandling**

There are many variations of the sad sack. The box office successes of Will Ferrell and Ben Stiller are largely due to their ability to create the lovable sad sack. Writer and actor Larry David morphed the sad sack into the schmuck by creating two unforgettable sitcom characters: his own alter ego on *Curb Your Enthusiasm,* and George of *Seinfeld.* The following are classic George Costanza lines.

 For I am Costanza, Lord of the Idiots.

I'm a great quitter. I come from a long line of quitters. I was raised to give up.

I can't carry a pen, I'm afraid it'll puncture my scrotum.

### The Drug Rebel

During Prohibition in the 1920s, the comedic performer who assumed a drunken posture was a popular nightclub, film, and campus entertainer. W.C. Fields was one of the first; then came others, like Joe E. Lewis, Robert Benchley, and Dean Martin. They frequently went on stage with drinks in their hands or would borrow one from a ringside table.

 Thou shalt not covet thy neighbor's house unless they have a well-stocked bar.

**—W.C. Fields**

The fascination with alcoholic clowns has turned into fascination with the druggie. When the druggie character emerged, this eccentric counterculture weirdo was a delight to college students and a disgust to the middle-aged. Comic Lenny Bruce was the guru of drug humor. Fellow comedian Robert Klein said that every modern comedian owes Bruce some debt of gratitude. Bruce claimed he entered the arenas of drugs, sex, and scatology to make a philosophical point. Don't believe it. He got in the smoking ring because it separated him from more erudite satirists like Mort Sahl.

 Marijuana is rejected all over the world. Damned. In England, heroin is all right for outpatients, but marijuana? They'll put your ass in jail. I wonder why that is? ... The only reason could be: To Serve the Devil—Pleasure! Pleasure, which is a dirty word in Christian culture.

**—Lenny Bruce**

George Carlin continued Bruce's legacy as a counterculture comedian. "The population segment I appeal to is the one that feels there is no hope for the human race," Carlin said. In the 1960s, his essential themes were drugs and rebellion, and he used hard-core words and ideas to shock his stunned audience to attention. Since that time, Carlin has dropped the druggie character, but he has continued to use dazzling word play as he viciously ridicules all parts of the Establishment. Following in Carlin's smoke are many others, including Emo Philips and Denis Leary.

 I used to do drugs. I still do, but I used to, too.

**—Mitch Hedberg**

Cocaine is God's way of saying you're making too much money.

**—Robin Williams**

I would never do crack. I would never do a drug named after a part of my ass, okay?

**—Denis Leary**

## The Intellectual

Before he shifted his focus to filmmaking, Woody Allen was the most successful erudite character. He played the mascot of the intellectuals for twenty years. His humor was based on the incongruity between his appearance and his material: the mousy physical look that disguised a secret sexual prowess, the very antithesis of the aggressive dominance of his peers, including Shecky Green, Jan Murray, and Jack Carter.

 I told my sexual experiences to Parker Brothers, and they made it into a game.

**—Woody Allen**

Stand-up comics who have been influenced by Allen include Steven Wright, whose act is one of abstract surrealism—illogical logic based upon literal interpretation. His onstage costume is always the same: jeans, work shirt with rolled-up sleeves, tennis shoes, frizzy hair, and a sullen face that never laughs. It gives him the appearance of an iconoclastic drifter.

I've never seen electricity. That's why I don't pay for it. I write right on the bill, "Sorry, I haven't seen it all month."

Today's reigning intellectuals include Dennis Miller and Lewis Black. Their characters are hip and sarcastic, frosted with a thick layer of sadistic hostility that belittles public figures and criticizes social and political trends.

 The radical right is so homophobic that they're blaming global warming on the AIDS quilt.

**—Dennis Miller**

Look, if New Jersey needs money, they could raise the sales tax on press-on nails. They'll make a killing!

**—Lewis Black**

Man, these things [solar-powered cars] are so ugly they are powered by humiliation.

**—Lewis Black**

### The Political Satirist

Satire is a humor maverick. Like topical humor, it has the life expectancy of a fly. One of the most famous satirical stylists, Mort Sahl, used to carry a rolled-up copy of the day's newspaper on stage as if he were ready to swat that fly. Satire reflects who and what are in the news at the very moment a joke is being told. The following week, the same material may be too old. On the other hand, some satirical commentary seems to illustrate the aphorism that the more things change, the more they stay the same.

 Liberals feel unworthy of their possessions. Conservatives feel they deserve everything they've stolen.

**—Mort Sahl**

Satire attacks both social and political targets, and therefore is risky when the audience is large and mixed. Will Rogers felt that if he could score a 50 percent "laugh rate," he was doing well. Until the explosion of cable networks, Mark Russell was the most prominent TV political satirist.

The Republicans have a new healthcare proposal: Just say no to illness!

**—Mark Russell**

Today, *Real Time With Bill Maher* and *The Daily Show With Jon Stewart* provide the uncensored cable forums with political satire. Jon Stewart and his collaborators also wrote the best-seller *America (The Book)*, a parody of a political science textbook. Examples of their satirical look at democracy include the following "Were You Aware?" factoids.

 The fact that the Magna Carta was written in 1215 is, by law, the only thing you are required to know about it.

Supreme Court justices fend off physical confrontations from lower court judges to maintain supremacy, much like silverback gorillas.

Ninety-six percent of congressional incumbents are reelected— which means the other four percent must really suck.

The public feels more tolerant toward print satirists like Art Buchwald, Russell Baker, and Ellen Goodman. Perhaps that's because, in performance, there's a second when the audience is thinking—not laughing. And for a performer, thoughtful silence is deadly.

 Would somebody please tell George W. Bush that he is not Commander in Chief of the Judiciary? No matter how "hot" he looked in his flight suit, black robes require a cooler demeanor.

**—Ellen Goodman**

## The Storyteller

There's a lot of characterization in the storyteller shtick. The story line is not a potpourri of one-gag anecdotes but is confined to one unique theme. The performer makes heavy use of strong critical comments that are strung out for as long as ten minutes (eventually, the comedian arrives at the point). Jokesters like Bill Cosby, Garrison Keillor, Richard Pryor, and David Sedaris don't flip from gag to gag. Instead, they share with the audience a universal experience and irritation. Like actors, they carefully rehearse and dramatize their stories. As a result, their material tends to stay away from current events and concentrate on standbys like family, business, and social situations.

 It's so much easier for me to talk about my life in front of two thousand people than it is one-to-one. I'm a real defensive person, because if you were sensitive in my neighborhood you were something to eat.

**—Richard Pryor**

Before broadcast humor, folk tales were the staples of frontier humor. They went with the territory—a world of yokels and rustics, where everything was tall. They had joke-telling contests, storytelling contests, and even awards for the biggest liars. Imagination was encouraged, and humor opportunities were limited only by the boundaries of the individual's mind. The antecedents of Western homespun fabulists were George Ades and Mark Twain (at the beginning of the twentieth century), and decades later, Danny Thomas, Buddy Hackett, and Alan King continued the tradition.

 If you want to read about love and marriage, you've got to buy two separate books.

**—Alan King**

Today, Garrison Keillor's radio program, *A Prairie Home Companion*, uses myth and exaggeration as its only story line; it emanates from fictional Lake Wobegon, "a small town that time forgot," located in a state of mind. It's a love poem to America's small towns, a universal birthplace for those who once lived (or would like to think they once lived) west of the Hudson, and who like to go home for a few hours each week. The audience warms to Keillor's mythical folk humor about a town "where all the women are strong, all the men are good-looking, and all the children are above average."

 Where I'm from we don't trust paper. Wealth is what's here on the premises. If I open a cupboard and see, say, thirty cans of tomato sauce and a five-pound bag of rice, I get a little thrill of well-being—much more so than if I take a look at the quarterly dividend report from my mutual fund.

Bill Cosby started out with a "one of the boys" routine on neighborhood characters (Fat Albert, Weird Harold). Now, he's so confident in his own material that he breaks the first commandment of comedy—push for a first, big laugh. He's a stand-up comic who prefers being a sit-down storyteller, chatting with his audience about a common problem, creating a facsimile of his family life. He calls it building a rapport. His stories start with a stock situation, and then he follows with exaggerations. He builds animated cartoons with words, not jokes. In storytelling, the big benefit is that if the audience doesn't laugh at what was supposed to be a funny line, it doesn't seem to matter unless it's the last line.

 As I have discovered by examining my past, I started out as a child. Coincidentally, so did my brother. My mother did not put all her eggs in one basket, so to speak: She gave me a younger brother named Russell, who taught me what was meant by "survival of the fittest."

**—Bill Cosby**

David Sedaris's wickedly jaundiced and funny observations push storytelling to a new level. With a brilliant deadpan delivery, he takes the audience on a surrealistic journey based on his eccentric life experiences. Part of his success is his unusual material, such as stories about working as an elf at Macy's. But Sedaris's true gift is his unique slant on topics like the perils of inter-elf flirtation, and doing drugs in his parents' house.

 After a few months in my parents' basement, I took an apartment near the state university, where I discovered both crystal methamphetamine and conceptual art. Either one of these things is dangerous, but in combination they have the potential to destroy entire civilizations.

One reason so few comedians adopt the storyteller mask may be that the seemingly extemporaneous style of storytelling requires a talented actor with exquisite timing and accent, skills that can only be perfected through years of careful character honing. Many young performers don't want to practice that hard. Another reason may be that in our frenzied tempo of communication, we just don't take the time to listen to long stories. It's a product of our credit card mentality—every hour today must be devoted to paying for the excesses of yesterday. Humor, like commercials, is judged in thirty seconds.

## The Rube

This country-boy humorist, tipping back in a cane-bottom rocker on the front porch of the general store with a hound dog at his feet, was a consistent hit with rural audiences. They felt comfortable laughing at some yokel less intelligent than they were. Over the past hundred years, there have been few costume changes for this character, except that the wide-brimmed farm hat was replaced with a John Deere cap.

 I have never been jealous. Not even when my dad finished fifth grade a year before I did.

**—Jeff Foxworthy**

In the 1970s, the most famous and (paradoxically) most obnoxious character on commercial TV was Ernest P. Worrell, a cavern-mouthed gangly redneck created by actor Jim Varney. Ernest spewed a fountain of overbearing, unsolicited advice, and he looked like the consummate Appalachian rube. Ernie gave his advice to his unseen friend ("Hey, Vern"), but then—to give the viewer a feeling of superiority and the satisfaction of revenge over his annoying character—he transformed his "Know what I mean, Vern" smugness to self-ridicule by going berserk and doing something incredibly stupid, like slamming a tailgate on his hand or electrocuting himself.

The country rube has spun off into two new characters: the NASCAR bubba and the urban idiot. Jeff Foxworthy and his *Blue Collar* buddies own the market on redneck-based comedy.

 Right now there's a bill in the Texas legislature that would speed up the execution process of those convicted of a heinous crime with more than three credible witnesses. If more than three people saw you do what you did, you don't sit on death row for fifteen years, Jack, you go straight to the front of the line. Other states are trying to abolish the death penalty. My state's puttin' in an express lane.

**—Ron White**

The movie *Dumb and Dumber* created a variation on the rube—the raging moron—and the movie's success ensured that future comedy films would feature at least one outrageous act of stupidity or lewdness.

---

## QUESTION & ANSWER

### HOW DO I FIND MY OWN SHTICK?

The most common advice given to beginning comedians is to be yourself. Writers receive similar advice when they are admonished to find their own voice. In theory, being yourself or finding your own voice are good ideas. However, in your quest for self-discovery, remember not to exclude the audience, the most important element of the MAP theory.

Audiences quickly—and unconsciously—stereotype performers into characters. Audiences understand and appreciate characters, not performers. If the audience cannot quickly identify a performer's character, there will be no emotional investment by the audience—and thus no laughs.

Character development relies on two elements of the THREES formula: realism and exaggeration. An effective character is an extension of the performer's personality, with exaggerated features. A comedic character is a caricature (because normal ain't funny).

Anyone can tell a joke, but a well-defined character makes it easier. Rodney Dangerfield's sad sack was so obvious that it could be summarized by a two-word catchphrase, No respect. A hidden benefit of creating a distinctive stage persona is that it reduces joke stealing by other performers.

---

## SHOWTIME

Develop a character and find your voice. Take a crash course in the history of comedy by completing the following exercises.

Watch performances of past and present comedians to understand the diversity of comedic characters. Keep a journal identifying the dominant characteristics of each character, and note how the masks of comedy changed over time.

Collect twenty jokes by past performers, and examine each joke for its content and style. Then, rewrite each joke for a contemporary audience.

Do a comparison of early sketch shows, such as *Your Show of Shows*, to *Saturday Night Live*. Note the differences between the main characters, sketch structure, and joke formulas.

Read the *Encyclopedia of 20th-Century American Humor* by Alleen Nilsen and Don Nilsen for a comprehensive overview of comedic trends.

Never stop writing.

## ESTABLISHING AN IDENTIFIABLE CHARACTER

If your character isn't instantly recognizable, the performance is off to a shaky start. Generally, there's no time to build a character the first time the audience meets you. Comedy demands that you get laughs within the first few paragraphs or within the first thirty seconds.

To make the audience feel secure, the performer must eliminate any threat of intimidation. The nebbish look of Woody Allen, the weirdo clothing of Emo Philips, and the squeaky voices of Jerry Lewis, Pinky Lee, and Paul Reubens's Pee-wee Herman were all carefully designed to let the audience feel superior. Just imagine the difference in perception if Ellen DeGeneres started wearing business suits and doing material on corporate America.

The mind plays tricks on you. You play tricks back! It's like you're unraveling a big cable-knit sweater that someone keeps knitting and knitting and knitting and knitting and knitting and knitting....

**—Pee-wee Herman**

Since we tend to feel sympathetic with the underdog, performers often try to make the audience care through a discourse on their misfortunes. But there's always the danger that no respect can lead to disrespect.

Once you find your character, you must stay in character. During one of the annual San Francisco International Stand-Up Comedy competitions, Jon Fox, a coproducer, reported that after Charles Cozart won a number of preliminary rounds with a take-off on a militant black, several of his competitors implied he wasn't versatile enough to do any other material. Cozart rose to the challenge, and in the next round did a completely different set. Unfortunately, his critics were right. He went down in flames, finishing dead last.

 Comedians as a group are a neurotic bunch. Most are immature and self-centered, insecure, and (at one time) at least three of the funniest were certifiably emotionally unbalanced.

**—Steve Allen**

Characterization can also be enhanced or accomplished using one or a combination of the following.

1. costume
2. props
3. voice
4. physical appearance

## Costume

A farcical costume is certainly one of the most visual ways to signal the audience that the performance is nonthreatening. It's the first thing the audience notices—that is, after they note whether the performer is male or female, and that's getting harder to tell every year.

To appear silly and nonthreatening, jesters of the Middle Ages wore floppy, belled caps; scalloped shirts and trousers; large, pointy-toed shoes; and carried a wand or scepter. Even today, baggy pants signal a comic character. Only a fool dresses like one.

 A scout is a boy who dresses like a schmuck. A scoutmaster is a schmuck who dresses like a boy.

Today, clowns carry on the same harlequin tradition. Mimes, whether on stage or street corner, have an established costume of top hat, white grease-painted face with red lips, black leotard, and soft black shoes. Their costume is so traditional you can spot them a quarter of a mile off: Caution—Mimes Ahead!

The outlandishness of Charlie Chaplin's Tramp, who sported a toothbrush moustache, a bowler, enormous trousers, and gigantic shoes, and who always carried a slender walking stick, was "a totemic figure of such deceptive simplicity that it can be imaginatively interpreted by everyone," wrote Luc Sante. Chaplin took several years to develop a character that was hapless, yet graceful; mischievous, yet chivalrous. In many respects, the Tramp was a descendent of Peter Pan. He played for tears as well as laughs.

 I had no idea of the character. But the moment I was dressed, the clothes and the makeup made me feel the person he was. I began to know him, and by the time I walked onto the stage he was fully born.

**—Charlie Chaplin**

A large black moustache was a comic symbol in the slapstick films of Ben Blue (among others), and the painted moustache was the comic trademark of Groucho Marx.

Steve Martin, after writing gags for the Smothers Brothers for several seasons, decided to go on stage himself. He played the jerk originally, but he struck out on the adult comedy circuit the first two years. Only after he went from witticisms to put-down humor and re-created his character as a wild and crazy show-off in a pure white three-piece suit, white shoes, and arrow through his head, did he find his audience with college-age kids.

I believe entertainment can aspire to be art, and can become art, but if you set out to make art you're an idiot.

**—Steve Martin**

Robin Williams's trademark is a printed Hawaiian shirt. Lily Tomlin always wears black trousers and color-splashed blouses. Her characters—militant feminists looking for intelligent life ("I'm against war, but if it weren't for Army surplus I'd have nothing to wear")—wouldn't permit her to wear dresses or frilly anything.

## Props

Effective props range from Denis Leary's dangling cigarette to Carrot Top's trunk of goofy items and Gallagher's mallet and watermelon. Groucho Marx's cigar, nose, moustache, and glasses are more often used as the symbol of comedy than the traditional clown mask.

 Groucho to TV quiz contestant: "Tell me, Mrs. O'Leary, how many children do you have?"

"I have fourteen, Groucho."

"How come so many?"

"Well, I love my husband."

"I love my cigar, too, but I take it out of my mouth once in a while."

George Burns commented: "I use my cigar for timing purposes. If I tell a joke, I smoke as long as they laugh. When they stop laughing, I take the cigar out of my mouth and start my next joke."

## Voice

Voice is certainly the most obvious physical instrument for conveying character. In some scripts, the words are written on music bars with pitch notes. Voice inflection, from malicious cackling to nasal whines, indicates personal characteristics not physically evident.

The right tone can portray ignorance, anger, sophistication, regional heritage, and even ethnicity. There are five major regional American accents: New York, New England, Southern, Appalachian, and Western. In addition, this country is rich in ethnic voices, such as Black, Yiddish,

Hispanic, Italian, and Indian. And finally, there is the personal character voice: the homosexual, the redneck, the gangster—and scores of others. While heavy dialect humor, on the national level, is becoming rare, character humor using regional accents, pauses, and grammatical levels is as popular as ever.

## Physical Appearance

Some comedians, like John Candy and Jackie Gleason, had such comic looks that you laughed just watching them screw up their faces. Buster Keaton, "the great stone face," learned at an early age that audiences enjoyed him more if he acted passively with every slapstick trick the heavy played on him.

 No man can be a genius in slap shoes and a flat hat.

**—Buster Keaton**

But cosmetic pride has killed off a lot of humor. Phyllis Diller for years ridiculed her face; her hair purposely looked as if she'd stuck her finger in an electrical socket. She could have played the witch in *The Wizard of Oz*—without makeup. One day she had a facelift, and then had to concentrate on exaggerated gown colors. She was funnier when she looked funnier. Jack E. Leonard was so big he was known as "Fat Jack." Then one year he went on a crash diet and lost one hundred and fifty pounds. This killed his act—his material had disappeared.

 Yeah, I'm overweight. Actually, it's due to water retention. Right now, I'm retaining Lake Erie. Once I laid down on a beach. I got harpooned twice and fourteen guys tried to drag me back into the water. I buy Hefty designer jeans, not at The Gap, at The Gorge.

**—Billy Elmer**

If you have big eyes (or if your client does), make them work for you as Marty Feldman and Carol Channing did in the seventies, and Eddie Cantor did in the thirties. Woody Allen made his eyeglasses a part of his act, particularly in films.

The performer must be honest as well as comfortable with the character. Makeup and lights can change looks. Props and costumes can emphasize the characterization—Tina Fey's glasses represent the serious anchorperson. But many things are almost impossible to change: age, color, height, and whether you're male or female (or both). Therefore, over the long haul, personality must coexist with character.

Beginning performers are well advised to try several characters before they settle on one. And that's when the real work begins.

## SHOWTIME

All successful sitcoms must have well-defined characters. And the public must know them intimately. Monica, Chandler, Ross, Joey, Rachel, and Phoebe never deviated from their *Friends* personas for more than ten years. Watch several sitcoms and complete an analysis of the main characters.

### TRICKS OF THE TRADE

There are a number of techniques stand-ups use to enhance their performances. Whether she needs to keep an audience laughing or respond to a sudden interruption, a good comedian is always prepared. Here are the most commonly used writing techniques in monologues and sketches.

#### Toppers

Getting an audience laughing from a dead start is like pushing a truck stuck in snow. It takes a great deal of effort and luck, and if you start by gunning the motor, you'll end up spinning your wheels. First, you've got to rock the truck (the audience) back and forth until the wheels catch. Then, when the weight is going forward, you keep momentum rolling with split-second timing. If it works, you're on your way.

One popular device that works to keep the energy up is the topper, a follow-up joke that builds on a previous laugh. Essentially, it's a second line that comes when the audience thinks the joke is already finished. The topper surprises them with an even funnier coda. The trick is to create a laughing roll—wait for the laughter to come down to about one-third or one-half of its peak volume, and then immediately start your next line.

 I'll tell you what I like about Chinese people. They're hanging in there with the chopsticks. You know they've seen the fork. They're staying with the sticks. I don't know how they missed it. Going out all day on the farm with a shovel. Come on. Shovel. Spoon. You're not plowing fifty acres with a couple of pool cues.

**—Jerry Seinfeld**

Jack Benny's writers used this device frequently because Benny's tightwad character was so strong, a laugh could come from every reference. Here, Benny uses a topper in a dialogue with a bum who begged for money.

 **BENNY:** Here's a quarter. Buy yourself a pair of shoes.
**BUM:** With a quarter? [small laugh, followed by a pause]
**BENNY:** You'll need laces, won't you?

Toppers can also be used in a number of the joke combinations discussed earlier. For example, here's an attempt to build a topper with a triple.

 **QUESTION:** Do you know the definition of fame?
**FIRST MAN:** Sure, fame is when I'm invited to the White House for a personal meeting with the president.
**SECOND MAN:** No, fame is when I'm invited to the White House, the phone rings, and the president ignores it.
**THIRD MAN:** No, real fame is when the president answers the phone, listens for a moment, and then says, "It's for you."

**—Robert Orben**

Comedy should be written so that each joke in the series is funnier than the previous one. Since the setup has already been established, the second, third, and fourth jokes are short, shorter, and shortest. You can keep the roll building with physical action. When the audience laughs, it's the equivalent of a home run with the bases loaded.

## QUESTION & ANSWER

### WHAT'S THE HOLY GRAIL OF LIVE COMEDY?

Hollywood's annual Academy Awards, one of the highest-rated TV specials, demands a comic for host—not for the stodgy attendees, who feel too superior to laugh at an outsider, but for the millions of pop-culture watchers who are being fed tedious acceptance speeches by actors, directors, and producers (who pathetically ad lib mandatory bons motes of depreciation). One of the first assignments of the show's producers is to find an MC whose humor appeals to the youth—cinema's present and future core audience.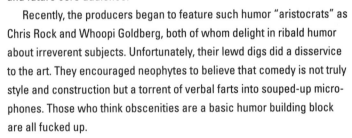

Recently, the producers began to feature such humor "aristocrats" as Chris Rock and Whoopi Goldberg, both of whom delight in ribald humor about irreverent subjects. Unfortunately, their lewd digs did a disservice to the art. They encouraged neophytes to believe that comedy is not truly style and construction but a torrent of verbal farts into souped-up microphones. Those who think obscenities are a basic humor building block are all fucked up.

### The Running Gag

A running gag (sometimes called a combo) is a line that comes early in a monologue and then is repeated as a payoff line for jokes scattered throughout the piece. Milton Berle's running gag was the "makeup" line. Every time Berle called "Makeup!" a man would run on stage and hit him in the face with a giant powder puff. The Russian-born comedian Yakov Smirnoff used a running gag in several of his stories.

 Soon after I came to America, I went to Tennessee. They are always checking your hearing there. They keep saying, "Now, you come back. You hear?" I can hear. Then a farmer played a practical joke on me. He told me to milk his bull. Now when you milk a bull you've made a friend for life. The bull kept running down the field yelling, "Now you come back. You hear?"

One of the most famous running gags was Jack Benny's joke about his parsimony. For years, he repeated the gag that resulted from a long pause after a robber demanded, "Your money or your life!" Finally, the robber asked, "Well?" And Benny would retort, "I'm thinking it over!"

## The Callback

A callback is a reference to something said earlier in a routine or sketch. The reference is usually a previous joke, but stand-up comics often use callbacks after interacting with the audience—an audience member's name will be inserted into a later joke. For a callback to work, the time between the original reference and the callback must be relatively brief. Repeated callbacks can be used (but never more than three times, of course). Audiences like callbacks because repeated references cause them to feel as if they are part of a shared experience.

## The Saver

The saver is a line used to save you when a joke bombs. Johnny Carson frequently used "I knew that joke wouldn't work." Others savers are "That's the last time I buy a joke from [the president of the club]" or "When did you all become members of a jury?" Comedy writers have to prepare a fistful of savers for their clients. The most dangerous time is when the fist is empty.

There are also savers for when a performance is interrupted by an unexpected event—which no professional performer ever fails to expect.

 A plane flies overhead: I hope it's one of ours.

Police siren: Here comes my ride home.

Electricity goes off: Call the power company and tell them the check is in the mail.

Someone enters late: That's okay. Let me tell you what you missed.

Attractive man or woman enters late: I thought I told you to stay in the tub.

Trip and fall to the platform: Now I'm ready to take questions from the floor.

The worst thing a performer can do in the event of an onstage emergency is publicly complain. A humorist should alleviate tension, not cause it.

### Switching a Joke

Woody Allen called the old switcheroo the big non sequitur. You start with a familiar story, then reverse (or switch) the ending. This is a popular technique because it catches the audience by surprise—especially if you don't overuse it.

 He carried a bullet in his breast pocket. Someone threw a Bible at him and the bullet saved his life.

**—Woody Allen**

### Working the Audience

Working the audience is a performance technique that requires a rare skill. The performer goes into the audience and asks questions, then makes brilliant insult rejoinders regardless of the target's answer. Audiences love it because the humor is at the expense of someone else. Tension is high: What if he comes over to me? Others don't mind being insulted as long as they're the center of attention.

While difficult, working the audience can be deconstructed like a magician's hocus-pocus. The performer must be in control at all times, only asking questions or picking on people for whom he has already prepared material. The questions are general—about hometowns, professions, clothing being worn, marital status, and size of family. Therefore, answers can be predictable. There are only so many states, professions, and colors of hair. Even our ages can be categorized.

Working the audience can be dangerous because it runs counter to the advice against threatening your audience, so this type of ad-lib performance requires a great deal of practice, and must be carefully plotted by the writer and the performer. Material should be tested repeatedly in performance situations.

 I love the complete fear when the curtain goes up. I never believe I am completely prepared.

**—Howie Mandel**

A beginning version of this technique uses the audience as a Greek chorus.

 **PERFORMER:** Hey, every time I ask you a question, yell back "Shit, no!"

**CROWD:** Shit, no!

**PERFORMER:** Having a good time tonight?

**CROWD:** Shit, no!

**PERFORMER:** Am I your favorite entertainer?

**CROWD [LOUDER]:** Shit, no!

**PERFORMER:** Are you going to get laid tonight?

**CROWD [VERY LOUD]:** Shit, no!

**PERFORMER:** Hell, I could have told you that!

# SHOWTIME

The only way to truly understand the unique dynamics of live performance is to perform live. Most comedy clubs hold open-mic evenings on Mondays for amateurs. Find out when your local open-mic nights are, then create and perform a five-minute routine. Even if you don't plan to become a stand-up comic, this experience will help you better understand how to write for performance.

### WHY IS THE SAME PERFORMANCE GREAT ONE DAY AND TERRIBLE THE NEXT?

Some psychologists believe outside factors account for the wide variety of responses to identical humor from different audiences. The rule is that you can neither hypnotize nor amuse an unwilling subject. External factors like bad weather, current events (terrorism alerts or attacks), or temporary physical irritations (the air conditioning broke down, or the show started late) increase audience tension and overcome their initial desire to take a vacation from reality. No performer wants to face an audience daring him to abruptly change their mood.

## MARKETING: SELLING YOUR HUMOR WRITING TO STAND-UP PERFORMERS

Most established comics will work only with freelance professionals— and a freelance professional is defined not as someone who is funny but as someone who is consistently funny for a living. It's not a waste of time to send your material to big-name entertainers—only a fool would refuse to look at new material. If the material is good, there's certainly a chance they'll buy it, but it's not easy to sell material this way.

Some entertainers are afraid that unknowns may not be sending original material. Although jokes cannot be copyright-protected, anybody can file a lawsuit for stealing material. Until a performer trusts you, you're in a catch-22 situation. One way to promote trust is to not waste the performer's time by submitting unusable material.

Many beginning writers are afraid of being ripped off. Sometimes they do get ripped off, but this doesn't happen as often as they fear it does. Performers are anxious to develop reliable sources of material, not to steal one joke. They are looking for consistency as well as quality, writers who can produce today, tomorrow, and next week.

One-joke sales are a thing of the past—no one buys them except *Reader's Digest*. But repetitive formats, like David Letterman's Top Ten List, are a freelancer's dream (this format, which Letterman fought to take with him from NBC to CBS, was submitted by a freelance writer from West Virginia).

The best strategy for selling your writing is to start locally and hang out at comedy venues. Attend performances, then linger in the bar to network with managers and performers. Don't push your material on anyone right away. Get a feel for the types of material that the performers use, and eventually ask if they will consider your work. Payment may not be much at first, but the experience will be invaluable.

Beginning and established comics will probably be members of the American Guild of Variety Artists. If there's a chapter where you live, it may be willing to put you in touch with a particular performer to whom you'd like to offer material.

When you submit material, send a collection of gags or routines, not just a single item. If the performer reads something she likes, she'll try to test it before purchase. A joke never tested cannot be funny; it can only be called a bit. (If it works, it's called a funny bit.)

# CHAPTER 14
## Print Humor: Columns, Articles, and Fillers

 Humor is a rubber sword—it allows you to make a point without drawing blood.

**—Mary Hirsch**

Magazine and newspaper editors are demanding more levity in their publications. Even in serious nonfiction pieces, they're anxious to lighten the load with humor. They realize there are few new stories, so they're looking for new ways of telling an old story. They also recognize that their readers want more humor. Studies show that the two most popular newspaper editorial features are both humorous—the editorial cartoon and the humor column. And material for *Reader's Digest* humor columns are requested in every issue.

 Writing a humor column beats honest work. It leaves mornings free for other projects, such as writing rare books. In my case, the books are extremely rare.

**—Art Hoppe**

Humor for print is written differently than for live performances. This chapter will describe humor-writing techniques for columns, articles, and fillers. Other forms of print humor, including Web sites, bumper stickers, T-shirts, and fortune cookies, will also be discussed.

## COLUMNS

Journalists call it the toy department—the editorial columns of a newspaper. Reporters dream about seeing their own columns. "If the editorial column is the land of Utopia," wrote writer Ed Cohen, "then the humor column is its capital city."

The humor column is a soapbox upon which clever writers can air their views. Humor permits them to take stands on issues of major and minor importance. Some of the most controversial subjects start out as humor pieces.

Bob Greene was an avid Coke drinker, and when Coca-Cola broke a ninety-nine-year tradition and changed the recipe, he wrote an outrageous humor column demanding that Coke bring back the old formula. He thought his temper in print would have no more sting than the usual political cartoon. Even he was surprised when his article helped snowball a national protest, and the public outcry forced Coca-Cola to bring back the old formula as "Coke Classic."

Frequently, humor columnists are discovered while they're writing for some other area of a paper, shuffling humor into their news articles. Erma Bombeck started out as an obituary writer for the *Dayton Journal Herald*. In 1963, she talked the editors into letting her have her own column. (She was paid three dollars apiece for her columns, but she claimed they were really worth twice that much.)

 Anybody can bring out your tears. That's a piece of cake. It is twenty times—no, make that fifty times—easier to make people cry rather than laugh.

**—Erma Bombeck**

For some time, the two most popular syndicated columns in newspapers were the personal advice columns written under the fictional names Abigail Van Buren and Ann Landers, both of whom were read as much for their humor as for their advice. For many years, the next in popularity were the four Bs: Erma Bombeck, Art Buchwald, Russell Baker, and Dave Barry.

 The only thing I was fit for was to be a writer, and this notion rested solely on my suspicion that I would never be fit for real work, and that writing didn't require any.

**—Russell Baker**

The average columnist works under deadline three times a week. Humor columns average 450 words, and rarely exceed 600. Humor columnists cannot make the reporter's standard excuse—that it was a slow news day. As a result, they frequently concentrate on the beat they know best: themselves. Humor columns often have a second life—Bombeck's columns were the source of several bestselling books, such as *The Grass Is Always Greener Over the Septic Tank*.

Some columnists work in rhyme, and nothing could be verse than that! This four-liner by Don Marquis, titled "Nothing to It," refers to his humor column.

 I do not work in verse or prose,
I merely lay out words in rows.
The household words that Webster penned—
I merely lay them end-to-end.

Russell Baker once ridiculed the Internal Revenue Service with a "Taxpayer's Prayer," a parody in the form of Biblical text.

 O mighty Internal Revenue, who turneth the labor of man to ashes, we thank thee for the multitude of thy forms which thou hast set before us and for the infinite confusion of thy commandments which multiplieth the fortunes of lawyer and accountant alike.

But verse or prose, column humor comes in five forms.

1. the anecdote
2. the one-line joke
3. overstatement
4. understatement
5. ironic truth

### The Anecdote

Humor in print demands a lighter touch than verbal humor. According to Roy Paul Nelson in his book *Articles and Features*, a light touch simply means a relaxed writing style—but not so relaxed it ends up cute. Rejection slips from editors often mention that an article could have used anecdotes to

illustrate generalizations. Generalizations include adjectives like *frugal,
tough, fast-thinking,* and *horny.*

There are two types of anecdotes: (a) a short, one-paragraph tale of
simple humor, and (b) a short, short story, rarely more than three paragraphs. Both types of anecdotes breathe life into any article and can
either precede or follow a generalization.

All anecdotes should:

1. sound true, or at least realistic
2. depict a common situation
3. start off with an attention-getting opening line
4. end with a one-line, bright response

Here are examples of short and long anecdotes. Note how they both have
the characteristics mentioned above.

 **SHORT ANECDOTE**

These days, ask a child a simple question, better be prepared
for a very honest answer. I was baby-sitting my six-year-old
granddaughter the other night and when we sat down for dinner,
I asked, "Nyika, at home do you pray before every meal?" And
she said, "No, grandpa, we don't have to. Mom is a great cook!"

**LONGER ANECDOTE**

As I was walking across campus yesterday, I saw one of my blind
students, Troy, being led by his seeing-eye dog to the campus gate.

I followed closely behind because I was curious to see how the
dog was going to get Troy safely across the street. At the busy
corner, they came to a stop when the light turned red. Then, as
soon as it turned green, the dog lifted his leg and urinated over
Troy's pants.

I watched in amazement as Troy bent down and called the dog
over and patted him on his head. Then he reached in his breast
pocket and took out a biscuit and put it in the dog's mouth.

I couldn't help saying, "Troy, that was the kindest act I've
ever seen."

"Kind, hell," retorted Troy, "I just wanted to find out where his head was so I could kick him in the ass."

—**Mel Helitzer**

Ultimately, it's more important for anecdotes to be humorous than to be true. Writers shade facts and edit true stories to save the punchline for last. When stories are made up, the readers should not be clued with lines like "This story may be apocryphal, but. ..." (Few readers know that word, anyway.)

Some anecdotes are obviously fictional; others may need a disclaimer. (But if you start with "One day, God, Jesus, and Moses were playing golf," don't bother using a disclaimer.)

 Three baseball umpires were arguing. Said the first, "I call balls and strikes exactly the way they come." (This man was an objectivist.)

Said the second, "I can't do that. I call them balls or strikes the way I see them." (This man was a subjectivist.)

But the third had ideas of his own. "They are neither balls nor strikes until I call them." (He was an existentialist.)

—**Nels F.S. Ferre**

## The One-Line Joke

One-liners are the backbone of humor writing. In print humor, one-liners inject humor without detracting from the message of the article or column.

It's important to remember that a joke is written differently for the printed page than it is for a performer. Columns and articles use a high percentage of cliché-inspired aphorisms. The printed page also permits more use of puns and double entendres, because homonyms are more understandable in writing.

 A pastor said to his congregation: To meet our budget deficit, I ask all of you to consider giving 10 percent of your income. Frankly, your church is fit to be tithed.

—**Herm Albright**

You'll find double entendres and puns all over the editorial pages. Puns are also a staple of newspaper headlines and photo captions. Within hours after a humpback whale got lost and mistakenly swam sixty miles up the Sacramento River into the middle of California, editors and T-shirt designers were having "a whale of a time." And when a luxury car fell into a giant pothole in Columbus, Ohio, even the *South China Morning Post* in Hong Kong ran the picture with the caption: "The hole truth—Mercedes bends."

A skilled columnist can turn an average one-liner into a thought-provoking observation—on life, children, husbands, even sports. Erma Bombeck filled her column "Wits End" with clever truisms that are as sharp today as they were when she first wrote them.

 I don't think women outlive men, it only seems longer.

There is nothing more miserable in the world than to arrive in paradise and look like your passport photo.

No self-respecting mother would run out of intimidations on the eve of a major holiday.

Before you try to keep up with the Joneses, be sure they're not trying to keep up with you.

The Rose Bowl is the only bowl I've ever seen that I didn't have to clean.

Columnist Dave Barry is the reigning king of pithy observations.

 Karate is a form of martial arts in which people who have had years and years of training can, using only their hands and feet, make some of the worst movies in the history of the world.

Life is anything that dies when you stomp on it.

Buying the right computer and getting it to work properly is no more complicated than building a nuclear reactor from wristwatch parts in a darkened room using only your teeth.

I have long contended that, however many zillion dollars the federal government costs us, we get it all back and more in the form of quality entertainment.

## Overstatement

Russell Baker is a cynic who sees the world as it is, instead of as it should be. In his column "An Idea That Must Be Unfolded Now," Baker used exaggeration to describe an early success of his "National Bumbershoot Academy."

 The pattern is familiar to us all. If you rise on a rainy morning and go to the closet for your umbrella, you find the umbrella gone. Usually it has gone to the office. If you go to the office on a clear morning, and it rains in the afternoon and you go to the closet for your umbrella, what do you find? Your umbrella is gone. Most cases it has gone home.

Another example of overstatement was Baker's attack on the Super Bowl, the Miss America pageant, and the Academy Awards as three American religious rituals.

 They are utterly boring, meaningless, pointless, and whatever happens doesn't make a goddam bit of difference to anything that is going to happen tomorrow. But when they run, the whole country comes together in some kind of great national town meeting.

**—Russell Baker**

## Understatement

Art Buchwald's ironic humor is so understated, the uninitiated reader thinks Buchwald is deadly serious. After the attorney general published a report recommending action against pornography, Buchwald wrote:

 I'd like to volunteer my services. One of my greatest fantasies has been to censor magazines and send those who sell them to jail. ... My qualifications? I've read many of the magazines the pornography commission finds objectionable. Secondly, I know exactly where in the store such reading materials are kept. ... I have done a lot of dry runs since the report was published. I know how to distinguish between literature with no redeeming value, as opposed to magazines which are just trying to give me a cheap thrill.

---

## HONE YOUR HUMOR WRITING

Erma Bombeck's legacy continues via the Erma Bombeck Writers' Workshop, held biennially at the University of Dayton. The conference is dedicated to the profession of humor writing and features workshops by famous humorists. Its Web site (www.humor writers.org) is a comprehensive humor-writing resource with articles, links, marketing tips, and writing contests.

---

## SHOWTIME

Select one of the five humor-writing techniques for columns, and compose a 500-word humorous column. Write about the subject, not yourself.

---

## ARTICLES

When writing jokes, you just want to be funny. When writing a humorous article, you want to inform and educate in a humorous way. Humor is appropriate in either of the two following situations.

**1. THE SUBJECT OF THE ARTICLE IS A PERSON KNOWN FOR HUMOR.** This makes humor in the article almost mandatory. The trick to profiling a humorist is to avoid trying to upstage the subject by forcing your own humor into the article. This is especially risky when you are

---

writing about humor professionals who've spent many years perfecting their lines, because you've got only a few days to perfect yours. You're bound to come off looking second-rate. Make use of the great lines the subject has created. Don't rewrite and don't compete.

**2. THE SUBJECT MATTER IS SERIOUS, BUT IT CAN BE MADE FUNNY.** Some article topics are inherently funny: a dog who sings along to rock music. Others are serious but can be treated in a humorous manner: an old lady who rides a motorcycle. It's obviously easier to produce humor when the subject itself is humorous, as is the case in the first example. The humor for the second type of subject, however, must be gentle, reassuring, and predictable. It should celebrate ordinary events in a new way. It should bring a smile of recognition rather than a hearty laugh. Its success is based upon genuineness of feeling and clarity of writing.

Even very serious subjects are more memorable when humor is added. In serious articles, humor works best as an opener. You can suck the reader into the story faster with a good anecdote. You'll find examples of this technique every day in front-page features in the *Wall Street Journal*. A humorous anecdote also works well as a sign-off.

## FILLERS

The term *filler*, which originated when type was set by hand or Linotype, refers to the one- or two-line tidbits editors used to quickly fill space at the end of a column or a page. A filler can be a joke, quote, short anecdote, or other small contribution. Today, fillers are more common in *Reader's Digest* than in daily newspapers.

There is no precise formula for a filler. "A good filler," wrote Betty Johnston, a former *Reader's Digest* editor, "is one that the reader will want to quote or read aloud to a colleague." Because most magazines have editorial deadlines four and five months in advance of publication, fillers need a certain timelessness and relevance—a quote or anecdote from the past must have some special application for today.

 My father, a retired Air Force pilot, often sprinkles his conversation with aviation jargon. I didn't realize what flying had meant to him, however, until the day he showed me the folder with his last will and testament. It was labeled "Cleared for departure."

**—Cheryl E. Drake**

Several staff editors at *Reader's Digest* review all humor anecdotes and fillers. Humor is read by at least two editors before being rejected so that the bad mood of one editor won't automatically eliminate a marginal possibility. Then, the magazine submits all material seriously being considered for publication to an index department, where it's checked for originality. (A beginning writer can ruin her reputation with a magazine by trying to pass off someone else's material as her own.) Finally, a research department checks original sources for verification.

Personal anecdotes are acceptable fillers, but anecdotes about famous people are particularly desirable because names make news (or the other way around).

Many general publications have taboos against bathroom humor, vulgarity, and stories that ridicule the handicapped. Put-down humor is acceptable when the joke is in the cleverness of the response to the put-down, so self-deprecating stories have a much greater chance of publication. A few magazines are also interested in reprinting good humor from other publications, and will pay readers handsomely for discovering it. *The New Yorker* delights in typos and short items with unintentional double entendres or weird phrasing.

Unlike a regular article, a filler is usually paid for only on publication. (Which means that if your piece is omitted at the last minute because they ran out of space, you'll get no check.) *Reader's Digest* gets thousands of submissions each month, many online (at www.rd.com), so they don't return material even if you include a self-addressed, stamped envelope (SASE). If they like your piece, you'll generally hear within three months—but sometimes they may take up to a year to respond. Keep this in mind when deciding whether to submit the same material elsewhere. (If you have sold the item elsewhere and any magazine's research department calls to verify, never lie. You'll win that game only once, and will be blackballed forever.)

## SHOWTIME

Write a letter to the editor of a local newspaper on a controversial subject—it's one of the easiest ways to get published. Remember, you'll have a better chance of getting published if you use humor and follow the writing guidelines previously described. For example, the annual swimsuit issue of *Sports Illustrated* prompts more letters from readers than many other issues combined. (It gets a lot of subscriptions renude.) Here's an example of a letter that got published because of a basic reverse technique.

 I was shocked at the display of flesh [that issue] contained. What legs! What chests! Where did you find those Sumo wrestlers?

## QUESTION & ANSWER

### HOW CAN I INCREASE MY CHANCES OF GETTING PUBLISHED?

The key to the sale of a column, article, or filler is the perfect marriage of quality humor with the periodical's subject matter and audience. Look through an annually updated directory—like *Writer's Market*, which lists hundreds of publications and their submission guidelines—and identify publications that match your specific areas of interest and accept humorous material. After you've selected several publications, go to a bookstore or library and look through them. Once you're certain that your material matches a certain magazine, follow the publication's submission guidelines.

Comedy writers Stef and Mary Kaiser Donev sell regularly to regional medical journals with small pieces like: "Hemorrhoids: They Won't Kill You—You Just Wish They Would," and "The One Sure Cure of Acne—Old Age." They claim that a 1,500-word article on a subject like hospital-room etiquette can contain up to eight humorous anecdotes or jokes and still be considered serious and informative.

## THE INTERNET

The humor-writing principles discussed in this book also apply to pieces posted on the Internet, with one exception: Internet pieces must be shorter than print articles. The physical layout of a Web page and the short attention span of the typical Web surfer both mandate concision. The title and opening of an Internet piece are critical—if surfers are not hooked by the first few lines, they'll click to the next site.

One of the most popular and well-written humor Web sites are *McSweeney's Internet Tendency* (www.mcsweeneys.net), *College Humor* (www.collegehumor.com), and *The Onion* (www.onion.com); a news source with factitious stories and funny takes on "real" news. Examples of headlines from *The Onion* are:

 Deadbeat Dads March on Las Vegas

Goth Kid Builds Scary-Ass Bird House

College Student Does Nothing for Tibet Over Summer

If you'd like to get published on an established Web site, review the submission guidelines on the site and follow their instructions. Many sites require sample submissions to the editor. You can also look for sites that hold writing contests for readers. Some of the more popular sites, like *The Onion*, for example, do not accept freelance material.

An alternative to getting published on an established site is to construct your own Web page. You can also post your best jokes, anecdotes, and stories in a personal blog (Web log). Setting up a blog is simple, and numerous

Web sites (including www.blogger.com) provide step-by-step instructions for creating your own humor space on the Internet.

## ABBREVIATED PRINT HUMOR: EVERYWHERE YOU WANT TO BE

Abbreviated humor copy appears in a wide variety of forms, from bumper stickers to window signs. They don't get written by themselves. For pros, such writing assignments are a great way to earn petty cash with material that doesn't fit anywhere else.

### Bumper Stickers: Put It on Your Rear

Bumper stickers publicly indicate the way we feel about ourselves. They are for adults what T-shirt humor is for adolescents. They are more popular than buttons and more socially acceptable than painted graffiti. Their form is very structured.

1. They must be short, rarely more than eight words.

 Cover me. I'm changing lanes.
    I brake for no apparent reason.

2. They are usually a play on words (POW).

 Archaeologists do it with any old thing.
    Where there's a will, I want to be in it.

3. Paired words are effective in this format.

 To make America work, Americans worked.

4. They frequently refer to specific interests and activities.

 I is a college student.
    Work is for people who don't know how to fish.

5. They are often nihilistic.

 Get a taste of religion. Bite a preacher.
    Learn from your parents' mistakes—use birth control.

6. They include a lot of put-down humor and insults.

 Watch out for the nut behind me.

Forget about world peace—use your turn signal.

Keep honking. I'm reloading.

## T-Shirts: Put It on Your Front

If there was ever a cottage industry in humor land, it's the T-shirt business. You can not only write the gags from your own kitchen, you can be in business in less time than it takes to marinate a steak. Typical of T-shirt success stories is that of Dan Gray, a high school dropout from Cleveland who went into business with an investment of six hundred dollars, and five years later was grossing six million dollars in sales under the name of Daffy Dan's T-Shirts.

T-shirt humor is written from the point of view of adolescents who have discovered that body language is the next step up from sticking out their tongues. T-shirt copy is frequently made up of in-jokes brazenly poking fun at some local happening: a current news event, sports event, or a success story ("I survived ..." is the most popular legend).

The writing techniques used most often for T-shirts are double entendres and reformed clichés. The only other requirement is that the copy be short. T-shirt manufacturers must get in and out of fads quickly because the humor is topical and very short-lived; three weeks is average, and a fad that lasts three months is a big winner. As a result, they welcome ideas and suggestions offered on spec (payment only if accepted, with no guarantee of acceptance). The only value, in this case, of an on-spec presentation is that a meeting may result in an assignment from the manufacturer to focus on a specific future happening.

T-shirts are popular premium giveaways for all types of commercial businesses. A dental practice might request T-shirts with the quip: "I got drilled by Dr. Allen," for instance.

T-shirt humor, like the T-shirt itself, gets dirty quickly. Sex teasers are one of the biggest commercial T-shirt successes.

Consume now before I'm all used up.

You can't win if you don't play.

Feel good all under.

Help with the fun raising.

### Fortune Cookies: Put It in Your Mouth

In most Chinese-American restaurants, guests are awarded a free fortune cookie at the end of a meal. Fortune cookies are unknown in China, although a few Chinese historians believe they were invented by revolutionaries during the Ming Dynasty (A.D. 1368–1644) who used the brittle folded cakes to pass secret messages. (No, one of them was not "Help! I'm a hostage in a fortune cookie factory.") Today, they are like the prize in the Cracker Jack box. Some restaurants even provide pornographic cookies on request.

Fortunes must sound like Confucius composed them.

 Success is relative. More success, more relatives.

Anger improves nothing except the arch of a cat's back.

In truth, they're written by gag writers who knock off fifty improbable predictions, bits of sage advice, and witticisms a day.

 Money not key to happiness, but unlocks interesting doors.

Chinese restaurant managers even have their own gag line for when a customer accidentally receives an empty cookie. Sara Wilson tells the story of the waiter who said to his customer, "Ah, very lucky. No news is good news."

## MARKETING ABBREVIATED PRINT HUMOR: PUT IT IN YOUR WALLET

If you're interested in producing your own ideas instead of selling them to a company, there are a number of do-it-yourself software programs that allow you to create your own products. Many printers also specialize in bumper stickers, T-shirts, and fortune cookies. Search the Internet for a current listing.

## SHOWTIME

Write a series of one-liners that could be used for bumper stickers, T-shirts, or fortune cookies. For example, write abbreviated copy for advertising your job, identifying your hometown, or promoting your sexual prowess (*that* won't take you long).

# CHAPTER 15
## Saw the Picture, Loved the Gag: Humor for Cartoons and Greeting Cards

 Now I'm getting paid for what I used to get in trouble for when I was in school—drawing in class.

**—Ben Sargent**

Even if your artistic skills are limited to stick figures, you can still work with visual humor. For the professional gag writer, cartoon and greeting card humor are no different than the basic one-liner—a play on words (POW), a reverse, exaggeration, or take-off. The cartoon (or the outside of the greeting card) is typically the setup, and the caption (inside of the card) is the punchline.

Most humor historians agree that the advent of *The New Yorker* in 1925 most influenced the development of the gag cartoon. This magazine made cartoons respectable, and according to English scholar M. Thomas Inge, it also "established the standard against which the works of all modern cartoonists are measured."

Prior to *The New Yorker*, humor cartoons consisted primarily of illustrations indicating a dialogue between two people, both of whom were identified by pronouns, names, or titles, as if the caption was a play script. Drawings were stylized and not intended to add much to the comedic impact. The narrative was expected to carry the full load.

 **GENTLEMAN CALLER TO MAID**: You might ask your mistress if she is at home?
**MAID**: It's no use, sir. She saw you coming.

Today, the formula is the same, but the style is different. The humor copy is shorter—pithy—and specialized. Because of the influence of *The New*

*Yorker*, the two-person dialogue has practically disappeared in favor of the one-line gag caption. Today's satirical cartoons demand an audience that's sophisticated and literate enough to be comfortable with the eccentricities of modern life.

The three major cartoon formats are single-panels, comic strips, and political cartoons.

## SINGLE-PANEL CARTOONS

You see these cartoons everywhere you look, from magazines as varied as *Cat Fancy*, *Skydiving*, and *Highlights for Children* to your local editorial page (we'll discuss political cartooning shortly). A single-panel cartoon is just that—a single, self-contained cartoon generally consisting of a short joke and an illustration. Your chances of succeeding in this field are greatest if you can provide both the verbal and visual components yourself.

### The Verbal Component

Single-panel cartoons generally include little or no text. At most, you may see three or four short lines. Since you don't have a lot of room to showcase your humor, technique is especially important. Some of the most common humor techniques for the verbal component of single-panel cartoons are one-liners, reverses, double entendres, and social commentary in the form of a spoof.

### The Basic One-Liner

The one-liner is the meat and potatoes of cartoon humor. Such gags combine a stereotype setup with a surprise caption. Since the caption can usually carry its own weight without a distinctive graphic, it can be successful in publications like *Reader's Digest* without any artwork at all.

 Girl introducing one beau to another: Albert, this is Edward. Edward, this is goodbye.

**—Leo Garel**

### The Reverse

The illustration is straight, but the caption is a reverse on a cliché.

Doctor, pointing to the X-ray of a beautiful girl: What's a joint like this doing in a nice girl like you?

—**Jack Markow**

More often, the caption is a reverse of a train of thought.

 Husband, watching TV, to wife at door: A walk in the moonlight? Sounds like a great idea. Take the dog with you.

—**Hagerman**

### Exaggerations: Ticks of the Trade

The jargon of every profession encourages double entendres and the simple (exaggerated) truth. They are especially valuable for trade magazines looking for customized humor.

 Bookseller, staggering under the load of a large, flat stone covered with hieroglyphics, to customer: Here's that first edition you wanted.

### Spoofs of Language, Habits, and Customs

Current habits and customs can be humorous when spoofed by super-sophisticated children, super-sprightly elders, aliens, and animals. Turns of phrase can also be humorous, especially when they don't fit the speaker.

 Two children, looking at a bent nail: I think it's called a dammit.

—**Burbank**

### The Visual Component

The visuals in a single-panel cartoon should not be complex. The illustration must take only a second to absorb, and must immediately be within the reader's intellectual grasp.

Even aspiring humorists who can't draw with much skill have a chance in this field if they can hone in on their own style.. "Most people can't draw anymore in the classical sense, and that can be oka," said Bob Mankoff, cartoon editor for *The New Yorker*. "I like to say to the people who can't draw: There's bad-bad drawing and bad-good drawing. Now when you look at Thurber, you see bad-good drawing. You see something that's easy and consistent and confident. I don't have a formula, but in a drawing that's simple, you want some sort of charm and personality to come through."

Most single-panel cartoons feature two characters, but usually only one character does the talking. Other basic illustrations range from one central character talking on the phone to cartoons showing small groups of three or four easily identifiable characters. The only purpose of the illustration is to communicate the basic context in which the reader should interpret the joke. The caption is about the only thing that surprises.

 Two chorus girls: I think a girl should marry for love. I'm going to fall in love with the first millionaire I meet.

Let's take a closer look at some of the most common visual techniques used in single-panel cartoons.

### This Is Balloony

Humor copy can be written in balloons above the speaker's head or as a caption underneath the illustration. The balloon doesn't even have to contain copy. In a cartoon by Randall Harrison, a man and woman are depicted with a balloons above their heads. The man's balloon is empty, while the balloon above the woman reads: "Richard, you're always so thoughtless."

### The Hidden Element

The basic gag in this type of illustration is that something is hidden from one of the characters. Everyone else, including the reader, knows what's taking place. For example, a scuba diver doesn't see what's coming up behind him; or a wife, looking out into the jungle, keeps talking to her husband, who's being swallowed by a python. Incongruity is fundamental in humor, and this type of cartoon is a perfect example of the superiority theory. We laugh because we know somebody else is about to become, in more ways than one, a fall guy.

### Understatement and Overstatement

Another type of cartoon juxtaposes an outrageous caption with a commonplace visual image, or an exaggerated illustration with mundane text below. When the illustration is exaggerated, the main character usually speaks in a way that indicates innocence, naïveté, or general stupidity.

Department store information clerk to flasher who has opened his raincoat: Men's department. Third floor center.

When the caption is exaggerated, the cartoon usually depicts a commonplace setting.

 Caveman to friend playing golf: I feel safe in saying that this game we've invented will be a calming and soothing influence on mankind for all time to come.

—**Bernhardt**

## Transformations

Transferring human characteristics to animals is called anthropomorphism. In humor, it is called transformation, and it has been a favorite cartoon device since the times of cavemen.

 One forest ranger to another as bear drives off in Jeep: I warned you about leaving the key in the ignition.

A popular practitioner of transformation is Gary Larson, creator of *The Far Side*. An example of Larson's style of humor shows a lady crouching down to feed squirrels. One squirrel says to the other, *"Oh I can't stand it! They're so cute when they sit like that!"*

Nowadays, transformations can be applied not just to animals but to such things as technology.

 A baby computer crawls up to a big computer and says: Data.

## Change of Time Frame

When today's customs, habits, or phrases are juxtaposed with those of another era, you have an opportunity for understated or overstated incongruity. Cartoonist Charles Addams's scene of a space rocket ready for launch being boarded by a long trail of animals, two by two, works visually and needs no caption.

## The Reverse

This technique, so popular in other forms of humor writing, can appear in cartoons in the illustration, in the caption, or in the interplay between the two. A visual example would be two horses playing horseshoes with a set of human shoes. In a caption, the reverse would work just like a standard reverse in humor writing.

 Woman talking to friend: I like sex in the morning—right after Bill goes to work.

When the reverse is in the interplay between the caption and illustration, it can go something like this.

 MC introducing beautiful girl to reunion dinner party: And now for the award to our former classmate who's changed the most since graduation. You may remember her better as Ed Furgeson.

—V.M. Yels

A frequent reverse formula is to apply new visual interpretations to a cliché. "Darling, they're playing our song" is a straight line when it's a caption under a picture of a couple dancing. It becomes a reverse when the illustration shows a stout couple on a luxury liner hearing the steward strike the dinner bell. It also works (without the word *darling*) when one mechanic shouts it to another as two cars smash into each other just outside of their garage.

## SHOWTIME

Check out *The New Yorker*'s cartoon collection online at www.cartoonbank.com. After you get a feel for cartooning techniques, find fifteen to twenty cartoons, illustrations, or photographs without captions and write a humorous punchline for each one.

### COMIC STRIP HUMOR: THE PLOT NEVER THICKENS

Comic strips, such as Jim Davis's *Garfield* and Scott Adams's *Dilbert*, differ from single-panel cartoons in that they contain three to six panels that work together to convey a single joke. The amount of text in each individual panel varies from nothing at all to two or three short lines. Since most comic strips are syndicated, freelancing in this area can be more difficult than finding work as a single-panel cartoonist. Here are a few tips for creating successful comic strips.

1. **KEEP THE SPOTLIGHT ON THE STAR.** The focus of humor should always be on your lead character. Just as in a sitcom or sketch comedy, the cast is there to support the central character. This is why there are never more than three main characters in any one panel.

2. **A CHARACTER IS A CONSTANT.** The star of the strip doesn't change. He always looks the same and wears the same basic expressions—and not too many of those, either. This character's actions are predictable.

3. **THERE IS NO PLOT.** The first frames are only the setup and background for a simple line of logic or illogic. Running gags are popular. Popeye's spinach and Dagwood's super sandwich are still working after more than fifty years.

4. **DIALOGUE IS ALWAYS SPARSE.** Sentences run four or five words per panel. There is much use of exclamations. The key words are repeated, as in this *Peanuts* example from Charles Schulz.

 **PANEL ONE:** Two kids sitting on steps watch Charlie Brown approach. Boy says to girl: Well! Here comes ol' Charlie Brown.
**PANEL TWO:** Charlie is next to them: Good ol' Charlie Brown. ... Yes, sir!
**PANEL THREE:** Charlie has just passed: Good ol' Charlie Brown ...
**PANEL FOUR:** Charlie is out of sight: How I hate him!

## POLITICAL CARTOONS: WHERE EVERYTHING'S BLACK AND WHITE

Political cartooning is an example of the use of hostility in humor—they are vicarious opportunities to bitch and gripe. Typically consisting of a single-panel image and a biting one-liner, these jewels of the editorial page offer readers a chance to blow off steam, a chance to say, "Yeah! Give it to 'em."

 What can be better than being able to draw, get pissed at people, and mouth off whenever you want to?

**—Mike Peters**

A political cartoon's value is as an irritant, lightning rod, or catalyst. As Garry Trudeau, creator of *Doonesbury*, observed, "We're not paid to be fair. In fact, if it were fair, then it would become something altogether different ... *once you say you may not exaggerate, you may not use hyperbole, you may not stretch the truth*, you take away all these tools, and you don't have satire at the end of the day."

Practitioners of political cartooning have been a powerful intellectual and political force. Benjamin Franklin drew the famous "Join or Die" cartoon that showed the colonies as separate pieces of a serpent. Thomas Nast created the Democratic donkey and the Republican elephant, and helped drive Boss Tweed and his Tammany Hall crowd from power in New York in the 1870s. Clifford Berryman's drawing of Teddy Roosevelt refusing to shoot a bear cub was the inspiration for doll manufacturers to create "Teddy's bear."

Today, in the golden age of political cartooning, hundreds of full-time editorial cartoonists, protected by the First Amendment, are daily lampooning the controversial issues and attitudes of our day.

 Most cartoonists like me—who like to attack—are like loaded guns. Every morning we start looking through the newspaper for a target to blast. That's our function. If you're trying to be fair, whatever you're putting across would have to be watered down.

**—Mike Peters**

Drawing heat for their work is the norm for political cartoonists. Cartoonists aren't positive they're getting their message across unless they're besieged with obscene mail, threatening phone calls, and petitions urging they be reassigned to the unemployment line.

 The dream of every editorial cartoonist is to get picketed.
It's got to be.

**—Mike Peters**

The single element all political cartoons must have in common is devastating wit. Their caricatures and situations raise smiles, laughs, whoops, and the desire to repeat the message to your associates. Increasingly, editorial cartoons not only expose the emperor's lack of clothes (or thought), but do it humorously.

Political cartoons are inherently more difficult than other types of cartoons. In order for the reader to get the joke, the visual metaphor in the cartoon must instantly conjure a well-known subject. "People must really understand what you're talking about before you start communicating," said cartoonist Hugh Haynie. Therefore, humor must make a biting point, not just play against the illustration. It can do this by either exaggerating the art or exaggerating the joke.

The real test is coming up with ideas day after day, so while they don't like to advertise it, political cartoonists are ripe markets for freelance humorists who know their style and are able to work off current headlines. Just send them the item. They'll do the drawing. You can draw the check.

### Exaggerated Art

Artwork for political cartoons is far more important than that for single-panel cartoons. For one thing, the ability to caricature famous personalities is a must. The best cartoons must hit you squarely in the jaw, so the artists look for a distinctive physical feature of each personality and exaggerate it. A stout woman becomes very fat. A tall man becomes a giant.

Another requirement is the use of stereotypical symbols. To some cartoonists, the CIA is a cloaked individual stealthily sneaking around corners. To others, it's Frankenstein's monster breaking down doors and crushing innocents.

The most frequent subject of caricature is the person who happens to be president. Richard Nixon, with his dark-shadowed face and beady eyes, was a political cartoonist's ideal target, and was pounced on with devastating force. Another popular target was Bill Clinton and his personal foibles.

 You know, with the Clinton years, reality was getting ahead of satire. I mean, you were almost just drawing what was happening, and it was hard to get ahead of it, and when that happens, that's very hard for a cartoonist. So I hope things are going to settle down and we can get to work on being satirists again, instead of having it done for us by the guy who's the object of it all.

**—Pat Oliphant**

Pulitzer Prize–winning political cartoonist Pat Oliphant usually engages his characters in a burlesque of some current controversy. And always, a wisecracking penguin comments on the action from a lower corner of the panel. Oliphant's style has been so widely copied that young cartoonists almost find it obligatory to insert smart-aleck animals of their own in the corners of their drawings. As cartoonist Mike Luckovich noted, "There wasn't a sense of fun in editorial cartooning, I think, before Oliphant."

## Exaggerated Text

Political cartoonists jump on names that lend themselves to double entendres. Cartoonist Bill Sanders told of a municipal court judge by the name of Christ T. Seraphim who "used to take his first name seriously and the Bill of Rights in vain."

To attack the high cost of health care, cartoonist Steve Kelley drew a scene of a patient in a doctor's office falling backwards off his stool after reading his bill. The doctor scribbles on his chart, "Reflexes normal."

 Outside of basic intelligence, there is nothing more important to a good political cartoonist than ill will. Cartoons are more likely to be effective when the artist's attitude is hostile, to be even better when his attitude is rage, and when he reaches hate, then he can really get going.

**—Jules Feiffer**

## BREAKING IN TO CARTOONS

Finding work in political cartooning can be difficult, especially if your goal is to see your work appear in a publication such as *The New Yorker*. Bob Mankoff, the magazine's cartoon editor and a cartoonist in his own right, receives more than 1,000 submissions each week, 980 of which he rejects. If you target your submissions carefully, however, and hone your skills by creating cartoons for publications that are more open to working with freelancers, your chances of success increase.

As recently as twenty years ago, it was common for a writer to write the caption and an artist to draw the illustration, but things have since changed. According to Mary Cox, editor of *Artist's & Graphic Designer's Market*, "You really need to be able to do both—or know a collaborator—if you're going to be successful in this field. It's rare for editors to set up artists and writers—especially if they're beginners with no track records."

While it may be easier to find work if you can handle both the visual and the verbal aspects of cartooning yourself, collaborations between a cartoonist or illustrator and a gag writer still exist. But the partnership is not equal. The illustrator gets three times as much money, 75 percent of the fee.

The lion's share of the money goes to the illustrator because editors usually contract for the services of the illustrator first. The artist, or his sales rep, comes in with a portfolio of material on spec. If the editor loves it, she'll try to work out some agreement, either exclusive or first-option, because each major cartoon market—magazines, newspapers, or syndicates—wants an individual look. You can achieve that in graphics more easily than with one-liners.

Once the job is assigned, it's up to the artist to produce the quality of humorous material demonstrated by his portfolio. Buyers don't care how it's done. The artist is the only one paid, and how the fee is split with the gag writers is none of the buyer's concern. As a result, the artist in need of ideas hires gag writers. An established artist can work through the mail with a dozen freelance writers on a "pay if used" basis.

In a sense, the cart is more valuable than the horse. Illustrations are not great works of art; most of them are stereotyped setups, and the fun is in the text. The gag writer does most of the creative work, and the artist gets most of the money. It doesn't sound fair, but it's not that different a setup from the one between on-stage performers and their gag writers.

The writer should submit each gag line on an individual index card. The back of the card should include contact information and the file number you assigned to that gag so it can be referred to in correspondence. Gag ideas are all the artist requires, unless the humor is the result of a unique illustration.

The National Cartoonist Society (www.reuben.org) offers comprehensive resources for the professional cartoonist. The annually updated *Artist's & Graphic Designer's Market* includes submission guidelines and contact information for hundreds of publications that accept cartoons from freelancers. Other recommended books include *The Big Book of Cartooning* by Bruce Blitz and *Everything You Ever Wanted to Know About Cartooning but Were Afraid to Draw* by Christopher Hart.

## GREETING CARDS: HUMOR IN THE MAIL

Personal sentiments, such as love and sympathy, have been incorporated into American greeting cards since the 1870s. When telephones became popular, there was fear in the greeting card industry that these brief missives would be one of Ma Bell's first victims. Au contraire! Letter writing is down, but greeting card sales continue to skyrocket. *Forbes* once estimated that half of all personal mail is now preprinted greeting cards— you can't put a phone call on the mantle.

Most cards are printed on one piece of 6' 3/4" x 9" stock folded once so it has a front cover (known as the *outside*) that opens to a double spread (known as the *inside*). Including multicolor printing, the cost of manufacturing the average greeting card (consisting of, say, four lines and a muted sunset) doesn't even approach the retail price. Even after adding the usual costs of distribution, sales, advertising, and overhead, the profits from greeting card publishing are enormous.

What is more significant for the world of humor writing is that every year buyers are willing to spend billions of dollars to have someone else write a funny (albeit mass-produced) message for one of their dear relatives or friends. This means that greeting card companies are a highly desirable market for budding humor writers. If you think receiving a greeting card is heartwarming, think how you'll feel receiving heartwarming checks for writing them!

Greeting card humor is no different from that in cartoons and one-liners—it's often based on a classic cliché gag. The opening (outside) is most frequently a cliché. The payoff line (inside) is a take-off, often another reformed cliché.

 **OUTSIDE**: You're the cat's meow.
**INSIDE**: Purrfect in every way.

Or the text may consist of a paired expression.

 **OUTSIDE**: You not only light up my life,
**INSIDE**: you light up the whole darned world.

For freelancers attempting to sell their humor to greeting card companies, there are six steps to follow.

1. Take a field trip.
2. Specialize.
3. Communicate.
4. Energize.
5. Revise.
6. Get real.

**1. TAKE A FIELD TRIP.** Go to all your local card shops, because most small retailers carry only one brand (Hallmark, American Greetings, or Gibson), and read. It's essential research. Read the back of each card to get acquainted with the styles of the different publishers. You may have a better chance of breaking in by targeting smaller card companies. For example, American Greetings and Hallmark do not accept unsolicited material from freelancers. But P.S. Greetings, for example, relies entirely on freelancers' submissions.

You can obtain writing and submission guidelines for most card companies by checking their Web sites or by requesting them via snail mail. Submission guidelines for more than thirty different card companies are also available online at www.WritersMarket.com, a subscriber-based Web site that's updated daily. Remember that the more informed you are about a publisher's needs, the greater your chances of success.

**2. SPECIALIZE.** Create a specific idea for a specific occasion. For example, as much as we rejoice in put-down humor, market studies indicate that sugarcoated "I love you" messages still account for 80 percent of total sales.

The vast majority of cards are sent for specific occasions, like New Year's, Christmas, Valentine's Day, and birthdays. The public may call them holiday and special occasion cards, but they are called everyday cards in the industry. Other specialty cards apply to situations in everyday life, like a death in the family, a wedding, the birth of a child, a severe illness, or a graduation. Thank you and congratulations cards are also standard.

 Get-well cards have become so humorous that, if you don't get sick, you're missing half the fun.
**—Earl Wilson**

**3. COMMUNICATE.** Greeting cards are a form of interpersonal communication. They must convey an intimate thought from the sender to the receiver. Slant the point of view for women because they buy the majority of all cards (with the exception of Valentine's Day cards—for that holiday, the male-female ratio is closer to fifty-fifty).

 Today is Valentine's Day—or, as men like to call it, Extortion Day!
**—Jay Leno**

Cards talk to the reader, telling them what they want to hear. They are not just opportunities for you to get a gag off your computer. When Peter Stillman began writing greeting cards, his first effort was a photocopy of a dozen dimes on the outside and a picture of a coin-operated dryer with socks spinning around in the window on the inside. The tag line: "These are the dimes that dry men's soles." Funny? Yes. Salable? No!

**4. ENERGIZE.** What sells a greeting card is the tag line, not the art. According to researcher Marcy Brown, many card publishers have their writers work in teams to encourage brainstorming. One easy way to encourage the creative process is by association—playing around with simple truths or tossing clichés around. (We'll discuss other brainstorming exercises shortly.)

**5. REVISE.** Your message must be conveyed clearly and with as much impact as possible. You must repeatedly go over your copy, asking if each word is necessary. Review is a continual process. Is there a clearer way to say what you want to say? What's the rhythm? Do you really need twenty-eight words on the inside?

Most copy can be tightened. Once you've sharpened a few cards, you'll see the difference and so will the editors. Editors do not want to do your work. If your copy takes too much editing, they'll toss it out.

 **OUTSIDE:** I'd like to tell you just how much I love you.
**INSIDE:** Have you got all night?

**6. GET REAL.** You have a set of twenty or more ideas you've fallen in love with and now you're ready to mail them off. Before you do, set them aside for a week—and then put them through a test suggested by Helene Lehrer, creative director at Oatmeal Studios.

1. Look at them again. Be honest with yourself. Are they still funny?
2. Would you personally spend a dollar for each and send them to someone you know?
3. How would you feel if you received them? How would you feel about the person who sent them?
4. Show them to your friends. Do they laugh? Would they buy it?
5. Are they true? Is there a grain of truth to make the receiver relate to them?

If you can't get a resounding positive answer for each question, it's back to the computer.

## HOW TO BRAINSTORM A GREETING CARD

Say you have to come up with a birthday card that would be sent from a boss to an associate. You start thinking about what a birthday really means: well, it's once a year, you get older, you get gifts, parties, and people are nicer than usual—*bingo*! When you hit "people are nicer than usual," an idea flashes. And you may come up with a reverse as in this Dale card.

 **OUTSIDE:** Enjoy how sweet, how thoughtful, how kind I'm being on your birthday.
**INSIDE:** Because tomorrow it's back to the same old shit.

Or say you want to write a birthday card focusing on fun. Birthdays are fun, but "Have a great time" and "Hope you enjoy yourself" are not salable. Again, you turn to associations: cake, drinks, hugs and kisses, the morning after—*bingo*! The morning after is generally a big letdown. It happens to everybody. Why not exaggerate and make it exceptionally lousy, as in this Hallmark card.

 **OUTSIDE:** (The cover art features a woman hiding under her covers, her arms wrapped around her pillow as the one last secure comforting thing in her bleary-eyed, headachy world.) The morning after your birthday celebration, pause and ask yourself ...
**INSIDE:** Who put the socks on all my teeth and how could I have slept through it?

You can also be creative with clichés. Keep an active mind. For an all-occasion card that tells someone how great she is, you might run through all the appropriate clichés, taking each word apart, doing verbal gymnastics, and hoping to find one that sparks. "You are the sunshine of my life ..." No. "How much do I love you? Let me count the ways ..." No. (Didn't someone else write that?) How about "Mere words can't describe how wonderful you are"? No. But wait! A sound there suggests a reformed homonym. Bingo! You're inspired, just like the person at Hallmark who got a check for this one.

**OUTSIDE:** Three men badly dressed in plaids, stripes, and spectacles are scratching their heads and looking obviously confused.

**MAN ONE:** You're so ... uh?

**MAN TWO:** No, you're more like ... ahhh?

**MAN THREE:** You have so much ... uhhh?

**INSIDE:** Mere nerds can't describe how wonderful you are.

Once you're on to a good idea, a whole series of cards can be assembled.

**OUTSIDE:** Same group of nerd characters.

**INSIDE:** Beware of geeks bearing gifts. Happy birthday.

A good rhyming dictionary and thesaurus are essential in humor writing, and many of the techniques we've already discussed can also be applied to greeting card humor. Once you know how to write humor, you'll see greeting cards as merely one of the most formalized humor formats.

### GREETING CARD TAKE-OFF

**OUTSIDE:** Some people might say that I think too highly of you but ...

**INSIDE:** I worship the water you walk on.

### GREETING CARD REVERSE

**OUTSIDE:** It's your birthday, so pucker up.

**INSIDE:** And kiss another year goodbye.

### GREETING CARD TRIPLE REVERSE

**OUTSIDE:** You're perverted, twisted, and sick.

**INSIDE:** I like that in a person.

### GREETING CARD PAIR

**OUTSIDE:** Happy birthday to a man who has it all.

**INSIDE:** From a woman who wants it.

### GREETING CARD INSULT

**OUTSIDE:** Sometimes, we get too smart for our own good.

**INSIDE:** But you don't appear to be in any danger at this particular time.

## BREAKING IN TO GREETING CARDS: DO YOU HAVE THE RIGHT STUFF?

It's not as easy as it may seem to break into the greeting card business as a full-time freelancer. Several larger companies, like Hallmark and American Greetings, prefer to work with in-house staff writers or a stable of trusted freelancers. But that doesn't mean that you're completely shut out. Start with smaller card companies and then set your sights on the major league companies.

The mechanics of sending out freelance material for consideration by greeting card publishers are rather simple. Most companies prefer submissions to be sent in batches of ten to twenty ideas typed individually on index cards with contact information listed on the back of the card. (Remember that each company has a specific set of guidelines, and be sure to double check the submission requirements before sending out your work.)

Be forewarned: Simultaneous submission of the same ideas to different companies is a major mistake. Because of the long time delay in receiving a response, however, it is impractical to just write twenty ideas, send them out, and then wait three months for an answer. You'll need to contact other publishers with additional ideas you didn't send to the first. The sales price for a card idea runs from twenty-five dollars and up, so you'll need volume sales to break even with your mailing costs.

Keep your submissions moving. Don't get discouraged after a few rejections. Persistence is the name of the game. And stop fearing that a company will copy your ideas before sending them back with a canned rejection letter. They're looking for reliable sources. And if you're close to the mark, they might send along a rejection letter with some helpful advice—and encouragement.

If they give you advice, take it. But more often, they will return your batch with a form letter, even though their rejection may be for no better reason than they're overflowing with birthday messages to grandma, and that's what you sent. You'll never know, and they won't answer your calls or letters to explain why.

These days, the large greeting card publishers are more leery of unknown writers than ever. What they fear most is a lawsuit from some amateur who spots a published card with an idea similar to one he claims he submitted years previously. It's hard to prove or disprove these claims. Most of all, it's expensive. Many lawyers instruct their publishing clients to return all unsolicited material unopened. Solicited material results from a favorable reply to your original query letter by a specific editor, who will then specifically request that you submit your material.

## SHOWTIME

Write twenty humorous greeting cards for special occasions, including graduations, birthdays, and anniversaries. Instead of buying brand-name cards, start sending out your own. Use software programs such as *Print Shop* to create personalized greeting cards that are close to professional. As a new father wrote to his wife, who had just given birth to a beautiful daughter:

 Sweetheart. Many Thanks. I knew you had it in you.

# CHAPTER 16
## The Scarce Comedy:
## Writing for TV Sitcoms

 There is so much comedy on television. Does that cause comedy in the streets?

**—Dick Cavett**

Sitcom writing is a seller's market for those writers who can consistently produce acceptable material—and, once again, the key word is consistently. Writers not only make good bread, they eat cake—with all the frosting. Each thirty-minute show needs a squad of approximately twelve writers to maintain quality while racing strict deadlines.

 Television is an invention that permits you to be entertained in your living room by people you wouldn't have in your home.

**—David Frost**

The standard salary per writer for a half-hour sit-com script is approximately twenty thousand dollars, but keep in mind that a portion of that salary goes to Uncle Sam, and another portion—10 to 15 percent—goes to an agent (agents are necessity in this field). For writers who have hyphenated titles like writer-director or writer-producer, it isn't unusual for salaries to average twice that amount. And, of course, TV reruns generate residual payments. There is never a time when reruns of such legendary hits as *All in the Family*, *M\*A\*S\*H*, *I Love Lucy*, and *The Jeffersons* aren't playing somewhere around the globe. In their old age, some writers will have nurses endorsing residual checks.

*Sesame Street Workshop* announced that they have laid off sixty workers. News of the firing was brought to the employees by the letters F and U.

**—Tina Fey**

Until they learn the importance of being earners, however, comedy writers start out very lean and hungry. To be a sitcom writer, you must reflect your world not through an ordinary mirror, but through what author Bert Andrews once called "a Coney Island mirror that distorts and makes amusing every little incident, foible, and idiosyncrasy."

 **BARNEY:** Hello, my name is Barney, and I'm an alcoholic.

**LISA:** Mr. Gumble, this a Girl Scout meeting.

**BARNEY:** Is it? Or is it that you girls can't admit you have a problem?

**—The Simpsons**

You must also be aware of the serious constrains of demographics on the creative process. A successful sitcom must satisfy the production company, the networks, the stars, the sponsors, the critics and—most importantly—a large enough segment of the viewing public to outdistance all competitive programming. That takes skill, then work, and then luck!

It might seem easy to please the audience, but the script must consider advertising demographics. The major consumer market is women between the ages of eighteen and forty-nine, and since men of brawn (and some brains) are attractive to this audience, macho types must get as much exposure as well-endowed young ladies in tight outfits.

## SHOWTIME

Study as many sitcoms as possible. You can find collections of scripts on the Internet and in the libraries of many colleges and universities, particularly those with large drama departments. Tape and analyze some of the many classic sitcoms now in syndication to develop a feel for pacing and a better understanding of how all the elements come together in performance.

---

## IT'S STILL THE SAME OLD STORY

One of the things you'll notice when watching both old and new sitcoms is that the same themes recur decade after decade. Successful shows like *Seinfeld* and *Friends* spawned many unsuccessful copies featuring groups of young city-dwellers.

> **ELAINE:** ... I know it's terrible, but I'm not a terrible person.
> **JERRY AND KRAMER:** No.
> **ELAINE:** No. When I shoo squirrels away, I always say, "Get out of here." I never ever throw things at them and try to injure them like other people.
> **JERRY:** That's nice.
> **ELAINE:** Yeah, and when I see freaks in the street I never, ever stare at them. Yet, I'm careful not to look away, you know, because I want to make the freaks feel comfortable.
> **JERRY:** That's nice for the freaks.
>
> *—Seinfeld*

*The Honeymooners* and *I Love Lucy* begat dozens of shows with bickering married couples (there was even a radio show called *The Bickersons* in the 1950s). Hillbillies, cops, show-biz professionals, and talking apparitions each go in and out of favor. But you can bet on one thing—they'll be back again someday to delight a new generation. (You'll also notice recurring story lines—review *TV Guide* to identify the crux of each story. By the way, unless you can summarize your plot in one simple sentence, it is probably too complex.) A number of years ago, comedian Beth Davidoff joked:

> I'm writing a new sitcom for HBO. It's called *Sex and the Suburbs*. It's about a five-minute show.

---

Today, *Desperate Housewives*, about sex in the suburbs, is a hit one-hour drama, and it's no joke—it's a big winner.

Humor is like magic. Any magician still uses the old tried-and-true tricks—the excitement comes from the new way in which these tricks are packaged. In sitcom writing, standard, audience-approved, funny situations must be portrayed in novel ways.

 **ROBERT:** I could of been a pretty good hockey player. I was big, I had the toughness, good hand-eye coordination.

**RAY:** Yeah, but eventually you would've had to let go of the side.

**—*Everybody Loves Raymond***

The heart of every sitcom is the *What if?* scenario (think back to chapter one). The plot is determined by the reaction of the main character when he is placed in a unique—frequently uncomfortable—situation. Not all sitcom dialogue is humorous. In fact, more than 65 percent of a sitcom's time is taken up with serious situations, which are highlighted by comic relief.

 Trouble? Who doesn't have any? If the experience is painful to you, don't block it out. Save it. Maybe in three days it will be funny.

**—Garry Marshall**

The following are ten of the most common recurring setups, popular with audiences since the beginning of motion picture production (the grandfather of all contemporary sitcoms). Most of these setups are just exaggerations of ordinary situations. In practical use, two or more of these themes may overlap or play out concurrently in a single sitcom episode.

1. family aggression
2. workplace aggression
3. mistaken assumptions
4. intrusions
5. heartbreak
6. moral and ethical conflicts
7. sympathy for the disadvantaged

8. physical mishaps

9. something of value

10. failure to cope

## 1. Family Aggression

People in close contact will eventually compete with and irritate each other. Husbands compete with wives, in-laws compete with married children, children compete with parents, and entire families compete with relatives and neighbors. The mother-in-law visit is still one of the hundred most common plots on TV. Laughter is created when characters interact with love, illness, jealousy, prejudice, death, and cream pies.

 **MARIE:** These breadsticks are old.

**FRANK:** Well, you are what you eat!

**MARIE:** Bobby, give your father his helping of Miserable Bastard.

*—Everybody Loves Raymond*

Someone in the family—or the entire family—must always be the fall guy, the target. The audience wants to watch the stupidity of others and feel superior.

 **GEORGE MICHAEL:** I like the family. I mean, if we leave, who's gonna take care of these people?

**MICHAEL:** I don't know. The state or the police. Maybe the Magician's Alliance will pick up some slack.

*—Arrested Development*

## 2. Workplace Aggression

Offices, factories, schools—even morgues—provide the setting for thriving antagonisms. Workers resent bosses and each other.

 **ELIOT:** Does this shade of red make me look like a clown?

**DR. COX:** No, it makes you look like a prostitute who caters exclusively to clowns.

*—Scrubs*

In every sitcom, close proximity produces enmity, and your story must reveal the farce around the friction.

**KAY:** Oh, good morning, my little worker ants! That's just a figure of speech; I would never compare you to insects. At least not after that sensitivity training seminar those maggots at the network forced me to attend!

—*Murphy Brown*

**DREW:** Oh, you hate your job? Why didn't you say so? There's a support group for that. It's called everybody, and they meet at the bar.

—*The Drew Carey Show*

Some of the on-the-job plots used frequently today include: Someone gives the boss a compliment that goes to his head, someone expects an important job promotion she's not going to get, someone is accused of being a crook or of trying to weasel out of work.

 **DR. COX:** Morning, class. As residency director, it is my pleasure to have both Surgical and Medical personnel here with us today. In fact, in this room we have enough brain power to light up a city! Not a real city, mind you, but definitely a tiny ant city whose government has recently passed a series of stringent energy conservation laws!

—*Scrubs*

## THE IMPORTANCE OF A NAME

Names and nicknames often express an important personality trait and keep the viewer focused on character expectations. The nickname "Hot Lips" was appropriate for the passion of Major Margaret Houlihan on *M*A*S*H*; Archie Bunker talked bunk; and "Hawkeye" Pierce sounded like the name of a rascal, not a Park Avenue doctor. And *Seinfeld* memorably introduced viewers to a controlling soup-shop owner with this.

**JERRY:** There's only one caveat—the guy who runs the place is a little temperamental, especially about the ordering procedure. He's secretly referred to as "the Soup Nazi."

*—Seinfeld*

## 3. Mistaken Assumptions

One essential ingredient in drama is that the audience be kept in the dark about something. In humor, it's just the reverse—the audience is clued in from the beginning, but one essential character is purposely not. *Three's Company* is a classic example of mistaken assumptions in action. In fact, if all the characters in a sitcom told the truth in the first three minutes, there would be no need for the other twenty. Examples are common: One character tries to hide his true ability, a body is hidden in a trunk, someone is hiding in the closet, a married couple pretend they're single, the boss is mistaken for a worker, a house painter is mistaken for a doctor, or someone has communication problems with a foreigner.

**STAN:** You guys, I'm getting that John Elway football helmet for Christmas.

**CARTMAN:** How do you know?

**STAN:** 'Cause I looked in my parents' closet last night.

**CARTMAN:** Yeah, well I sneaked around my mum's closet too and saw what I'm getting. The Ultravibe Pleasure 2000.

**STAN:** What's that?

**CARTMAN:** I don't know, but it sounds pretty sweet.

*—South Park*

## 4. Intrusions

Anything that disturbs the status quo heightens emotions and creates conflict. Relatives, friends, objects, and events cropping up at inconvenient times and places disturb the equilibrium, and the attempted cover-up provides the humor.

**GEORGE SR.:** Don't get involved. Believe me. When I thought your first wife was pulling us apart, I did not make a stink.

**MICHAEL:** You complained all the time, and she was my only wife. And she died.

**GEORGE SR.:** Yeah, well. See? Things have a way of working themselves out.

—*Arrested Development*

Examples of intrusions are workmen in the house, a pest of a kid coming for a visit, a surprise birthday party held at the wrong time, a house suddenly appearing to be haunted, or an unexpected visit by a famous celebrity.

 **JACK:** Kevin Bacon's stalker log, 6 p.m. eastern stalker time. My heart is racing and so am I. Moving in for a closer look! [Jack runs up to the window, which is open a crack.]

**JACK:** Hmm, new plant in living room. Must be gift from studio wooing "La Bacon" to do *Hollow Man II*. Note to self: See if I can get a job applying body makeup. [Jack pushes open the window and feels the drapes.]

**JACK:** Satin! Soft! Manly! Must remember this for fantasy dream later! [Jack climbs in and lands on the floor.]

[Kevin Bacon enters the room, talking on the phone.]

**KEVIN:** [on phone] Honey, I got it!

[Jack runs around in circles.]

**JACK:** Abort! Abort! Abort!

—*Will and Grace*

## 5. Heartbreak

Heartbreak is the oldest of all emotions—next to love—and frequently runs in tandem with it. In humor, it must focus on absurdities: an American GI falls for a Korean aristocrat; an old flame is discovered but is already married; or a doctor must tell a patient the truth about her illness.

 **GEORGE:** I get the feeling when lesbians are looking at me, they're thinking: "That's why I'm not heterosexual."

—*Seinfeld*

**RAY:** You're already planning the wedding?

**DEBRA:** I've been planning it since I was twelve.

**RAY:** But you didn't meet me until you were twenty-two.

**DEBRA:** Well, you're the last piece of the puzzle.

*—Everybody Loves Raymond*

## 6. Moral and Ethical Conflicts

These scenarios—so obvious and predictable—are the kindergarten of original satirical humor. The protagonist is a lone dissenter, or wants to go to a class reunion without a date, or tries to crash a celebrity party. Deeper issues include fighting for women's rights; single-parent families; and unique professional, business, or religious practices.

**LISA:** Dad, we did something very bad!

**HOMER:** Did you wreck the car?

**BART:** No.

**HOMER:** Did you raise the dead?

**LISA:** Yes.

**HOMER:** But the car's okay?

**BART AND LISA:** Uh-huh.

**HOMER:** Alright, then.

*—The Simpsons*

*All in the Family* was the first sitcom to address racial issues and racism.

**ARCHIE:** If your spics and your spades want their rightful share of the American dream, let 'em get out there and hustle for it like I done.

**MIKE:** So now you're going to tell me the black man has just as much chance as the white man to get a job?

**ARCHIE:** More, he has more. ... I didn't have no million people marchin' and protestin' to get me my job.

**EDITH:** No, his uncle got it for him.

*—All in the Family*

Lighter plots involving moral and ethical issues include finding money, a lost lottery ticket, or jewelry; calling the police to report a crime commit-

---

ted by a well-known person; purposely ignoring new rules; and trying to hide something from a friend.

 **LISA:** Oh, Mom, are you sure you want to sell a family heirloom to pay the gas bill? I mean, what would grandma say?

**MARGE:** I'm sure she'd be proud that her descendants had piping hot tap water and plenty of warm, dry underwear.

—*The Simpsons*

## 7. Sympathy for the Disadvantaged

Sitcom plots are getting into more and more delicate areas. Humor plots that deal with handicapped people, victims of crime, those with sexual disabilities, or the elderly are common.

 **JAY:** Lady, don't take this the wrong way, but you're nuts!

**OLD LADY:** Oh, you sound just like the toaster.

—*The Critic*

The audience instinctively feels for the underdog if there is some other fall guy on which to focus the humor.

 **BART:** Dad, how would you like it if you were sold to an ivory dealer?

**HOMER:** I'd like it fine.

**BART:** Even if they killed you and made your teeth into piano keys?

**HOMER:** Of course. Who wouldn't like that, being part of the music scene?

—*The Simpsons*

## 8. Physical Mishaps

This is a variation on the previous theme, but the plot conclusion generally indicates that an accident caused only a temporary disability: amnesia, broken bones, or impotency. These are the vaudeville shticks of slipping on a banana peel, falling down a manhole, and getting a pail of water flung in your face. No slapstick plot is more popular than two or more characters getting locked together in a room and not being able to get out.

**CHANDLER:** [while stuck in the ATM vestibule, voice-over]
*Oh my God, it's that Victoria's Secret model. Something ...*
*something Goodacre.*

**JILL:** [on phone] Hi Mom, it's Jill.

**CHANDLER:** *She's right, it's Jill. Jill Goodacre. Oh my God. I am*
*trapped in an ATM vestibule with Jill Goodacre! ... Is it a*
*vestibule? Maybe it's an atrium. Oh, yeah, that is the part to focus*
*on, you idiot!*

**JILL:** [on phone] Yeah, I'm fine. I'm just stuck at the bank, in an
ATM vestibule.

**CHANDLER:** *Jill says vestibule ... I'm going with vestibule.*

**JILL:** [on phone] I'm fine. No, I'm not alone ... I don't know,
some guy.

**—Friends**

## 9. Something of Value

Everybody wants money, promotions, awards, or material goods, and
many will create havoc to get it. The more oddball the need, the better.
The audience even identifies with get-rich-quick schemes if the hero
needs money—his own or someone else's.

 **RALPH:** This is probably the biggest thing I ever got into.

**ALICE:** The biggest thing you ever got into was your pants.

**—The Honeymooners**

## 10. Failure to Cope

These plots are based on the inability of the lead character to handle a
new situation at home, on the job, in a social event, or at a new school.

 **LOIS:** They have a special program for gifted children. They have
advanced textbooks and devoted teachers and all sorts of good
things they don't wanna waste on normal kids.

**—Malcolm in the Middle**

Becoming unemployed is one example; others are getting a divorce and
explaining the facts of life to a child.

**NORM:** It's a dog-eat-dog world, and I'm wearing Milk-Bone underwear.

—*Cheers*

## SCRIPT MECHANICS

Scripts are decided upon six months before airdate, and final taping takes place three to six weeks before airing. Therefore, writers must be thinking of what the world might be like up to a year in the future. That's normal. (What happens if the show you're working on gets cancelled? That's normal, too!)

Scripts must be timed precisely. In most cases, playing time is less than twenty-four minutes in every half-hour. Commercials take up four and a half minutes; opening and closing titles may take more than a minute. In addition, a certain amount of time is set aside for a promo of next week's show.

 Dictum on television scripts: We don't want it good— we want it Tuesday.

—**Dennis Norden**

The first drafts of scripts are written with minimal stage directions. Only the final scripts are blocked (separately for actors, cameramen, and sound-effect specialists). Script format should follow the Writers Guild guidelines.

### Make a Scene

As you get used to timing, you'll develop a feel for the logical number of characters, sets, and scenes in any given show. You can't allow the plot to get too complex in a sitcom. Your story is really no more than a good excuse for your characters to interact in a humorous situation.

 **DEWEY:** And then the monster started growling at me, so I threw rocks at him, and I killed him, and then he started flying around on rocket boost, and I got to ride inside his head, and now the monster's my friend, and we went—and we went to get Slurpees.
**REESE:** You did not. You just lied.

**HAL:** Reese, if that's what Dewey says happened, there's no reason to argue about it.

**REESE:** No one believes I beat the last level in Mortal Kombat.

**HAL:** Because that's just ridiculous. No one beats Sub-Zero.

*—Malcolm in the Middle*

Scenes usually start sensibly but get silly before ending abruptly with a cut to the next scene. Each scene may run two to three minutes, so in a half-hour show there may be eight to ten scene changes.

When you've decided on one or more of your *What if?* ideas, expand them into a one-page outline. Then, with a collaborator, brainstorm your ideas. How would the characters react? Who would take the lead in resolving the conflict? Who would obstruct the action? Why?

Break the idea down into the various scenes. You only have three sets to work with, so don't jump all over the globe. Your work will be filled with false starts, weak dialogue, and then finally—sudden brilliance. Think of the rewriting process as a mandatory luxury, probably the only luxury in a writer's life that never seems to end.

## Create Characters

The biggest mistake beginning sitcom writers make is writing in new characters who share (or hog) the spotlight. For many good reasons, the stars of a sitcom demand 80 percent of the dialogue. The audience, too, has been conditioned to see the whole show as a vehicle for the stars they love. Don't fight it.

 **RICHARD LEWIS:** Can't we have lunch or something and discuss this?

**LARRY:** I can't.

**RICHARD:** Why not?

**LARRY:** I've been auctioned off for some charity.

**RICHARD:** What is this, *Roots*?

*—Curb Your Enthusiasm*

It used to be that the lead characters in a sitcom always supported moral goodness—a throwback to the American film code that insisted that crime—at least on film—should not pay. More recently, characters fight for their rights, but their beliefs as to what constitutes right and wrong may vary. Overprotective parents are all right, because they are just looking out for their children's well-being. The audience may allow sitcom characters to get away with more, because the characters are goofy and lovable, but never wicked. Remember, *The Sopranos* is not a sitcom.

No matter how tense the situation becomes within one episode, your story should end happily. This construction is reassuring for the audience, who looks forward to a familiar situation each week. But although your ending resolves the immediate problem, it rarely resolves the basic conflict of the series. That's the cliffhanger.

### Develop Your Own Style

TV is a visual medium, so what we see must be even more entertaining than what we hear. If this weren't true, radio soap operas would still be popular. Characters must wear unusual clothing and flash signals with their face, hands, and body. You must incorporate physical humor—even slapstick—into your script: Audiences never seem to tire of seeing the wall of a house fall on a character—who, when the dust clears, is standing unscathed in the space left by a window frame.

 **TODD:** That was a compliment. Why won't any women talk to me?
**NURSE:** Because you're slimy, and you turn everything into a double entendre.
**TODD:** Not true! ... I'd like to double her entendre.

*—Scrubs*

It is not the mark of a poor writer to write in one particular style, but to be a successful sitcom writer you must write in the style that works for the show. You must learn from every comedian and every show. If you're writing for an existing show, that's the formula you must use.

 **LUCILLE:** Get me a vodka rocks.
**MICHAEL:** Mom, it's breakfast.
**LUCILLE:** And a piece of toast.

*—Arrested Development*

Only when you are conceiving your own show idea (success is about a ten-thousand-to-one shot these days!) can you establish your own characters and style.

 **FRASIER:** I'm deep enough to realize I'm shallow.

*—Frasier*

## MARKETING A SCRIPT

*Daily Variety* (www.variety.com) and *The Hollywood Reporter* (www.hollywoodreporter.com) list shows in production and the names of producers to contact for script submission. You can also watch a show's rolling credits for the name of the executive producer. *TV Market List* publishes the names of shows in development. But your best—and frequently only—bet is through is an agent.

The names of agents, with notations on who will (and who won't) look at unsolicited manuscripts, are available through the Writers Guild of America, West and East (www.wga.org and www.wgaeast.org) and through *Literary Market Place* (www.literarymarketplace.com). You don't have to submit a script for a show in production—submitting your script for an oldie in syndication permits agents to evaluate your ability and sales potential.

Other resources include *Writing Television Comedy* by Jerry Rannow, *Successful Sitcom Writing* by Jurgen Wolff, and *Writing Television Sitcoms* by Evan S. Smith.

## SHOWTIME

One of the best ways to attain skill in sitcom writing is to write for an existing show. It's not likely that you'll sell the script, especially since you'll be competing with a dozen pro writers who sweat the show weekly, but you'll provide yourself with a benchmark for evaluating your work.

You learn by doing it. I only learned by doing. I just kept writing and writing. I failed a lot. Then I found out I was in great company.

**—Selma Diamond**

Find a show that reflects the type of humor you feel comfortable with. Watch as many different episodes as you can, noting plot treatment, character development, set locations, timing, and running gags. Record the program for review and use an audiocassette to remember where you—and the laugh track—laughed. And then, write your masterpiece.

# CHAPTER 17
## We Mean Business

 The difference between the right word and almost the right word is the difference between lightning and the lightning bug.

**—Mark Twain**

Most neophyte humor writers believe that, in order to be commercially successful, they need to be writing material for stage, TV, or film. Nothing could be further from the truth. The biggest purchaser of humor material today is not the entertainment industry but the business community. Humor is a powerful means of communication in advertising, speeches, newsletters, sales meetings, fund-raising efforts, business publications, Web sites, and even voice mail. And corporations are hungry to find people who have the ability to use humor as a persuasive tool.

### THE SALESPERSON: DO I HAVE A GOOD ONE FOR YOU!

It is traditional for a salesperson to break the ice with a customer by telling a joke. For this technique to help with the sale, however, the a salesperson should use the joke to create an opportunity for the customer to state, "I've got a better one."

 I had a customer who broke my arm in two places, so we don't go to those places anymore.

One of the best compliments you can pay anyone is, "You know, you've got a terrific sense of humor."

An astute salesperson tells a joke about an area likely to interest the customer—like golf, fishing, grandchildren, a specific sport, etc. Once you determine the customer's interest, tell jokes on that subject during each subsequent visit. By the third visit, the customer will hardly be able to wait to get in her contribution, and the salesperson must laugh enthusiastically before writing the order.

### Double Your Pleasure: The Roll Out

Business humor, like that in a courtroom, is often chastised with remarks like "Quit your kidding, this is serious!" To find out whether your customer is open to humor, try a combination known as a roll out. The roll out follows the punchline of a joke with a pause (not to last longer than two or three seconds), then follows the pause with a topper. Both punchlines get a laugh—or at least a smile—and the pause promotes a bigger laugh for the second line because the listener doesn't expect it—unless, of course, it's telegraphed.

 Company president to nervous employee: I can only make one person happy a day, and today ... is not your day. [Pause] And tomorrow doesn't look good either.

In this example, the second line is telegraphed by the opening sentence, so the roll out is unsuccessful.

 Surgeon to patient: I have two pieces of good news. The first is that I've never done this life-or-death operation before, but I slept at a Holiday Inn last night. [Pause] And we won't explain the procedure since you'll be awake throughout the operation. The anesthesiologist is on vacation.

If you don't get a laugh or at least a smile from such a surefire technique as a roll out, than stick to business (because if at first you don't succeed, maybe your wife was right).

## ADVERTISING: A WORLD GONE AD

The congestion of modern advertising messages makes it more and more difficult to get an audience's attention. Advertising research claims that nearly a thousand ads vie for our attention each day, and our attention spans get ever shorter from exposure to a plethora of distractions. If you can remember one ad from yesterday, you are not only very perceptive, you are unique.

 Humor advertising is like marriage. There may be a better way, but what is it?

The advertising business does not have the right to bore the blazes out of 250 million Americans. The public has been beaten about the ear with a baseball bat of hard sell for so long that it is difficult to get the message through the scar tissue.

**—Stan Freberg**

Advertising is first a business and second an art form. Product success is measured at the cash register, and your personal success is measured at the bank. Positive reviews are meaningless if the product doesn't sell.

 You can fool all the people all the time if the advertising is right and the budget is big enough.

**—Joseph E. Levine**

There are eleven common creative techniques in advertising.

1. testimonials
2. humor
3. plays on words (POWs)
4. mnemonic devices
5. unique selling propositions (USPs)
6. product comparisons
7. problem solving
8. sexual innuendo
9. new product introductions
10. sale prices
11. musical jingles

The use of humor as an advertising technique has been growing in popularity to become one of the most effective methods of persuading a target audience to remember and to try a product. Of the forty-five commercials in a typical Super Bowl telecast (each of which may cost a million dollars to produce), 30 percent are intended to be humorous. But humor is also one of the most difficult of all advertising concepts. It is very subjective, elusive, and in a constant state of flux. Give a hundred creative directors the same humor assignment with the same set of facts, and you will get a hundred different campaigns. Without being able to test them all, it is impossible to predict which one would score best with the audience. And just when you think you've come up with a general rule, such as "Humor commercials should be created to appeal to a sense of enjoyment rather than a sense of logic," someone will break the rule and achieve a smash hit.

Skeptics of humor as an effective advertising technique abound.

 All the world may love a clown but nobody buys from one.

**—David Ogilvy**

Humor doesn't have much stature because there's not one funny line in the two best sales books of all time: the Sears catalog and the Bible.

**—Andy Rooney**

Expensive commercial production costs must be amortized, so spots must run often over the length of the marketing campaign without inducing viewer fatigue. If the humor is predictable, the commercial will have a short life expectancy and soon will not be funny at all. "Humor always works, and unexpected humor works particularly well," said Bob Lachky of Anheuser-Busch. Unpredictable, fresh, or surprising ad humor will continue to make you grin over the lifetime of the campaign.

There must, however, be a balance between the message and the humor. If too much humor is used, it can ultimately be counterproductive for a number of reasons.

1. Laughter can distract from the sales message.
2. Humor attracts attention, but then when the sales message comes on, the public can resent having been tricked into listening to a pitch.
3. A favorable attitude toward the product can be negated by humor of questionable taste.

Creative advertising is increasingly expensive, and marketing a product is so costly that the prospect of failure is terrifying. Humorous commercials, unlike straight commercials, have two opportunities to fail: They can be unfunny and irritating, or they can be so funny that the product name and value is lost in the humor.

 **ONE MAN TO ANOTHER:** I saw a very funny commercial yesterday. This guy tells his friend at a bar what lines to use to pick up a girl, and when he mistakenly repeats a few words about the cost of a beer (which his friend is actually asking the bartender), the girl knocks him on his ass.

**SECOND MAN:** Sounds great. What was the name of the product?

**FIRST MAN:** I don't remember, but it was as funny as hell.

Humor should never be at the expense of the product or the heavy user. The product and the advertiser must come off as likeable. And the facts of the product must be emphasized over the humor.

### TV Commercials: Air This

Advertisers who need to reach the influential target market of women aged eighteen to forty-nine should be impressed by the value of humor in commercials to this demographic. According to a survey by Oxygen Media, 93 percent of women in that age group not only enjoy humor commercials the first time they see one but enjoy watching the ads repeat; 88 percent claimed they would be less likely to change the channel during a commercial break if the ad was funny. When future generations open today's buried time capsules, they'll feel positive that every major decision in our lives was made in thirty seconds. They may be right.

 Humor advertising transforms a yawn into a yearn.

If Moses brought down the Ten Commandments today, *CNN Headline News* would probably broadcast the event this way.

 Today, in the Middle East, Moses carried God's Ten Commandments down from Mount Sinai. We'll be back with the three most important commandments after this vital message from Hartz Mountain cat food.

The seven most effective subjects and formats for humor commercials are, logically, also the most popular.

1. cartoons
2. anthropomorphic animals
3. physical slapstick
4. the underdog
5. celebrity comedians as spokespersons
6. plays on words (POWs)
7. children

Other formats and subjects are used less frequently because they are fraught with problems. The one-joke commercial wears thin too quickly; sex jokes can gross out the public and regulatory agencies; absurd situations can be too juvenile; and mistaken identity makes fun of the purchaser.

### Humor in Print

Only 15 percent of all print ad readers actually take the time to read a full ad. Therefore, 85 percent of the impact of an ad is the responsibility of the headline and illustration. If they don't stop a reader's eye, they won't stop her from turning the page.

Humor is one of the concepts that seem to do the job best. It also is a refresher. Manufacturers of products that have been on the market for many years (beers in particular) often use a short humor campaign as an effective way to breathe new life into the product and make it more memorable.

There are five major creative techniques in which print advertising utilizes humor.

1. POWs or puns in the headline
   • God is like Bayer aspirin: He works miracles.
   • God is like Coke: He's the real thing.
   • God is like Hallmark cards: He cares enough to send the very best.

- God is like General Electric: He brings good things to life.
- God is like Scotch tape: You can't see him, but you know he's there.

2. use of an anecdote in narrative copy
3. professional comedians in testimonials
4. humorous or sexy photographs (Grin and Bare It)
5. cartoons or multipanel comic strips (Peanuts for MetLife)

## Humor on Radio: The Gang's All Hear

The four most common formats for radio advertising are:

1. the straight pitch
2. an ad-lib fact sheet to be used by the DJ
3. the jingle
4. skit humor

Obviously, humor works best as a skit. Skit humor reached its peak popularity in the 1970s and 1980s when Dick Orkin and Bert Berdis produced numerous Clio award-winning spots for Concertina tomato paste, and *Time* magazine and Stan Freberg created humor spots for Chun King Chow Mein. These conflict-and-resolution skits ran sixty seconds in length, were brilliantly cast with comedic teams—like Jerry Stiller with Anne Meara; Bob and Ray—playing humorous characters in abnormal situations. This technique encouraged listeners to believe they were eavesdropping on a private conversation. The absurdity had the rare property of making listeners both laugh and buy.

To succeed, radio humor requires clever writers and clients with a strong sense of humor. Skits never make fun of the product, but they do have fun *with* the product—a difference most copywriters fail to see.

"There really isn't anything you can't sell with humor," claims Berdis, and to prove it, he did commercials for a cemetery "located just six feet under Cleveland."

The formula for skit comedy is very structured.

1. Because radio is a medium that is used as a background companion, attention-getting words or sound effects must be used in the first five seconds.

2. The first three to five seconds must also clearly establish the locale and the major characters. Radio commercials usually feature stereotyped characters, because there's no chance for a confused listener to go back to the head of the script.

3. Listeners must immediately empathize with the characters and the plot ("Oh, I've been in that situation myself"). The script must build on an embarrassing situation. Humor will depend on the surprise ending.

4. The humorous part of the commercial must be concentrated together in one part of the ad. The fall guy is easily identified and slowly winds the rope, which is about to hang him.

5. The commercial must sell product, not just entertain. In a sixty-second spot, the brand name should be mentioned four or five times. And the ad must be realistic. The fact that performance humor is often based upon a suspension of disbelief doesn't mean that humor advertising can benefit from fictional association.

6. The commercial punchline should generally be no more than a few words—certainly no more than one or two lines. It must resolve the conflict.

7. The commercial must end properly. Strangely, not enough copywriters know how to write a goodbye ending that doesn't just pass out. The last line is one last chance to establish the commercial's most persuasive sales point.

Underlining all these points is that the fact that a listener's imagination is perfect. You can take them anywhere at any time in history. Notice how all the above points are made in this sixty-second gem.

 **ANNOUNCER:** Stiller and Meara for Blue Nun wine.
**STILLER:** Good evening, miss. Will you be dining alone?
**MEARA:** [in tears] Yes!
**STILLER:** What can I get you?
**MEARA:** Manicotti.
**STILLER:** Oh, I'm sorry, we're all out.

**MEARA:** No, I meant Carmine Manicotti. He just broke our engagement. He had his mother call me.

**STILLER:** Oh, the swine.

**MEARA:** No, she was very sweet about it.

**STILLER:** No, I meant Carmine. Anyway, may I suggest the surf and turf?

**MEARA:** Is that some new singles bar?

**STILLER:** No, surf and turf is our new delicious combination of lobster tail and filet mignon. And to raise your spirits, a very special wine.

**MEARA:** But no wine goes with seafood and meat.

**STILLER:** Certainly. May I bring a little Blue Nun to your table?

**MEARA:** I'm sure she'd be very sympathetic, but I'd rather be alone.

**STILLER:** No, miss. Blue Nun is a wine. A delicious white wine that's correct with any dish. It goes as well with meat as it does with fish. And perhaps after dinner, cantaloupe.

**MEARA:** I don't see cantaloupe on the menu.

**STILLER:** No, that's me. Stanley Cantaloupe. I get off at eleven. Maybe we could go out on the town.

**ANNOUNCER:** Blue Nun, the delicious white wine that's correct with any dish. Another Sichel wine, imported from France.

**MEARA:** Fabulous! Why didn't I know about this before?

**STILLER:** You mean me?

**MEARA:** No, the Blue Nun!

## COMEDIANS AS SPOKESPERSONS: BRAND-NAME LIP SERVICE

One of the most expensive broadcast humor techniques is using established comedians as spokespersons. While the benefits seem obvious, the pitfalls are many.

Comedy stars will fight to get their own humor writers to do the material. Their reputation is built on their particular brand of funny, and they properly feel that their own writers know their style best. Ultimately, they will endorse anything short of leprosy if they get to endorse the check first. But what is more important to them is the need to satisfy their fans. Therefore, they will fight for laugh lines in the copy whether or not it's beneficial to the product.

 I've been chewing Beechnut gum for twenty-five years. Its price never changed. It is either a big bargain now, or it was a big gyp then.

—**Bob Hope**

Some critics claim that comedians are risky spokesmen because they can't be taken seriously. They are also so memorable in the public mind that they can overwhelm the product. For eleven years, actor and comedian Jonathan Winters, dressed in an all-white sanitation outfit, did commercials for Hefty bags, but the Glad bag continued to rank number one.

 Trouble was people kept asking me if I liked doing those Glad bag commercials. It tells you something about the bag, or it tells you something about me.

—**Jonathan Winters**

Yet, despite the fact that radio is a powerful medium for humor, there are few nationally sponsored spots. This means that most commercials are locally written for local clients. And since small local agencies are rarely expert with humor, skit comedy on radio has become rare—and no longer well done.

## THE DREAM MERCHANTS

National or local, humor advertising must be written by specialists. Satirical humor has as many varieties as Heinz foods, but it is not a panacea for inferior creativity. On the other hand, humor wins more awards at annual best-of-advertising competitions, and it is the fastest route to critical acclaim.

The guy you've really got to reach with great humor advertising is the creative director of your chief rival's ad agency. If you can terrorize him, you've got it licked.

**—Howard Gossage**

Beginners have two wonderful venues in which to practice their humor without fear of commercial failure: their local college's radio station and newspaper. Local advertisers generally welcome student attempts at unique creativity. But the bar keeps getting higher each year. If you prove yourself truly adept at writing humor, you can get a job at any advertising agency in the world.

## NEWSLETTERS: HOW'S IT GLOWING?

All public relations college graduates know that one of the first assignments they'll be responsible for at their first job will be to write or edit the company newsletter. Humor can make the text more readable and the information more memorable in newsletters to employees, newsletters to the sales staff, and newsletters to wholesale or retail customers.

Regardless of the target audience, humor can be included via POWs in headlines and captions. Humor can improve morale when it is injected into the CEO's otherwise staid opening letter; when it accompanies photographs in personnel feature stories; when it is used in letters to the editor; and when it is applied to fortune cookie advice columns.

Employees love to see their own names in print. Newsletters can fulfill this need and incorporate humor by publishing employee-submitted anecdotes and jokes.

As *Fortune* magazine reported, newsletter stories about executives who take their product seriously, not themselves, always get a good reception.

## SHOWTIME

Office humor can start with your voice mail message. Make your basic message humorous.

Please leave your name, phone number and VISA card number—that'll help—and I'll get right back to you.

By infusing voice mail messages with humor, you immediately establish your character and your ability while making your message memorable. By making every word count, you can keep the message to ten seconds. When you do call back and identify yourself, you can almost see the smile on the caller's face. They already know that speaking to you—even about business—is going to be fun. Popularity breeds success.

Writing voice mail messages is also among the best humor warm-up exercises. Since you can erase and change messages easily, you have innumerable opportunities to find the messages that get the best reactions. And this is one business communication that doesn't cost a cent.

 When the beep sounds, leave me a short message and I'll get back to you as soon as possible, unless you're inviting me to dinner, in which case I'll get back to you immediately.

If you're my mom, please send another check tomorrow. If you're my new girlfriend, please spell your last name carefully. And if you're my professor wanting to know where I've been for the past week, I've got a communicable disease from your friggin' class.

Thanks for calling the psychic hotline. I'm not in, but leave your number and what you think of when you hear the following: kumquats, mother, and unicorn. Also leave a brief history of your current diseases. Thank you.

Hi, I'm not in. Now you say something.

# CHAPTER 18
## Teach, Learn, and Laugh

 It's not what's taught, but what's caught. And if we can get our students' mouths open for laughter, we can slip in a little food for thought.

—Virginia Tooper

Humor is a proven tool for improving instruction and increasing retention. Studies show that humor enriches learning by increasing student interest and attention—making even the driest subjects come to life. Humor also reduces anxiety concerning challenging subjects and makes difficult concepts clearer and more memorable. More importantly, humor ultimately promotes creativity, exploration, and critical thinking—skills that students can carry with them for a lifetime.

The appropriate use of humor also creates a positive classroom environment that opens minds, fosters communication, and encourages active participation. And it allows teachers to model and reinforce a critical educational lesson—learning is fun.

The growing interest in educational humor affords new opportunities for humor writers. Publishers of educational and business training materials—such as books, online courses, and instructional videotapes—are increasingly seeking writers whose light touch can change dreaded subjects into interesting and memorable ones. John Cleese of Monty Python fame uses humor to teach management principles in his highly successful line of business training videotapes. His instructional philosophy is simple.

 He who laughs most, learns best.

—John Cleese

# A CLASSROOM IS NOT A COMEDY CLUB

Audiences expect comedians to be funny and entertaining. Students expect instructors to be scholarly and boring. The expectation that learning will be dull lowers the humor threshold. Simpler forms of humor that would bomb in a comedy venue—such as puns and riddles—can work in educational humor. Students appreciate any attempt at humor, and studies show that teachers who use humor are considered more enthusiastic and engaging.

Keep in mind, however, that while the planned, systematic use of humor can enhance instruction, humor can be either an educational lubricant or irritant. When used appropriately, as noted above, humor can reduce student anxiety, enhance comprehension, and promote critical thinking. But humor that is derogatory or ridiculing has no place in an educational setting, and too much humor is distracting and unnecessary. The judicious, developmentally appropriate, and timely use of humor makes learning memorable and enjoyable. Humor must address a specific instructional goal. Unless a joke is appropriate to the subject, students are more likely to remember the joke than the concept.

 A teacher in Oklahoma is in a lot of trouble for operating on a cat during class. Particularly since he's the math teacher.
**—Conan O'Brien**

## The PC Hall Monitors

Educational humor must be inclusive and avoid any appearance of ridiculing others or stereotyping groups. Sexist, racist, derogatory, or obscene humor is never appropriate. Even a flippant remark might be viewed as offensive.

 As a teacher it's important to be politically correct. I've learned not to tell a student they're failing my class, but rather that they will have another semester in which to get to know me better.
**—Bonnie Cheeseman**

Given the double-edged nature of humor, the safest target is always the instructor. Self-deprecating humor puts students at ease and avoids belittling or alienating others. The "Oops, that was a stupid remark!" response to a mistake by the teacher allows students to view the instructor as more human.

 Some of you might have heard that I am unfair, rigid, and boring. For those of you who have not talked to my wife ...

Most topical subjects and community targets are appropriate targets, but they must be carefully selected.

## MAP the Students

The audience ingredient of the MAP theory is critical in educational humor. The material must be student-oriented and factor in cultural, gender, and age differences. A joke that works in one setting for one student group may fail in another. But the humor must also fit the subject and reflect the teacher's personality.

It's also critical to recognize developmental differences in humor appreciation. Children in kindergarten through sixth grade delight in wordplay such as puns, comic verse, and riddles. The cornier the joke, the better the response.

 How did the Vikings send secret messages?
By Norse code!

What is the fruitiest lesson?
History, because it's full of dates!

Knock Knock
Who's there?
Ada!
Ada who?
Ada burger for lunch!

The same humor for older children might produce the "teacher is an idiot" stare. Satire, parody, and irony are more appropriate for high school students and adult learners. Older students will appreciate the irony-based "Murphy's Laws of Applied Terror," for instance.

When reviewing your notes before an exam, you'll discover that the most important ones are illegible.

Eighty percent of the final exam will be based on the one lecture you missed.

If you're given an open-book exam, you'll forget your book.

If you're given a take-home exam, you'll forget where you live.

When possible, the demographics and interests of the students should be identified before attempting humor. This can be challenging, given the diversity of the typical classroom, and is almost impossible for distance learning, such as correspondence or Internet courses.

## TEACHERS DO IT AT THE PODIUM

Effective lectures, presentations, and workshops follow the same principles as speeches. Whether you're speaking to third-graders about social studies, to tenth-graders about economics, or to corporate employees during a manager's training session, you have to stay on-message. Use humor to supplement your message—not overshadow it. Here are a few techniques you can use when you're up at the podium.

### Open With a Bang

Students will quickly stereotype teachers. Opening with a joke or humorous anecdote sends the message "this will be fun."

 I will never forget my first day of school. My mom woke me up, got me dressed, made my bed, and fed me. Man, did the guys in the dorm tease me.

**—Michael Aronin**

I had a terrible education. I attended a school for emotionally disturbed teachers.

**—Woody Allen**

I knew school was back in session because I saw a postman buying ammunition from a New York City schoolboy.

**—David Letterman**

Other possible openers include a funny subtitle, a visual or cartoon with a humorous caption, inserting funny factitious names in the roll call, exaggerated unit objectives, a reformatted quote, or a witty remark introducing the subject.

 Today's lecture will be an experiment—half of you will get real information, while the other half will get a placebo.

**—Matt Coleman**

Our topic today is déjà vu: Stop me if you've heard this before.

A fun icebreaker that works at any level and ensures group interaction is the *Find Someone Who* activity. Prepare a handout that requires students to obtain classmates' names based on physical features (someone who is taller, someone who has the same color hair) and personal preferences (someone who likes the same music or lives in the same neighborhood). Also include humorous items (someone who took a shower this week) and items that pertain to the class subject.

## Bridge the Gap

When eyes begin to glaze over, it's time to shift gears. As a transitional device, humor affords students a mental break. The trick is to "sandwich" the humor: Teach a concept, use humor to regain student attention, and summarize the principle. To be effective, humor transitions need to be short. If you use an anecdote, remember to keep it brief. If the transition takes too long, it can be difficult to calm students down and return to the topic.

 I used to substitute teach. The worst. I will never forget this second-grade class where I was subbing for a teacher named Susan. All day long these annoying little children would say, "Susan doesn't do it that way. Susan lets us play, Susan gives us gum. Susan is prettier than you." "Oh, really? Susan's dead."

**—Cathy Ladman**

## The Unexpected One-Liner

Teachers can prepare one-liners for when a class is interrupted by an unexpected event. (These are similar to savers prepared for speeches and live performances.)

 Police siren: I knew I shouldn't have parked in the principal's space.

A plane flies overhead: Here's my ride.

AV equipment fails: That's what happens when you buy from eBay.

Student enters late: I guess I'll have to repeat my lecture ... not!

School bell rings prematurely: Your prayers have been answered.

Cell phone goes off: For me?

## Leave 'Em Laughing

Longer humor pieces, such as humorous exercises, are best suited for wrapping up a subject lesson or at the end of the day. A popular closer is a top-ten list.

 **TOP TEN EXCUSES FOR SUBMITTING A LATE HOMEWORK ASSIGNMENT**

10. I thought Groundhog Day was a national holiday.
9. My pit bull ate my ferret, which ate my homework.
8. After watching Oprah, I realized that homework lowers my self-esteem.
7. I was too wrapped up in the latest *Survivor* episode.
6. I think I'm ADD.
5. My assignment was confiscated by Homeland Security officials.
4. The answers for the assignment were not in the CliffsNotes.
3. My mom didn't have the time to complete my homework.
2. I accidentally drank a six-pack of beer and thought I had already graduated.
1. Hey, President Bush was a C student.

## CREATE GROUP HUMOR

Humor in the classroom can be more than a joke here and an anecdote there. It can be an innovative approach. Group exercises, for example, invite lively interaction by their very nature. When humor is added into the mix, the exercises become even more engaging and the lessons more memorable. For example, you can spice up a reading scenes from Shakespeare's *Romeo and Juliet* by having the class perform it as a rap, or you can transform the Gettysburg Address into a Dr. Seuss–type story.

Other group activities with a humorous spin include:

- developing a class Web page with students' jokes, tongue twisters, riddles, funny anecdotes, and nonsense poems and songs
- drawing an event or theory as a comic strip, comic book, or group mural
- holding mock trials for notorious historical figures
- acting out the functions of different body parts
- creating a POW bulletin board or scrapbook with homonyms, euphemisms, double entendres, and Tom Swifties

Even junk food can lend itself to the educational process: The T.W.I.N.K.I.E.S. Project (www.twinkiesproject.com) teaches the scientific method via experiments with Twinkies. The experiments consist mostly of abusing Twinkies in extreme situations (dropping them from a skyscraper, bombarding them with radiation).

### Written in Fun

Creative writing exercises allow for more opportunities to introduce humor into the classroom and can make a mundane assignment fresh and fun. For example, students who are asked to create humorous—yet factually accurate—news headlines for past scientific discoveries will not only learn to appreciate a subject in a new way but also hone their critical-thinking (and headline-writing) skills.

Additional creative writing exercises with a humorous flair include:

- modifying proverbs, nursery rhymes, or maxims with subject-related names and principles

- composing a dictionary of fictitious definitions for topical terms
- creating funny words or phrases for remembering course concepts
- adding new captions for textbook illustrations and photos
- writing intentional malaprops for famous quotes
- transforming conceptual principles into a *Sesame Street* spot
- generating crazy predictions based on existing theories or principles
- writing funny last words, nicknames, bumper stickers, *Wanted* posters, fortune cookies, or resumes for historical figures.

The two most important words in humor writing, *What if?* can also breathe life into the dullest of homework assignments: the essay. The *What if?* prompt can be used to inspire original and humorous creative writing assignments that encourage students to look at their subjects in a new light. For example, what if:

- fairy-tale creatures appeared before Judge Judy (say, Pinocchio, for slander)?
- maps were relabeled with funny names for geographic locations and landmarks?
- children's stories were forced to be politically correct (Hansel, Gretel, and the co-dependent nonbiological mother)?
- animals could talk?
- children had written the Bill of Rights or the school rules?

Blending humor into a writing assignment has a hidden benefit for the teacher—it provides humorous material for future courses. (Unless you're Art Linkletter or Bill Cosby, and then you can turn all this material into a book.)

### Show and Tell

Visual humor—such as cartoons, illustrations, and photographs—works especially well in the classroom; it seems mandatory that every teacher display at least one *Far Side* cartoon. Captions that accompany the visual (or visuals that accompany a caption) can be reformatted as punchlines. When discussing the difficulty of an exam, show a picture of comically frightened people and state, "And this is how students often feel after the test." A visual doctored with editing software can also produce humorous results. Digital cameras are increasingly popular for producing humorous instructional vignettes.

 Good teaching is one-fourth preparation and three-fourths theater.
**—Gail Goodwin**

Props such as puppets, stuffed animals, or costumes can enliven a lecture. Teachers with a theatrical flair can dress and play the part of a historical figure—Abe Lincoln discussing the Civil War, for instance, or Albert Einstein explaining physics.

## COURSE MATERIALS

Humor can add spice to syllabi, handouts, overhead transparencies, and other materials. Examples of POWs include silly names, funny titles or headings, oxymorons, and factitious terms or definitions. Exaggerated humor examples include self-effacing humor; distorted numbers, concepts, or phrases; and outrageous theories or studies.

 I like a teacher who gives you something to take home to think about besides homework.
**—Lily Tomlin**

Periodicals such as the *Journal of Polymorphous Perversity* (www.psych humor.com) and *Annals of Improbable Research* (www.improb.com) offer a rich selection of exaggerated theories and studies, including the following.

 The Theory of Gravy
Inducing Religion in Sea Monkeys
Electron Band Structure in Germanium, My Ass

### Pass, Fail, or Laugh
Humor can lighten the pressure of examinations in several ways.

 In high school, I could not pass a math test. I couldn't pass a drug test either. There may be a correlation.
**—Lynda Montgomery**

Test directions can include a whimsical remark, ridiculous answers can be added to multiple-choice questions, student names can be incorporated into test questions, and trivia or goofy questions can be added to the exam. The test can also end with a humorous final question.

 The exam is over and you

    A. hope this was a bad dream

    B. should have read the book

    C. should have at least bought the book

    D. wonder if it's too late to drop the course

## YOU'VE GOT MAIL

At the college level, adding humor to online communication with students is another way to build rapport. Students frequently repeat the same questions, such as whether certain information will be on the exam. Teachers can prepare canned e-mail responses with a funny quote ("As Shakespeare once said …") that pertains to the question.

Discussion boards and chat rooms afford additional opportunities to use humor. Students should be encouraged to participate in class humor by posting jokes, collecting funny comments concerning the course, or identifying links to humorous Web sites.

## LIVE ON THE INTERNET: A CASE STUDY

Humor works as an instructional strategy, and it isn't just for kids. Mark Shatz and his colleagues Frank LoSchiavo and Matt Coleman completed the first study of the efficacy of humor when it is integrated into an online college course. Students in a humor-enhanced section of introductory psychology—as compared to students in a traditional section—viewed the class as more interesting and interacted more often. The following examples were used in an online context and are psychology-based, but they illustrate the wide-ranging potential of humor as an instructional strategy.

Lecture modules contained a sprinkling of fictitious items based on wordplay.

 **DEFINITIONS**

Independent variable: doesn't need other variables to feel good about itself

Double-blind experiment: both the researcher and subjects are blindfolded

**MEDICATIONS**

Anti-flunkotic: a major relaxant for forgetting a really bad test score

Cramonol: a stimulate for pulling all-nighters

**BOOKS**

*Stalking, Locating Spies, and Other Practical Uses of Paranoid Disorders*

*Overcrowding: The Internal Life of a Multiple Personality*

Unit closers included extended humor pieces using exaggeration.

 **QUESTIONS YET TO BE ANSWERED BY PSYCHOLOGISTS**

Does drinking Pepsi Blue cause depression?

How does the metric system impact the self-esteem of inchworms?

**DREAMS OF FAMOUS PEOPLE**

Al Gore: Florida was never granted state rights

Martha Stewart: Designing the new fall orange jumpsuit line

**THE REAL WARNING SIGNS OF OBESITY**

The only number on your speed dial is Pizza Hut

Seven times daily you say, "Super-size, please!"

Triples included the following.

 You probably will not pass this class if you think a hard drive involves an SUV, if you go to the bathroom to matriculate, or if you wonder why all college principals are named Dean.

Seldom-used yet practical applications of hypnosis include training men to ask for directions, forgetting your last test score, and convincing your parents that completing a college degree takes seven years.

## SHOWTIME

The steps for writing educational humor are the same as for writing any other joke. Let's write a joke with the setup *Sigmund Freud's Pet Peeves*.

Start by listing things associated with Freud: the couch, patients freely associating or looking at ink blots. Then, identify the opposite of each item: clients sleeping instead of talking, clients drawing on the ink blots. By combining the associations and disassociations, you'd able to create the following triple.

 Sigmund Freud's major pet peeves were patients who fell asleep on the couch, drew on the inkblots, and complained about being charged for free association.

The joke is no gut-buster, but it does meet the criteria for effective educational humor—it relates to the topic, avoids offending anyone, and emphasizes three professional terms.

Now you try it. Select a familiar subject and write a series of jokes that are topic-related and student-oriented.

# CHAPTER 19
## That's a Wrap

 I think everybody is entitled to my opinion!

**—Victor Borge**

Any intelligent person can learn humor, work at it, and even produce it. The problem is that the commercial world won't pay enough for second best to allow everyone to make a living. In humor, good enough is no longer good enough. Only a small percentage of those who study humor go on to become professional humorists, but the same is true in many professions. Since you're only as good as your last joke, there's a great deal of insecurity in comedy writing—and a great deal of turnover. There are four ways that you can improve your chances of succeeding as a professional humor writer.

## 1. WORK WITH OTHERS

Write with a partner whenever possible. Despite the added difficulty of scheduling, teams of two or three writers spark each other's wit, and test and refine each other's ideas. "I love working with other writers," wrote humorist Phil Lasker. "I have learned to appreciate surrounding myself with talent. Others may have better lines than you or better story points. You have to listen to those you respect, and it's also fun to notice that the great writers are listening to you."

As Eric Idle of the six-member Monty Python group observed:

 Getting six guys to agree on what's funny is easy. We read it aloud. If we laugh, it's in; if we don't, it's out. If four guys think something's funny and two guys think it's not, we solve that very simply: We take the two guys out and kill 'em.

Often a student will point out that the most famous comedies were written by one person—Charlie Chaplin or Neil Simon. Well, if you're as good as Chaplin or Simon, you can do it alone, too!

## 2. HIRE AN AGENT

Agents are a great example of a catch-22 situation. The big agents won't touch unknowns, but beginners can't become known without an agent. There are many exceptions, however, and your job is to find them. Playwright Abe Burrows said he thought of his agent as family. When Burrows paid his agent 10 percent, he didn't think of it as a commission, but as sending money home to mother.

Names and addresses of agents can be obtained by searching the Internet. Just never give a new agent your wallet to hold when you go on stage.

## 3. TEST, TEST, TEST

Humor can't be tested in a vacuum. You need an audience, and it must be an audience receptive to humor. If you can't find an audience, try your jokes out on another humor professional—writer or performer. Don't walk up to a stranger and ask, "What d'ya think of this?" The only thing worse than that is trying your humor out on your friends, spouse, parents, or children. They are too subjective, too critical, and—instead of just relaxing and enjoying it—they turn into pseudo-analysts.

 There are a hell of a lot of jobs that are scarier than live comedy. Like standing in the operating room when a guy's heart stops, and you're the one who has to fix it.

**—Jon Stewart**

Only one out of every ten jokes will probably work the first time out. And no joke will ever please every person in the audience. It's impossible. Getting laughs from 50 percent of the audience is doing very well.

If you're writing material for public speaking, put thirty seconds of new material at the very beginning of a tested speech. The first thirty seconds are the toughest because that's when the audience is most skeptical, but if the new material goes over then, you know it has merit.

Jokes are like machine-gun bullets. They don't all hit the target, but if you shoot enough of them accurately at the audience, you'll kill 'em. Count one point for a twitter of laughter, two points for a solid laugh, and three points for applause. If a a joke doesn't score any points after it has been tried at least three times, throw it out. If it gets only one point, try rewriting it, so your score is constantly going up. Don't fall in love with your own material, and don't blame failure on the performer or the audience. Once you learn about flop sweat yourself, you'll never write bad material for a client.

 If I get big laughs, I'm a comedian. If I get little laughs, I'm a humorist. If I get no laughs, I'm a singer.

**—George Burns**

## 4. WRITE, WRITE, WRITE

Writing humor is an all-day assignment, because new ideas can pop into your head anytime, anyplace. Some feel humor can be conceived even when they dream, so keep a notebook by your bed.

Once you've learned the basic techniques, don't let anybody talk you out of writing your own way. Humor styles change with each generation and, while formulas rarely vary, standard subject matter, formats, fads, and characterizations are constantly being challenged. New ideas are the lifeblood of comedy, as they are of most businesses. And most new ideas take at least several years to germinate.

There are two other essential elements to comedy success—luck and perseverance. Some claim they go together—that the luckiest people are those who work the hardest. In any case, you must be your own publicist. That means having confidence in your own material and ability. The business is so competitive that self-effacing writers rarely make it. Have the confidence to sell yourself and a few sheets of paper covered with jokes—without gagging.

### Rest in Piece or Whole

In addition to luck and perseverance, your success as a humor writer depends on:

**1. WATCHING.** Look for the absurdities of life. Notice the physical actions that bring a smile to people's lips.

**2. READING.** If you read something funny, make a note of it. Notice the construction. Keep adding to your joke file.

**3. LISTENING.** Try to remember how people phrase things, what Mel Brooks calls "the rhythm of human speech." Things that look good on paper don't always perform well. We don't speak in full sentences, we often skip words, and we almost always use contractions.

**4. SPEAKING.** Do your own stand-up. Don't hesitate to deliver your own material in a meeting, at private parties, or to dinner guests. You'll notice how audiences differ, how your performance differs, and how important it is to have the right material for the right audience.

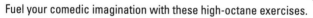

## SHOWTIME

Fuel your comedic imagination with these high-octane exercises.

Write a funny ...
- letter to the IRS defending an outrageous deduction
- set of directions for using a common personal hygiene product (soap, toothpaste)
- application letter for an unusual job (mortician, proctologist)
- "I'm out of the office" e-mail message
- top-ten list of your pet peeves
- list of new cable TV networks or shows
- weather forecast
- obit for roadkill
- travel guide for your local neighborhood
- insurance policy, will, or tax return

- scene for a silent film
- movie, play, or music review
- set of fake news headlines
- list of new car models
- short story of your worst dating experience
- roast for yourself, family members, or pet
- short story about how turkeys feel on Thanksgiving
- fairy tale about animals with mental disorders
- song or poem
- guide for parenting
- dress code for the office or home
- list of Internet domain names
- set of captions for old family photos
- fax cover sheet

# APPENDIX

# APPENDIX
## Glossary

**AMBIVALENCE THEORY**: A theory of comedy that stresses conflicting emotions, such as love and hate, toward a person, object, or idea.

**APHORISMS**: Concise expressions that contain truth or wisdom.

**ASSOCIATIONS**: A creative-writing technique that is used for discovering humor from unexpected relationships and creating POW jokes.

**BRAINSTORMING**: A humor-writing strategy that involves listing all available ideas.

**CONFIGURATION THEORY**: A theory of comedy that states we laugh when disjointedness falls into place, for example, when we solve a mystery or figure something out.

**DOUBLE ENTENDRE**: An ambiguous word or phrase that allows for a double interpretation of words, images, and associations.

**EVOLUTIONARY THEORY**: A theory of comedy that emphasizes that laughter is an instinct.

**EXAGGERATION**: A comedic device, used in conjunction with realism, to distort to an outrageous degree.

**INCONGRUITY THEORY**: A theory of comedy that emphasizes the logical but unconventional pairing of actions or thoughts.

**IRONY**: The use of sarcastic statements that generally mean the exact opposite of what's being expressed.

**MALAPROPS**: The use of twisted language that is innocently spoken by an ignorant person.

**MAP:** An acronym for material, audience, and performer. This theory postulates that the material must fit the persona of the writer or performer and the interests of the audience.

**MASKS OF HUMOR:** A comedic characterization that can be used to enhance humor.

**NON SEQUITUR:** An illogical statement that is humorous because of the juxtaposition of two elements.

**OBSERVATIONAL HUMOR:** A type of humor in which the humorist focuses on a realistic action or logical thought with the intent of destroying it.

**OVERSTATEMENT:** A comedic device to produce exaggerated humor.

**OXYMORON:** An incongruous double entendre that combines two contradictory terms in a humorous fashion.

**PAIRED ELEMENTS:** In the form of paired phrases, sentences, words, or statistics, this comedic device has a simple parallel structure that is craftily repeated by reversing the order at the end.

**POW:** An acronym for a play on words, which is a twist on common expressions, such as clichés or metaphors.

**PSYCHOANALYTICAL THEORY:** A theory of comedy presented by Freud that states that humor is therapeutic and allows people to express inhibited, perhaps childlike, tendencies in a socially acceptable manner.

**REALISM:** A comedic device, used in conjunction with exaggeration, meaning to state what is acceptable or true.

**REFORMING:** A comedy tactic that alters either the word order of a cliché or the spelling of words and substitutes a homonym or rhyming variation.

**RELEASE THEORY:** A theory of comedy that emphasizes that laughter is a planned event, a voluntary reduction of stress triggered by a conscious effort to unlock life's tensions and inhibitions.

---

**REVERSE:** A comedic device that adds a contradictory tag line to the opening line of a cliché, thus changing its point of view.

**RUNNING GAG:** A line that comes early in a monologue and then is repeated as a payoff line for jokes scattered throughout the routine.

**SAP HUMOR TEST:** An acronym given for the three parts of most comedic bits—setup, anticipation, and punchline.

**SATIRE:** A form of humor in which the comedian ridicules the vices of another, especially those in political or social positions.

**SAVER:** A line that is used to save "face" when a joke bombs.

**SIMPLE TRUTH:** A comedy tactic that takes the explicit meaning of a key word in an idiom and interprets it literally.

**STRETCH-BAND THEORY:** The theory that relates humor to a rubber band—the more it can be stretched, the more useful it is.

**SUPERIORITY THEORY:** A theory of comedy that involves comparing ourselves with others we consider inferior by ridiculing their intelligence, their social standing, and their physical infirmities.

**SURPRISE:** A theory of comedy suggesting that we laugh at the unexpected and to hide our own embarrassment.

**TAKE-OFF:** A technique that starts off with a common interpretation of a cliché followed by a bizarre reference. The take-off implies something that is not explicitly stated, making it the opposite of the simple truth.

**TEE:** An acronym for truth, emotion, and explicitness—the three criteria that determine whether a premise properly sets up the punchline.

**TELEGRAPH:** This occurs when a beginner gives too detailed an introduction to a story, making the setup so obvious that the audience can anticipate its ending.

**THREES FORMULA:** An acronym for the six essential elements of humor: target, hostility, realism, exaggeration, emotion, and surprise.

**TOPPERS:** A comedy tactic that involves a series of punchlines, each related to the previous one, especially used when the audience is on a roll.

**TRIPLES:** A comedic device used to build tension by using a triad grouping of examples or a sequence of three actions, comments, or categories.

**UNDERSTATEMENT:** A comedic device in which the humorist uses subtlety or shows a lack of emphasis in expression.

**USAGE BLUNDERS:** A tactic comedians use, on purpose or accidentally, which involves making spelling and grammatical errors.

# INDEX

hiding, 132
*Hite Report on Male Sexuality, The*, 39
Hite, Shere, 39
Hobbes, Thomas, 19
homographs, 78
homonyms, 62, 64, 74, 77, 78-83, 140, 142, 256
homophones, 78
*Honeymooners, The*, 289
hook. *See* persona.
Hope, Bob, 16, 68, 228
hostility, 36, 42-51, 54, 164-165, 274, 291
Hubbard, Elbert, 4
humor
  benefits of, 3-4, 10-11, 19
  comedy vs., 4
  as criticism, 37, 24, 44, 274-277
  entre-nous, 33-34
  ethnic, 24, 49-50, 183, 185, 242-243
  as group experience, 29, 31, 49-50, 216, 321
  as learnable skill, 1, 7-9
  localizing, 207, 208-209
  nihilistic, 44, 264
  paradox as, 51
  physical, 62, 160-161, 296-297, 300
  print, 99, 308-309
  put-down, 265, 284, 316
  recipe for, 36
  self-deprecating, 203, 209, 230, 316-317, 323
  shock, 189, 191, 192-195, 197
  sick, 33-44
  slapstick, 62, 296-297, 300
  in speaker introductions, 202-203
  in speeches, 199-221
  theories of, 19-21
  visual, 268, 322-323
  the what and why of, 36
  at work, 3-4, 10-11, 12, 303-304, 313-314

humor and duration principle, 96
humor writing
  careers in, 12-13
  for cartoons, 278-279
  courses in, x, 3
  for greeting cards, 280-281, 283-286
  for live performance, 250-251
  markets for, ix, 214-221, 222-223, 250-251, 315
  for print, 252-267
  sitcoms, 287-290, 298-302
  for speeches, 214-221
  tips, 327-331
humor, abbreviated print, 264-267
hyperbole. *See* exaggeration, overstatement.

**I**

*I Love Lucy*, 170-171, 287, 292
ideas
  generating, 16-17
  as targets, 38, 41
  *See also* material.
imagery, 158
imagination, 8
incongruity, 21, 22, 27-28, 52, 271, 272
inferiority, 24-25
  *See also* superiority.
Inge, M. Thomas, 268
instinct, 21, 26-27
intellectual, 232-233
Internet humor, 220, 263-264, 324-326
ironic truth, in columns, 254
irony, 4, 68

**J**

*Jeffersons, The*, 287
jerk, 241
jester, 228-230
Johnston, Betty, 260
joke on the way to a joke, 161

jokes
  originality of, 4-5, 261
  restricting number of, per topic, 71, 154
  world's funniest, 32
  *See also* material.

**K**

Katz, Mark, 42, 218
Kaufman, George S., 196-197
Kean, Edmund, 94
Keaton, Buster, 243
Keillor, Garrison, 157, 234, 235-236
Keith-Spiegel, Patricia, 21
Kelley, Steve, 277
Kennedy, John F., 218
KISS approach, 212
Klein, Robert, 231

**L**

Landers, Ann, 253
Lang, William, 152
Larry the Cable Guy, 222
Larson, Gary, 272
lateral thinking, 51-52
LaughLab, 32
laughter, as instinct, 26-27, 29
Leacock, Stephen, 52
Leary, Denis, 232, 242
Leno, Jay, 4, 15, 226
Leonard, Jack E., 243
Letterman, David, 4, 12, 41, 134, 204, 225-226, 251
Lewis, Jerry, 239
Lewis, Joe E., 231
Lewis, Richard, 230
Liebman, Wendy, 229
Linkletter, Art, 98, 322
listing, 115-122
live performance, 222-223, 239-251, 330
localizing humor, 207, 208-209
Luckovich, Mike, 277

**M**

MacDonald, Dwight, 187
malaprops, 62, 70-72

Mankoff, Bob, 270, 278
MAP, 13-15, 37, 225-226, 238,
   317-318
   shock humor and, 194
   in speech-writing, 206-212
Martin, Steve, 12, 224,
   231, 241
Marx Brothers, 182
Marx, Groucho, 241, 242
masks of comedy, 226-238
material
   generating, 16-17, 20, 61
   organizing and tracking,
   16-17
   originality of, 4-5, 261,
   289-290
   targeting to performer and
   audience, 13-14, 15, 37
   testing, 74, 200, 225-226,
   328-329
McMahon, Ed, 215
*McSweeney's Internet*
   *Tendency*, 263
Meara, Anne, 309-310
Meir, Golda, 203
Mencken, H.L., 37
Miller, Dennis, 232
Mindess, Harvey, 25
misdirection, 22, 125-126
money, as source of hostility,
   43, 45-46
Monty Python, 177, 315
Morley, John, 4, 200
Mostel, Zero, 182

**N**

names
   funny, 182-184
   nick-, 292-293
Nast, Thomas, 275
*National Lampoon*, 44
Nelson, Bob, 160-161
Nelson, Roy Paul, 254
Nessen, Ron, 197
*New Yorker, The*, 261, 268-
   269, 270, 273, 278
newsletters, 313-314
nihilistic humor, 44, 264

non sequiturs, 100-101, 174
nonsense, exaggeration as,
   170-171
Noonan, Peggy, 220
numbers
   exaggerating, 172-173
   funny, 186
   paired, 146-147
   understating, 174-175

**O**

obscenity, 34, 43-44, 67-68,
   69, 186-195, 246, 261, 316
Oliphant, Pat, 277
Olivier, Sir Laurence, 54
one-liners, 64, 254, 256-258.
   268, 269, 280
*Onion, The*, 263
online humor, 263-264,
   324-326
Orben, Robert, 110, 208, 220
overstatement, 166, 167, 175-
   176, 254, 258, 271-272
   *See also* exaggeration.
oxymorons, 62, 73

**P**

paired elements, 138-149,
   280, 284
   in aphorisms, 138, 147-148
   numbers, 146-147
   omitting second element
   of, 140
   phrases, 138-140
   reverses in, 139, 140
   sentences, 138-140
   take-offs in, 139, 142
   words, 141-145
paradox, as humor, 51
Parker, Dorothy, 52
parody, 4
Paulos, John Allen, 100
pauses, 55, 97, 175, 304
*Peanuts*, 274
Perelman, S.J., 62, 104,
   174, 182
performance, live, 222-223,
   239-251, 330

performer, matching audi-
   ence and material to,
   13-14, 15, 37
   *See also* MAP, persona.
Perret, Gene, 57, 111
persona, 14, 15, 37, 54, 191,
   223-244
Philips, Emo, 127-128,
   232, 239
phrases, paired, 138-140
physical appearance, 240,
   243-244
physical humor, 62, 160-161,
   296-297, 300
places
   as targets, 38, 41
   funny-sounding, 184-185
plays on words, 22, 61-87,
   89-108, 264, 268, 305,
   308, 313, 323, 325
   brainstorming, 109-124
   clichés and
   daffy definitions, 75-76
   double entendres, 62, 63,
   65-70, 74, 77, 92-93, 98-
   99, 182-183, 256, 257,
   265, 269, 270, 277
   groupings in, 145
   malaprops, 62, 70-72
   oxymorons, 62, 73
   paired elements in, 138-149
   in print vs. spoken aloud, 82
   puns, 62, 63, 74-77, 78,
   104, 256, 257
   reforming, 62, 77-83, 83-87,
   197, 104
   simple truths, 64, 89-102
   take-offs, 64, 90, 102-107,
   139, 268, 280, 284
plots, sitcom, 290-298
political cartoons, 269,
   274-276
political satirist, 233-234
POW. *See* plays on words.
Powers, Austin, 62
practicing, 225-226, 328-329
*Prairie Home Companion,*
   *A*, 235

print ads, 308-309
*Producers, The*, 93
products, as targets, 38, 41
profanity. *See* obscenity.
props, 240, 242, 323
Pryor, Richard, 43-44, 69, 234
punchlines, 152, 310
  creating, first, 122-123,
    135, 139, 149
  placement of, 104-105,
    114, 119, 131, 256
*Punk'd*, 27
puns, 62, 63, 74-77, 78, 104,
  256, 257
put-down humor, 265,
  284, 316
puzzle-solving, 21, 30

**Q**
Quayle, Dan, 71
questions, using, to build
  emotion, 55-56

**R**
Rackham, Marty, 16
radio commercials, 309-311
*Reader's Digest*, 192, 251,
  260-261, 269
Reagan, Ronald, 205, 207,
  218-219
realism, 36, 51-53, 97,
  112, 163, 165, 169-170,
  238, 310
  balancing, with exaggera-
    tion, 167-168, 176-178
recipe for humor, 36
reforming, 62, 77-83, 104
  and shock humor, 197
  split-, 79-81
  step by step, 83-87
Reiner, Carl, 12, 38
release, 21, 29
remember, 11
researching, 17-18, 239, 273
  for greeting cards, 280-281
  performers, 224-225
  for sitcoms, 288, 302
respect, 10-11, 34

reverses, 110, 125-137, 248,
  268, 269, 272-273, 284
  anecdotal, 129-130
  of clichés, 135
  misdirection in, 125-126
  in paired elements, 139, 140
  setting up, 125-126
  surprise in, 127-128
  telegraphing, 130-131
  triples as, 151, 153
  uses for, 133-134
revision, 113-115, 123-124
  *See also* economy of words.
reward, 12
Richards, Ann, 218
Richards, Michael, 15
Rivers, Joan, 229
Rock, Chris, 4, 12, 15, 188,
  225-226, 228, 246
Rogers, Will, 5, 233
roll outs, 304
Romano, Ray, 15
Rs, three, 9-13
rubber-band theory, 166
rube, 237-238
Rudner, Rita, 4, 15, 225, 229
running gags, 246-247

**S**
sad sack, 230-231
Sahl, Mort, 231, 233
sales, humor in, 303-304
Sanders, Bill, 277
SAP formula, 152
sarcasm, 4, 68
satire, 4
satirist, political, 233-234
*Saturday Night Live*, 136,
  142, 197, 227
savers, 247-248
scenes, sitcom, 298-299
Schulz, Charles, 274
Sedaris, David, 234, 236
*Seinfeld*, 15, 32, 39, 231, 289,
  292-293
Seinfeld, Jerry, 12, 15, 176
self, as target, 38
self-censorship, 9

self-deprecating humor, 203,
  209, 230, 316-317, 323
sentences, paired, 138-140
sentences, varying the
  length of, in speeches,
  205, 213
setups, 152, 159, 168-169, 268
  sitcom, 290-298
  TEE formula for, 168-169
sex
  as source of hostility, 43
  as target, 38-40
Shandling, Garry, 12, 230
shock humor, 189, 191, 192-
  195, 197
  *See also* obscenity.
shtick. *See* persona.
sick humor, 33-34
Simmons, Marty, 44
Simon, Neil, 29, 181
simple truths, 64, 89-102
  double entendres in, 98-99
  mispronunciation-based, 98
  non sequiturs, 100-101
  in physical comedy, 93
  toppers and , 97
single characters, 226-238
single-panel cartoons, 268-
  273, 274-275
sitcoms, 287-303
sketch comedy, 222-223
skits, 227-228, 309, 312
slapstick, 62, 296-297, 300
Smirnoff, Yakov, 15, 246
sounds, funny, 181-182
speeches, 201-221
  booking, 221
  closing remarks of, 213-214
  and introduction of
    speaker, 202-203
  introductory remarks of,
    203-204, 212
  length of, 212
  political, 217-220
  preparation of venue
    before, 216
  rehearsing, 215
  researching, 212